Teacher's Edition
Grade 1
Here We Go!

D1283366

Back to School

Senior Authors J. David Cooper, John J. Pikulski

Authors Patricia A. Ackerman, Kathryn H. Au, David J. Chard, Gilbert G. Garcia, Claude N. Goldenberg, Marjorie Y. Lipson, Susan E. Page, Shane Templeton, Sheila W. Valencia, MaryEllen Vogt

Consultants Linda H. Butler, Linnea C. Ehri, Carla B. Ford

HOUGHTON MIFFLIN

BOSTON • MORRIS PLAINS, NJ

California • Colorado • Georgia • Illinois • New Jersey • Texas

Literature Reviewers

Consultants: **Dr. Adela Artola Allen**, Associate Dean, Graduate College, Associate Vice President for Inter-American Relations, University of Arizona, Tucson, Arizona; **Dr. Manley Begay**, Co-director of the Harvard Project on American Indian Economic Development, Director of the National Executive Education Program for Native Americans, Harvard University, John F. Kennedy School of Government, Cambridge, Massachusetts; **Dr. Nicholas Kannellos**, Director, Arte Publico Press, Director, Recovering the U.S. Hispanic Literacy Heritage Project, University of Houston, Texas; **Mildred Lee**, author and former head of Library Services for Sonoma County, Santa Rosa, California; **Dr. Barbara Moy**, Director of the Office of Communication Arts, Detroit Public Schools, Michigan; **Norma Naranjo**, Clark County School District, Las Vegas, Nevada; **Dr. Arlette Ingram Willis**, Associate Professor, Department of Curriculum and Instruction, Division of Language and Literacy, University of Illinois at Urbana-Champaign, Illinois

Teachers: **Shirley Ferguson**, Lakota Elementary School, Lakota, North Dakota; **Susan Flanagin**, Mt. Jumbo School, Missoula, Montana; **Robin Holland**, Windsor Academy, Columbus, Ohio; **Maureen Mack**, Lawn Manor Elementary, Oaklawn, Illinois; **Amy Shisako**, Harding Elementary, El Cerrito, California; **Deborah Lopez Young**, Navajo Elementary School, Albuquerque, New Mexico

Program Reviewers

California Reviewers: **Maureen Carlton**, Barstow, California; **Karen Cedar**, Gold River, California; **Karen Ciraulo**, Folsom, California; **Marilyn Crownover**, Tustin, California; **Cheryl Dultz**, Citrus Heights, California; **Beth Holguin**, San Jose, California; **Sandi Maness**, Modesto, California; **Muriel Miller**, Simi Valley, California; **Jean Nielson**, Simi Valley, California; **Sue Patton**, Brea, California; **Jennifer Rader**, Huntington, California; **Bea Tamo**, Huntington, California

Supervisors: **Judy Artz**, Middletown Monroe City School District, Ohio; **James Bennett**, Elkhart Schools, Elkhart, Indiana; **Kay Buckner-Seal**, Wayne County, Michigan; **Charlotte Carr**, Seattle School District, Washington; **Sister Marion Christi**, St. Matthews School, Archdiocese of Philadelphia, Pennsylvania; **Alvina Crouse**, Garden Place Elementary, Denver Public Schools, Colorado; **Peggy DeLapp**, Minneapolis, Minnesota; **Carol Erlandson**, Wayne Township Schools, Marion County, Indianapolis; **Brenda Feeney**, North Kansas City School District, Missouri; **Winnie Huebsch**, Sheboygan Area Schools, Wisconsin; **Brenda Mickey**, Winston-Salem/Forsyth County Schools, North Carolina; **Audrey Miller**, Sharpe Elementary School, Camden, New Jersey; **JoAnne Piccolo**, Rocky Mountain Elementary, Adams 12 District, Colorado; **Sarah Rentz**, East Baton Rouge Parish School District, Louisiana; **Kathy Sullivan**, Omaha Public Schools, Nebraska; **Rosie Washington**, Kuny Elementary, Gary, Indiana; **Theresa Wishart**, Knox County Public Schools, Tennessee

Teachers: **Carol Brockhouse**, Madison Schools, Wayne Westland Schools, Michigan; **Eva Jean Conway**, R.C. Hill School, Valley View School District, Illinois; **Carol Daley**, Jane Addams School, Sioux Falls, South Dakota; **Karen Landers**, Watwood Elementary, Talladega County, Alabama; **Barb LeFerrier**, Mullenix Ridge Elementary, South Kitsap District, Port Orchard, Washington; **Loretta Piggee**, Nobel School, Gary, Indiana; **Cheryl Remash**, Webster Elementary School, Manchester, New Hampshire; **Marilynn Rose**, Michigan; **Kathy Scholtz**, Amesbury Elementary School, Amesbury, Massachusetts; **Dottie Thompson**, Erwin Elementary, Jefferson County, Alabama; **Dana Vassar**, Moore Elementary School, Winston-Salem, North Carolina; **Joy Walls**, Ibraham Elementary School, Winston-Salem, North Carolina; **Elaine Warwick**, Fairview Elementary, Williamson County, Tennessee

English Language Learners Reviewers: **Maria Arevalos**, Pomona, California; **Manuel Brenes**, Kalamazoo, Michigan; **Susan Dunlap**, Richmond, California; **Tim Fornier**, Academia de Español Elementary School, Grand Rapids, Michigan; **Connie Jimenez**, Los Angeles, California; **Diane Bonilla Lether**, Pasadena, California; **Anna Lugo**, Patrick Henry School, Chicago, Illinois; **Marcos Martel**, Hayward, California; **Carolyn Mason**, Yakima School District, Yakima, Washington; **Jackie Pinson**, Moorpark, California; **Jerilyn Smith**, Salinas, California; **Noemi Velazquez**, Jersey City, New Jersey; **Dr. Santiago Veve**, JM Ullom School, Las Vegas, Nevada

Credits

Front and Back Cover Photography
by Tony Scarpetta.

Front and Back Cover Illustrations
by Nadine Westcott.

Acknowledgments

Grateful acknowledgment is made for permission to reprint copyrighted material as follows:

Theme 2
"The Giants" by Isabel Carley, from *Music for Children Orff-Schulwerk® American Edition, Primary 2, Revised Edition.* Copyright © 1977 by Schott Music Corp. Reprinted by permission of the proprietor Warner European American Music, 15800 NW 48th Avenue, Miami, FL 33014. All rights reserved.

Student Writing Model Feature

Special thanks to the following teachers whose students' compositions appear as Student Writing Models: **Cheryl Claxton**, Florida; **Patricia Kopay**, Delaware; **Susana Llanes**, Michigan; **Joan Rubens**, Delaware; **Nancy Schulten**, Kentucky; **Linda Wallis**, California

Theme 2

Surprise!

Kindergarten Review

Phonemic Awareness blending phonemes

Phonics consonants *d, w, l, x, y, k, v, q, j, z;* blending short *o,* short *e,* and short *u* words

Reading Strategies phonics/decoding; question; monitor/clarify; summarize

Comprehension noting details; fantasy and realism; story structure

High-Frequency Words recognize high-frequency words

Grammar capitalizing names; naming words; action words

Writing alliteration; writing about animals, bugs

Spelling and Phonics write words with *d, l, y, v, j, z,* short *o,* short *e,* and short *u*

Vocabulary number words; fun things; opposites; foods; days of the week; homographs

Listening/Speaking/Viewing sharing information; compare and contrast; main idea and details; conflict resolution; retell/summarize; reader's theater

Information and Study Skills following instructions

Theme 2

Surprise!
Literature Resources

Theme Read Aloud Jack and the Beanstalk page R3

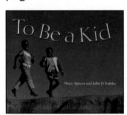

Books for Small-Group Reading

Other Theme Resources

Decodable	Easy	On Level / Challenge

Phonics Library

Dot Fox
Lesson, page T29

Bob Pig and Dan Ox
Lesson, page T41

Once Upon a Dig
Lesson, page T71

I ♥ READING BOOKS
Books 10–14
Review Books 5–14

On My Way Practice Reader

Five Big Boxes
by Irma Singer
Lesson, page T32

On Level Theme Paperback

"What Is That?" Said the Cat
by Grace Maccarone
Lesson, page T33

Challenge Little Big Book

To Be a Kid
by Maya Ajmera and John D. Ivanko
Lesson, pages T34–T35

Phonics Library

Not Yet!
Lesson, page T89

Big Ben
Lesson, page T101

Get Wet, Ken!
Lesson, page T135

I ♥ READING BOOKS
Books 15–18
Review Books 10–18

On My Way Practice Reader

The Pet
by Maria Cara
Lesson, page T92

On Level Theme Paperback

The Pet Vet
by Marcia Leonard
Lesson, page T93

Challenge Little Big Book

Minerva Louise at School
by Janet Morgan Stoeke
Lesson, pages T94–T95

Phonics Library

The Bug Kit
Lesson, page T153

Quit It, Zig!
Lesson, page T165

Rug Tug
Lesson, page T197

I ♥ READING BOOKS
Books 19–22
Review Books 15–22

On My Way Practice Reader

Where Is Tug Bug?
by Oscar Gake
Lesson, page T156

On Level Theme Paperback

Spots
by Marcia Leonard
Lesson, page T157

Challenge Little Big Book

Jasper's Beanstalk
by Nick Butterworth and Mick Inkpen
Lesson, pages T158–T159

Other Theme Resources

 **Audiotapes** *for Surprise!*

Literature Resources
Grade 1

Bibliography

Books for Independent Reading

Choose books from this list for children to read, outside class, for at least twenty minutes a day.

Key

 Science

 Social Studies

 Multicultural

 Music

 Math

 Classic

 Art

Very Easy

Good Night, Gorilla
by Peggy Rathmann
Putnam 1996 (32p)
In a comical, almost wordless story, a gorilla and other zoo animals follow their keeper home.

 Hop, Skip, Run
by Marcia Leonard
Millbrook 1998 (32p) also paper
When a boy who likes to hop and two girls who like to skip and run meet, they're in for a surprise.

 Loose Tooth
by Margaret Yatsevitch Phinney
Lee & Low 2000 (8p)
A girl wonders when her loose tooth will come out.

Hot Dog
by Molly Coxe
Golden 1998 (32p) also paper
A dog finds a way to cool off on a hot summer day.

Goldilocks and the Three Bears
by Betty Miles
Simon 1998 (32p) also paper
Three bears return home to find an unexpected visitor in their house.

Easy

Wash Day
by Charnan Simon
Millbrook 1999 (32p)
While their dad naps, two brothers help out by washing floors and rugs and clothes and walls.

Fox Trot

Fox Trot
by Molly Coxe
Golden 1999 (32p) also paper
Fox's plans for a delicious dinner are spoiled by a band he hires to entertain his guests.

A Beasty Story
by Bill Martin Jr
Harcourt 1999 (32p)
In a dark wood in a dark house, the mice Nick and Hank plan a surprise.

Cat Traps
by Molly Coxe
Random 1996 (32p) paper
Cat sets a trap for a snack, but catches everything except what he wants to eat.

Big Egg
by Molly Coxe
Random 1997 (32p) paper
Hen wakes to find a gigantic egg in her nest, but does it belong to Fox as he claims?

On Level

Turnover Tuesday
by Phyllis Root
Candlewick 1998 (32p) also paper
When Bonnie Bumble eats turnovers for breakfast one morning, her whole world turns upside down.

Tumble Bumble
by Felicia Bond
Front Street 1996 (32p)
After a walk, a bug and his friends end up napping in a boy's bed.

Surprise!
by Charnan Simon
Millbrook 1999 (32p) also paper
Two brothers prepare a surprise for their mom's birthday.

Pig Picnic
by Patricia Hubbell
Golden 1999 (32p) also paper
A group of pigs share their picnic with an unexpected guest—a wolf.

Sheep in a Shop
by Nancy Shaw
Houghton 1991 (32p) also paper
Five sheep shop for the perfect gift.

Challenge

 The Cat in the Hat
by Dr. Seuss
Random 1957 (60p)
Chaos ensues when the Cat in the Hat pays a visit to Sally and her brother.

Surprise Puppy
by Judith Walker-Hodge
DK 1998 (32p) also paper
Twins Jessica and Sam are surprised with a puppy for their birthday.

 **Little Red Riding Hood**
by Harriet Ziefert
Viking 2000 (32p) also paper
Red Riding Hood meets up with a hungry wolf.

The Surprise Garden
by Zoe Hall
Scholastic 1998 (32p)
Three siblings plant unmarked seeds and watch to see what grows in their garden.

Books for Teacher Read Aloud

The Pig Is in the Pantry, the Cat Is on the Shelf
by Shirley Mozelle
Clarion 2000 (32p)
Eight mischievous farm animals make a mess in Mr. McDuffel's house while he's away.

Possum's Harvest Moon
by Anne Hunter
Houghton 1996 (32p) also paper

The beautiful harvest moon inspires Possum's busy friends to go to his party.

The Pigs' Picnic
by Keiko Kasza
Putnam 1988 (32p) also paper
Miss Pig doesn't recognize Mr. Pig when he dresses up to impress her.

A Birthday Basket for Tía
by Pat Mora
Simon 1992 (32p)

Cecilia prepares a special birthday gift for her great aunt. **Available in Spanish as *Una canasta de cumpleaños para Tía.***

I Like Your Buttons
by Sarah Marwil Lamstein
Whitman 1999 (32p)

Cassandra's compliment sets off a chain reaction of small kindnesses.

Bearsie Bear and the Surprise Sleepover
by Bernard Waber
Houghton 1997 (40p)
Bearsie Bear ends up with a house full of company on a cold night.

The Very Hungry Caterpillar
by Eric Carle
Putnam 1984 (32p)
A hungry caterpillar eats his way through the days of the week and changes into a beautiful butterfly.

Who Took the Cookies from the Cookie Jar?
by Bonnie Lass and Philomen Sturges
Little 2000 (32p)

Skunk and his friends try to solve the mystery of the missing cookies.

Mouse Mess
by Linnea Asplind Riley
Scholastic 1997 (32p)
In this funny rhyming story, a mouse creates chaos in the kitchen as he fixes himself a nighttime snack.

Technology

Computer Software Resources
- **The Cat in the Hat** *CD-ROM. Broderbund*
- **Arthur's Birthday** *CD-ROM. Media Basics*

Video Cassettes
- **Good Night, Gorilla** *by Peggy Rathmann. Weston Woods*
- **A Birthday Basket for Tía** *by Pat Mora. Spoken Arts*
- **Goldilocks and the Three Bears** *by James Marshall. Weston Woods*
- **Red Riding Hood** *by James Marshall. Weston Woods*

Audio Cassettes
- **Sheep in a Shop** *by Nancy Shaw. Houghton*
- **Mr. Rabbit and the Lovely Present** *by Charlotte Zolotow. Weston Woods*
- **The Elves and the Shoemaker** *by Paul Galdone. Weston Woods*
- **Ride a Purple Pelican** *by Jack Prelutsky. Listening Library*
- **Audiotapes for *Surprise!*** *Houghton Mifflin Company*

Technology Resources addresses are on page R36.

Education Place
www.eduplace.com *Log on to Education Place for more activities relating to Surprise!*
Book Adventure
www.bookadventure.org *This Internet reading incentive program provides thousands of titles for students to read.*

Theme at a Glance

Theme Concept: *Things don't always turn out the way you expect.*

✓ **Indicates Tested Skills**

Learning to Read

	Phonemic Awareness; Phonics/Decoding	High-Frequency Words	Comprehension Skills and Strategies
WEEK 1 **Big Book** **To Be a Kid** **Anthology** **The Box** **Wigs in a Box** **Poetry Link** **Phonics Library** *Decodable stories*	✓ Consonants *d, w, l, x*, T26–T29, T41, T71 ✓ Short *o*, T27 ✓ Blending Short *o* Words, T27–T29, T41, T71 **Phonics Review: Words with Short *i*, T52–T53**	✓ High-Frequency Words, T40–T41 Word Pattern Board, T30, T40, T42, T72	✓ Noting Details, T22, T38–T39, T47, T49, T50, T51, T59, T61, T62, T63, T64, T65, T70 **Cause and Effect, T50, T61, T64; Compare and Contrast, T49, T62, T64** **Strategy Focus: Question, T22, T47, T49, T50, T59, T61, T63**
WEEK 2 **Big Book** **Minerva Louise at School** **Anthology** **What Can a Vet Do?** **Hot Fox Soup** **Music Link** **Phonics Library** *Decodable stories*	✓ Consonants *y, k, v*, T86–T89, T101, T135 ✓ Short *e*, T87 ✓ Blending Short *e* Words, T87–T89, T101, T135 **Phonics Review: Blending Short *o* Words, T114–T115**	✓ High-Frequency Words, T100–T101 Word Pattern Board, T90, T100, T102, T136	✓ Fantasy and Realism, T82, T98–T99, T107, T110, T112, T121, T123, T125, T127, T129, T134 **Noting Details, T109, T110, T111, T123, T125; Cause and Effect, T109, T123, T125, T128** **Strategy Focus: Monitor/Clarify, T82, T107, T109, T111, T121, T126, T127**
WEEK 3 **Big Book** **Jasper's Beanstalk** **Anthology** **A Hut for Zig Bug** **The Rope Tug** **Poetry Link** **Phonics Library** *Decodable stories*	✓ Consonants *q, j, z*, T150–T152, T165 ✓ Short *u*, T151 ✓ Blending Short *u* Words, T151–T153, T165, T197 **Phonics Review: Blending Short *e* Words T178–T179**	✓ High-Frequency Words, T164–T165 Word Pattern Board, T154, T164, T166, T198	✓ Story Structure, T146, T162–T163, T171, T173, T175, T176, T185, T187, T189, T196 **Fantasy/Realism, T173, T187; Noting Details, T188, T191** ✓ **Strategy Focus: Summarize, T146, T171, T173, T175, T185, T187, T189**
Theme Resources	**Spiral Review,** T199A–T199B **Reteaching,** R4, R6, R8, R10, R12, R14 **Challenge/Extension,** R5, R7, R9, R11, R13, R15	**Spiral Review,** T199A–T199B **Reteaching,** R16, R18, R20 **Challenge/Extension,** R17, R19, R21	**Spiral Review,** T199A–T199B **Reteaching,** R22, R24, R26 **Challenge/Extension,** R23, R25, R27

Pacing	Multi–age Classroom	Technology 
• This theme is designed to take approximately 3 weeks, depending on your students' needs.	**Related themes —** • **Kindergarten:** *Let's Count!* • **Grade 2:** *Silly Stories*	**Education Place: www.eduplace.com** Log on to Education Place for more activities relating to *Surprise!* **Lesson Planner CD-ROM** Customize your planning with the Lesson Planner.

Word Work		Writing & Language			Centers
Spelling and Phonics	**Vocabulary**	**Writing**	**Grammar, Usage, and Mechanics**	**Listening/ Speaking/Viewing**	**Cross-Curricular Content Area**
Words with *d, w, l, x,* and Short *o*, *T30, T42, T54, T66, T72*	Number Words, *T54* Fun Things, *T66*	Independent Journal Writing, *T31* Shared Writing: A Class Letter, *T43* Using Alliteration, *T67* Coached Writing, *T73*	Capitalizing Names, *T55* Word Order in Sentences, *T73*	Sharing Information, *T31* Compare and Contrast, *T73*	**Phonics and Language:** Word Booklets **Writing and Technology:** A Friendship Book **Creative Arts:** Making Puzzles **Social Studies:** Playing a Game
Words with *y, k, v,* and Short *e*, *T90, T102, T116, T130, T136*	Opposites, *T116* Foods, *T130*	Independent Journal Writing, *T91* Shared Writing: A Class Message, *T103* Writing About Animals, *T131* Coached Writing, *T137*	Naming Words, *T117, T137*	Main Idea and Details, *T91* Conflict Resolution, *T137*	**Phonics and Language:** Word Booklets **Writing and Technology:** Make a Label Book **Creative Arts:** Sock Puppets **Math:** How Many Make 12?
Words with *q, j, z,* and Short *u*, *T154, T166, T180, T192, T198*	Days of the Week, *T180* Homographs, *T192*	Independent Journal Writing, *T155* Shared Writing: A Diary, *T167* Writing About Bugs, *T193* Coached Writing, *T199*	Action Words, *T181, T199*	Retell/Summarize, *T155* Reader's Theater, *T199*	**Phonics and Language:** Word Booklets **Writing and Technology:** Make a Story Sequel **Creative Arts:** Make a Beanstalk **Science:** Watching Things Grow
			Spiral Review, *T199A–T199B*		**Information and Study Skills:** Following Instructions, *R28*

Planning for Assessment

Use these resources to meet your assessment needs. For additional information, see the **Teacher's Assessment Handbook.**

Baseline Group Test　　　**Emerging Literacy Survey**

Lexia Quick Phonics Assessment CD-ROM

Diagnostic Planning

Continue to assess informally children's progress in phonemic awareness and phonics/decoding skills in order to plan your class and individual instruction. Retest children you have concerns about, using the assessments below as appropriate.

If you are concerned that some children may need intervention, you might want to assess their letter-naming or word-reading fluency. See the **Teacher's Assessment Handbook**, page 27.

Baseline Group Test
- Indicates the amount of reading support individual children will need

Emerging Literacy Survey
- Assesses phonemic awareness, concepts of print, letter naming, word recognition, word writing, and sentence dictation
- Identifies areas of strength and need, including the need for early intervention

Lexia Quick Phonics Assessment CD-ROM
- Identifies children who need more help with phonics

Leveled Reading Passages Assessment Kit
- Can be used to determine reading level and instructional needs

Theme Skills Test
- Various subtests can be used as a pretest to find which skills children know prior to instruction and to plan levels of support for meeting individual needs.

Comprehension Checks

Ongoing Informal Assessment

Day-to-day informal measurement of your children's progress should be performed as an integral part of your instructional plan. Your observations, recorded on checklists and in anecdotal records, will complement the informal measures listed below.

Phonemic Awareness/Phonics and High-Frequency Words
- **Practice Book**, pp. 53–59, 62–63, 71–75, 78–79, 86–89, 92–93
- Reading Check, pp. T71, T135, T197

Comprehension
- Selection Comprehension Checks, **Practice Book**, pp. 65, 67, 81, 83, 96, 98

Writing
- Student writing from lessons or activities in this theme

Observation Checklist

Ongoing Informal Assessment *continued*

Other Informal Assessment

- Diagnostic Checks, pp. T28, T39, T40, T49, T53, T62, T72, T88, T99, T100, T112, T126, T136, T152, T163, T164, T176, T188, T198, R4, R6, R8, R10, R12, R14, R16, R18, R20, R22, R24, R26
- Student Self-Assessment, pp. T51, T63, T113, T127, T177, T189
- Observation Checklist, **Teacher's Resource Blackline Masters**

End-of-Theme Assessment

Integrated Theme Test

Theme Skills Test

Use the following formal assessments to help you measure children's progress in attaining the theme's instructional goals.

Integrated Theme Test

- Tests in a format that reflects instruction
- Tests phonics, comprehension strategies and skills, high-frequency words, spelling, grammar, writing, and listening comprehension

Theme Skills Test

- Tests discrete skills: phonics, comprehension skills, and high-frequency words

Periodic Progress Assessment

Benchmark Progress Test

Periodically throughout the year, evaluate your children's progress compared to other children's at the same grade level.

Benchmark Progress Test

- Assesses student progress in reading and writing, two to four times a year

Assessment Management

Technology

Learner Profile™ CD-ROM by Sunburst Technology

This software can help you record, manage, and report your assessment of children's progress.

Learner Profile™ CD-ROM

- Records children's achievement of instructional goals
- Has companion software, **Learner Profile to Go™**, that allows you to record each child's information on a handheld computer device

Theme 2
Theme Resources

Houghton Mifflin Reading includes a wide variety of resources for meeting the needs of all students. The chart below indicates features and components of the program and the students for whom they are appropriate.

Universal Access: Reaching All Students

	On Level Students	English Language Learners	Challenge Students	Extra Support Students	Inclusion/Special Needs
Big Books	★	★	○	★	★
Anthology					
• Get Set to Read	★	★	○	★	★
• Poetry Links	★	★	★	★	★
Audiotape	○	★		★	★
Teacher's Edition					
• Teacher Read Aloud	★	★	○	★	★
• Universal Access notes		★	★	★	★
• Theme Resources	★	★	★	★	★
• Theme Project	★	○	★	○	○
Practice Book	★	★	★	★	★
Books for Small-Group Reading					
• Phonics Library (Decodable)	★	★	○	★	★
• I Love Reading Books (Decodable)	★	★	○	★	★
• On My Way Practice Readers (Easy)	★	★	○	★	★
• Theme Paperbacks (On Level)	★	○	★	○	
• Little Big Books (Challenge)	★	○	★	○	○
• Literature Resources	★	○	★	○	○
* **Challenge Handbook**	○	○	★		
* **Extra Support Handbook**		○		★	★
* **Handbook for English Language Learners**		★		○	○

* See Universal Access Plans, pp. T17A–T17B, T77A–T77B, T141A–T141B

KEY: ★ = highly appropriate   ○ = appropriate

T10 THEME 2: **Surprise!**

	On Level Students	English Language Learners	Challenge Students	Extra Support Students	Inclusion/Special Needs
Home/Community Connections	★	★	★	★	★
Classroom Management Handbook	★	★	★	★	○

Technology

	On Level Students	English Language Learners	Challenge Students	Extra Support Students	Inclusion/Special Needs
Education Place	★	○	★	○	○
Lexia Quick Phonics Assessment CD-ROM				★	★
Lexia Phonics CD-ROM: Primary Intervention				★	★
Published by Sunburst Technology*					
• Tenth Planet®: Vowels: Short & Long	★	★	○	★	★
• Tenth Planet®: Blends and Digraphs	★	★	○	★	○
• Tenth Planet®: Word Parts	○	○	★	○	
• Curious George® Pre-K ABCs	○	○		★	★
• First Phonics	★	★	○	★	★
• Reading Who? Reading You!	○	○	★	○	
• Sunbuddy® Writer	★	★	★	○	
Published by The Learning Company					
• Dr. Seuss®'s ABC	★	★	○	★	○
• Paint, Write & Play!™	○	○	★	○	
• ¡Vamos a Jugar, Pintar y Escribir!™		★			

Launching the Theme
for *Surprise!*

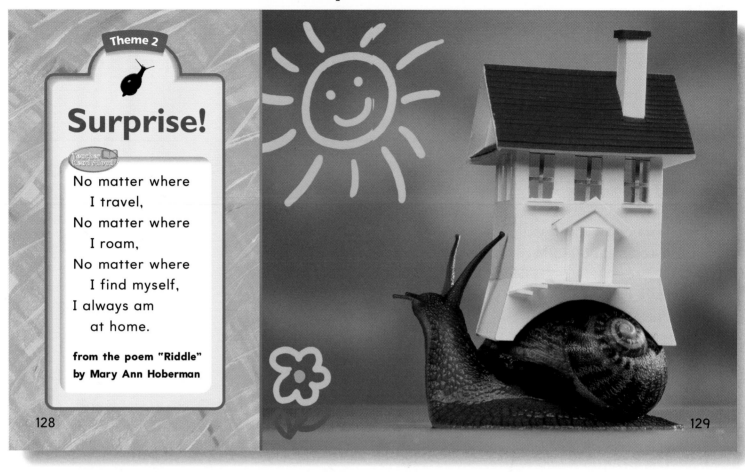

Theme 2

Surprise!

Teacher Read Aloud

No matter where
   I travel,
No matter where
   I roam,
No matter where
   I find myself,
I always am
   at home.

**from the poem "Riddle"
by Mary Ann Hoberman**

128   129

▶ Using the Theme Opener

Have children open their Anthologies to pages 128–129. Read aloud the theme title *Surprise!* Tell children to look closely at the picture, and ask what's surprising in it. Then tell children you are going to read aloud part of the poem "Riddle" by Mary Ann Hoberman. Tell them to listen carefully to solve the riddle. Then ask

- *Who do you think is speaking in the poem?* (Sample answer: a snail)

- *How do you know?* (Sample answer: Snails carry their homes on their back.)

Discuss the kinds of stories children think they will read in *Surprise!,* suggesting that the stories might be surprising.

Multi-age Classroom

Related themes:

Kindergarten . . . . Let's Count!

▲

Grade 1 . . . . Surprise!

▼

Grade 2 . . . . Silly Stories

▶ Using the Teacher Read Aloud

MATERIALS • *Jack and the Beanstalk*, R3 •

Read aloud the Teacher Read Aloud *Jack and the Beanstalk* to develop children's oral comprehension and listening skills. After reading, use the following questions to discuss how the story relates to the theme *Surprise!*

- *How was each of the characters surprised?* (Jack's mother: when the beanstalk grew overnight; Jack: when he saw the castle, the giant, and the hen that spoke and laid golden eggs; the giant: when Jack ran off with the hen and when Jack's mother chopped down the beanstalk)

- *What surprised you most?* (Answers will vary.)

Reading aloud is an important part of daily instruction. You may want to choose books from the Bibliography on pages T4–T5 to read aloud.

Theme Project

"Surprise Door" Have children follow these steps to make a Surprise Door:

- *Fold an 11-inch x 17-inch sheet of paper in thirds.*

- *Draw and label an animal in the middle box of the paper.*

- *Fold over the right flap and write a one-word clue that tells about the animal.*

- *Fold over the left flap and write another one-word clue about the animal.*

Partners can share their Surprise Doors and try to guess the animal from the clues.

Create an apartment building of "Surprise Doors" as a bulletin-board display.

Challenge Children can make Surprise Doors to hide a favorite word, writing synonyms as clues on each of the folds.

green hops

frog

Technology

Education Place
www.eduplace.com
Log on to **Education Place** for more activities relating to *Surprise!*

Lesson Planner CD-ROM
Customize your planning for *Surprise!* with the Lesson Planner.

Home Connection

Send home the theme letter for *Surprise!* to introduce the theme and suggest home activities. See **Teacher's Resource Blackline Masters**.

Home Community Connection

For other suggestions relating to *Surprise!*, see **Home/Community Connections**.

Literature for Week 1
Different texts for different purposes

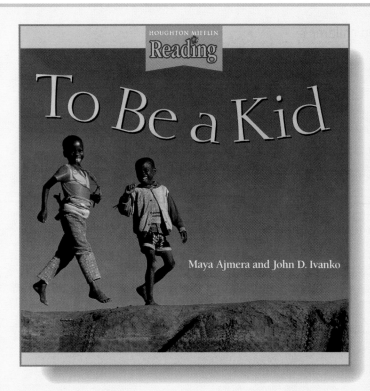

Decodable Text

The Box

written by Andrew Clements
illustrated by Cynthia Fisher

Decodable Text

Wigs in a Box
by Valeria Petrone

Big Book

Purposes

- oral language development
- reading strategies
- comprehension skills

 ### Awards

- ⭐ Notable Children's Trade Book in the Field of Social Studies
- ⭐ *Early Childhood News* Director's Choice Award

 Also available on audiotape

 Also available on audiotape

Challenge
Little Big Book

Purposes

- vocabulary development
- reading fluency
- application of phonics/decoding and comprehension skills

Anthology: Main Selections

Purposes

- reading strategies
- comprehension skills
- phonics/decoding skills
- high-frequency words
- critical thinking

 ### Award Winner

- ⭐ Books by Clements have received numerous children's choice awards including the Rebecca Caudhill Young Reader's Award, the William Allen White Children's Book Award, and the Rhode Island Children's Book Award; his work has also received the Christopher Award and been named to the *Horn Book*'s Fanfare list.

Anthology: Get Set to Read *The Box*

Anthology: Get Set to Read *Wigs in a Box*

Purpose

• applying phonics skills and high-frequency words

Anthology: Poetry Link

Purposes

• skill: how to read a poem
• critical thinking; discussion

Decodable Text

Phonics Library

Purposes

• applying phonics skills
• applying high-frequency words

Also available in take-home version

I ❤ READING BOOKS

Purposes

• applying phonics skills
• applying high-frequency words

Books for Small-Group Reading

Use these resources to ensure that children read, outside class, for at least twenty minutes a day.

On My Way Practice Reader

Easy

Five Big Boxes
by Irma Singer
page T32

Theme Paperback

On Level

"What Is That?" Said the Cat
by Grace Maccarone
page T33

Education Place

www.eduplace.com
Log on to Education Place for more activities relating to *Surprise!*

Book Adventure

www.bookadventure.org
This Internet reading-incentive program provides thousands of titles for students to read.

Instructional Goals

	Day 1	**Day 2**

Learning to Read

Strategy Focus: Question

✓ **Comprehension** Noting Details

Phonemic Awareness: Blend Phonemes

✓ **Phonics** Consonants *d, w, l, x;* Short *o;* Blending Short *o* Words (CV, CVC)
- Additional lessons for phonics skills are included in the *Extra Support Handbook* and *Handbook for English Language Learners.* (See Universal Access Plans.)

Phonics Review: Words with Short *o*

✓ **High-Frequency Words:** *five, four, in, once, three, two, upon, what*

90–110 minutes

Day 1

Opening Routines: *T20–T21*

Reading the Big Book
To Be a Kid, T22–T25

Phonemic Awareness
- Blend Phonemes, *T26*

Phonics Instruction, Practice, Application
- Consonants *d, w, l, x, T26; Practice Book, 53–56*
- Short *o, T27; Practice Book, 57*
- Blending Short *o* Words, *T28; Practice Book, 58*
- Phonics Library, *Dot Fox, T29*

Day 2

Opening Routines: *T36–T37*

Rereading the Big Book
To Be a Kid, T38–T39

Comprehension Skill Instruction
- Noting Details, *T38–T39*
- *Practice Book, 61*

High-Frequency Words
- Instruction, *T40*
- *Practice Book, 62-63*

Phonics Application
- Phonics Library, *Bob Pig and Dan Ox, T41*

Word Work

Spelling and Phonics: Words with *d, l, w, x,* and Short *o*

Word Pattern Board: High-Frequency Words; Words with Short *o*

Vocabulary: Number Words; Fun Things

30–40 minutes

Day 1

Spelling and Phonics
- Instruction: Letters and Sounds *d, l, T30*
- *Practice Book, 60*

Word Pattern Board
- Words with Short *o, T30*

Day 2

Spelling and Phonics
- Instruction: *w, x, T42*
- *Practice Book, 64*

Word Pattern Board
- High-Frequency Words, *T42*

Writing & Language

Grammar: Capitalizing Names

Writing: A Class Letter; Using Alliteration

Listening/Speaking/Viewing: Sharing Information, Compare and Contrast

30–40 minutes

Day 1

✏ **Writing**
- Independent Journal Writing, *T31*

Listening/Speaking
- Sharing Information, *T31*

Day 2

✏ **Shared Writing**
- A Class Letter, *T43*

Teacher's Notes

📖 **Books for Small-Group Reading, T28–T29, T32–T35, T41, T53, T71**
For reading outside class and homework

Technology

Lesson Planner CD-ROM
Customize your planning for the week with the Lesson Planner.

Day 3

Opening Routines: *T44–T45*

Preparing to Read *The Box*
- Building Background, *T46*
- Get Set to Read, *T46*
- Strategy/Skill Preview, *T47*

Reading the Anthology *The Box*
- Comprehension/Critical Thinking, *T49, T50*
- Strategy Focus, *T49, T50*
- Responding, *T51, Practice Book, 65*

Phonics Application/Review
- Anthology: *The Box, T48–T51*
- Review/Maintain: Words with Short *o*, *T52–T53*

Spelling and Phonics
- Words with *d, w, l, x,* and Short *o*, *T54*

Vocabulary
- Number Words, *T54*

Writing
- Response Activity, *T51*

Grammar Skill Instruction
- Capitalizing Names, *T55*

Day 4

Opening Routines: *T56–T57*

Preparing to Read *Wigs in a Box*
- Building Background, *T58*
- Story Vocabulary, *T58, Practice Book, 66*
- Get Set to Read, *T58*
- Strategy/Skill Preview, *T59*

Reading the Anthology *Wigs in a Box*
- Comprehension/Critical Thinking, *T61, T62, T63*
- Strategy Focus, *T61, T63*
- Responding, *T64, Practice Book, 67*

Reading the Poetry Link
- "Here Is the Beehive," *T65*

Phonics Application
- Anthology: *Wigs in a Box, T60–T63*

Spelling and Phonics
- Word Wheels with Short *o*, *T66*

Vocabulary
- Fun Things, *T66*

Writing Instruction
- Using Alliteration, *T67*
- *Practice Book,* 69

Day 5

Opening Routines: *T68–T69*

**Revisiting the Literature:
Comprehension Skill Instruction**
- Noting Details, *T70*

**Reading Skills Check:
Phonics Application, Assessment**
- Phonics Library, *Once Upon a Dig, T71*

Spelling and Phonics
- Spelling Words with Short *o*, *T72*

Word Pattern Board
- High-Frequency Words, *T72*

Writing
- Independent Writing Prompt, *T69*

Grammar Review
- Word Order in Sentences, *T73*

Viewing
- Compare and Contrast, *T73*

Daily Writing: Opening Routines, T21, T37, T45, T57, T69

See Universal Access Planning Chart on the following pages.

Week 1

Universal Access Plans
for Reaching All Learners

Grouping for Instruction

Day 1 | Day 2

30–45 minutes

With the Teacher

Extra Support
Teach—Use Extra Support Handbook

Day 1	Day 2
Preteach Phonics: Consonants *d* and *l* **Preteach** Phonics: Blending Short *o* Words **Preview** *Dot Fox* ▪ Extra Support Handbook pp. 46–47	**Preteach** Preteach Comprehension: Noting Details **Preview** *Bob Pig and Dan Ox* ▪ Extra Support Handbook pp. 48–49

Working Independently

On Level
Use Classroom Management Handbook

Challenge
Use Challenge Handbook

English Language Learners
Use Classroom Management Handbook or Challenge Handbook

Day 1	Day 2
Independent Activities For each group, assign appropriate activities—your own or those in the handbooks listed below. Then get students started on their independent work. ▪ Classroom Management Handbook pp. 26–33 ▪ Challenge Handbook pp. 16–19	See plan for Day 1 **Monitor** Answer questions, if necessary.

30–45 minutes

With the Teacher

English Language Learners
Teach—Use Handbook for English Language Learners

Day 1	Day 2
Preteach Where We Live **Preteach** Big Book, *To Be a Kid* **Preteach** Phonics: Consonants *d, w, l, x* ▪ Handbook for ELL pp. 50–51	**Preteach** Time of Day **Preteach** Get Set to Read; *The Box* **Preteach** High-Frequency Words: *in, once, upon, what* ▪ Handbook for ELL pp. 52–53

Working Independently

On Level
Use Classroom Management Handbook

Challenge
Use Challenge Handbook

Extra Support
Use Classroom Management Handbook

Day 1	Day 2
Independent Activities Students can continue their assigned activities, or you can assign new activities from the handbooks below. ▪ Classroom Management Handbook pp. 26–33 ▪ Challenge Handbook pp. 16–19	See plan for Day 1 **Monitor** Partner Extra Support students, if needed.

Independent Activities

Classroom Management Handbook
- Daily Activities
- Grouping
- Management

Resources for Reaching All Learners

Extra Support Handbook
- Daily Lessons
- Preteaching and Reteaching
- Skill Support

Handbook for English Language Learners
- Daily Lessons
- Language Development
- Skill Support

Challenge Handbook
- Independent Activities
- Instructional Support

Day 3

Reteach High-Frequency Words
Preview The Box

- Extra Support Handbook   pp. 50–51

See plan for Day 1

Check in
Reinforce instruction, if needed.

Preteach Ownership
Preteach Get Set to Read; Wigs in a Box
Reteach High-Frequency Words: two, three, four, and five

- Handbook for ELL   pp. 54–55

See plan for Day 1

Check in
Reinforce instruction, if needed.

Day 4

Reteach Phonics: Consonants d, w, l, x
Reteach Phonics: Blending Short o Words
Preview Wigs in a Box

- Extra Support Handbook   pp. 52–53

See plan for Day 1

Check in
Regroup English learners, if needed.

Preteach Jobs
Reteach The Box and Wigs in a Box
Reteach Phonics: Blending Short o Words

- Handbook for ELL   pp. 56–57

See plan for Day 1

Monitor
How well are challenge projects progressing?

Day 5

Reteach Comprehension: Noting Details
Revisit Dot Fox, Bob Pig and Dan Ox, The Box, and Wigs in a Box

- Extra Support Handbook   pp. 54–55

See plan for Day 1

Build confidence
Reinforce successful independent work.

Preteach Pulling It All Together
Reteach Grammar: Capitalizing Names

- Handbook for ELL   pp. 58–59

See plan for Day 1

Share work
Allow students time to share work.

Managing Small Groups

Small-Group Resources

Books for Small-Group Reading

Decodable

- Phonics Library
- I Love Reading Books

Easy

- On My Way Practice Reader

On Level

- Theme Paperback

Challenge

- Little Big Book

Other Resources

- Literature Resources, Grade 1
- Level 1.1–1.2 Practice Book

Center Activities

▶ Word Booklets   ▶ Making Puzzles

▶ A Friendship Book   ▶ Playing a Game

Sample Small-Group Schedule

Independent Work

▶ Independent Reading

▶ Phonics Library Stories

▶ Center Activities

▶ Practice Book pages

Teacher-Led Group

▶ Books for Small-Group Reading

▶ Vocabulary Speed Drills

Daily Fluency Building

Children need to read leveled texts fluently before moving on to higher levels of challenge. Daily Fluency Building, as supported by the Little Big Book lesson on T34–T35, facilitates the successful application of reading strategies and consolidates skills, allowing children to move toward independence in reading.

Suggestions for Daily Fluency Building		
Extra Support	**On Level**	**Challenge**
DAY 1 **Partner Reading** • Reread Anthology, Phonics Library, and I Love Reading Books selections	**Teacher-Supported Reading** • Phonics Library	**Independent Reading** • Books from Bibliography • Literature Resources
DAY 2 **Teacher-Supported Reading** • On My Way Practice Reader: *Five Big Boxes*	**Partner Reading** • Books from Bibliography • Literature Resources	**Partner Reading** • Reread the Little Big Book: *To Be a Kid*
DAY 3 **Independent Reading** • Reread On My Way Practice Reader: *Five Big Boxes* • Reread Anthology, Phonics Library, and I Love Reading Books selections	**Teacher-Supported Reading** • On Level Theme Paperback: *"What Is That?" Said the Cat*	**Independent Reading** • Check in with teacher after reading the Little Big Book: *To Be a Kid*
DAY 4 **Teacher-Supported Reading** • Phonics Library	**Independent Reading** • Reread On Level Theme Paperback: *"What Is That?" Said the Cat* • Reread Anthology selections	**Independent Reading** • Reread Anthology selections • Literature Resources
DAY 5 **Partner Reading** • Books from Bibliography • Literature Resources	**Independent Reading** • Books from Bibliography • Literature Resources	**Teacher-Supported Reading** • Phonics Library

Technology

Education Place

www.eduplace.com
Log on to Education Place for more activities relating to *Surprise!*

Book Adventure

www.bookadventure.org This Internet reading-incentive program provides thousands of titles for students to read

Management Routine

Workboards Use an Activity Workboard to show the activities children can work on if they are not meeting with you in a group. Workboards can be written on the board or created from pocket charts, velcro, and magnets.

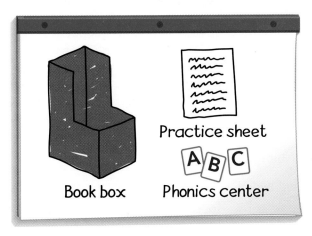

Book box

Practice sheet

A B C

Phonics center

Instructional Routine

Word Booklets Copy and cut out **Blackline Masters** 199–200. Use the word *pig* to show children what to do.

- Write the word *pig* on the first line.
- Draw a picture of a pig to illustrate the word.

Tell children to make several words with short *i* and illustrate them. Then children can bind the pages together to make their own Word Booklets. Children may choose to make separate booklets for each short vowel.

Center Activities

Phonics and Language

Word Booklets Have children work independently to make the Word Booklets. They can use **Blackline Masters** 199–200 to create their own pages. Once their booklets are completed, children can get together with partners or in small groups to share them.

Materials
- **Blackline Masters 199–200**
- safety scissors
- crayons
- pencils

Writing and Technology

A Friendship Book Children can staple or tie several sheets of paper together to make their own blank Friendship Books. Children can pass the books to their friends for autographing and message-writing.

Materials
- drawing paper (cut into fourths)
- crayons or markers
- stapler

Creative Arts

Making Puzzles Children can surprise friends with homemade puzzles. Children cut large pictures from magazines, mount them on oaktag, and then cut up the pictures to form puzzle pieces. Caution children to put paste on every part of the picture when mounting it so that the oaktag will stick when they are cutting their picture into puzzle pieces.

Materials
- magazines
- safety scissors
- glue or paste
- oaktag

Social Studies

Playing a Game Suggest that children play games with their friends. They might play a board game or a card game. Talk with children beforehand about how to take turns politely. After children play, have them report the results. Encourage them to tell not only how they played the game but also what courtesies they observed.

Materials
- classroom board or card games

Day at a Glance

Learning to Read

Reading the Big Book, *T22–T25*

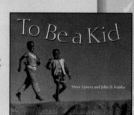

✓ **Comprehension:**
Noting Details

• **Reading Strategy:**
Question

Phonics Instruction, Practice, Application
T26–T29

✓ **Review** *d, w, l, x*

✓ **Blending Short** *o* **Words**

• **Phonics Library:** *Dot Fox*

• **I Love Reading Books: Books 10–14**

Word Work

Spelling and Phonics, *T30*

• **Letters and Sounds:** *d, l*

• **Penmanship**

Word Pattern Board, *T30*

Writing & Language

Independent Journal Writing, *T31*

Listening and Speaking, *T31*

• **Sharing Information**

Opening

Daily Message

Note: Beforehand, hide the Big Book *To Be a Kid* in a box. After reading the Daily Message, have children guess what the surprise is.

Use the Daily Message for a quick review of high-frequency words, phonics, and language skills.

■ Read the message aloud, pointing to each word as it is read.

■ Call on a few children to find and circle examples of consonants *d, l,* and *x.* Have children tell where in the word—beginning, middle, or end—each of these consonants appears.

■ Have children find and underline the high-frequency words *a, and, have, the,* and *Who.*

> Good Morning, Children! Today is a new day, and I have a surprise for you. My surprise is in the box. I hope you will like it. Who can guess what the surprise is?

Count Them!

Have children count the number of sentences in the Daily Message.

123

Concepts of Print

Emphasize through modeling:
• where one sentence ends and another begins
• end punctuation
• capital letters to begin new sentences

Routines

Daily Phonemic Awareness

Blending Phonemes: Blend the Rhyme

- Say: *I'm going to say a rhyme. Listen carefully to the last word of the rhyme! I will say the sounds in it. You blend the sounds together and say the word.*

- Say: *Mike is <u>big</u>. He drives a / r // ĭ // g /. Blend the sounds. Raise your hand when you know the word.* (rig)

- Continue with the following rhymes:

  Jack and <u>Jill</u> went up the / h // ĭ // l /. (hill)

  Peculiar <u>Pam</u> eats lots of / h // ă // m /. (ham)

  Do not <u>stop</u>. Let's reach the / t // ŏ // p /. (top)

  I can <u>tap</u>. I can / r // ă // p /. (rap)

  Put the <u>pin</u> in that / b // ĭ // n /. (bin)

Daily Independent Reading

Daily independent exploration and reading of books will increase children's experiences with print.

- Bibliography, pages T4–T5

  Choose books from this list for children to read, outside class, for at least twenty minutes a day.

- Little Big Book *To Be a Kid*

- Reread I Love Reading Books, Review Books 5–9

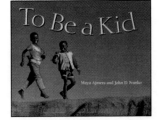

Daily Prompt for Independent Writing

Use the prompt below, or allow children to write about a topic of their choice. Encourage them to use what they know about letters and sounds to record their ideas.

I like to race trucks.

- Draw and write about something you like to do with your friends.

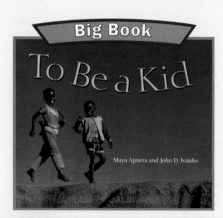

Big Book

To Be a Kid

Maya Ajmera and John D. Ivanko

Purpose • oral language development
• reading strategies • comprehension skills

Selection Summary:
This photo-essay explores how children from all over the world are alike in many ways. Children go to school, play, have friends, and interact with families.

Key Concept:
• **Kids all over the world have similar needs and wants.**

Reaching All Students
English Language Learners

English language learners may have difficulty with the gerunds and the idioms in the selection. As you read, pause to discuss the *-ing* word that follows *means* on each page. Explain idioms such as *spending time* (p. 8), *dancing your heart out* (p. 16), and *goofing off* (p. 20). Explain that the verb *last* on page 22 means "continue."

Reading the Big Book
Oral Language and Comprehension

▶ **Building Background**

Introduce the Big Book by reading aloud the title and the names of the authors. Explain that this book is about children all over the world.

Strategy Preview:
Question

Teacher Modeling Read aloud the Strategy Focus question on Big Book page 5: *What would you like to find out from this story?* Model how to use the question strategy.

Think Aloud

Before I read To Be a Kid, *I think about what I want to find out as I read. I ask myself, "Where do all the children in the story live?" As I read, I'll look for answers to this question. I'll also ask more questions about the children.*

Have children look at the first few pages of the story and ask questions about things they want to find out from the story.

✓ **Comprehension Skill Preview:**
Noting Details

Show children a few more of the photographs in the Big Book. Point out that all the photographs in this book were taken in different parts of the world. Children should pay special attention to the photos as you read the text.

▶ **Teacher Read Aloud**

Have children look at the pictures and listen as you read. Allow them to chime in and allow time for children to note details in the photographs.

Concepts of Print (Big Book, pages 8-9) Point to the labels and explain that each picture on pages 8–9 has a label. The label names the country where the people in the picture live.

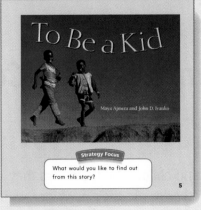

To Be a Kid

Maya Ajmera and John D. Ivanko

Strategy Focus

What would you like to find out from this story?

5

Big Book page 5

To be a kid in . . .

7

Big Book pages 6–7

To be a kid means being carried by those who love you and spending time with your family.

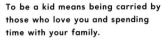

Senegal

Nepal

Portugal

United States

Israel

Canada

Philippines

8   9

Big Book pages 8–9

To be a kid means going to school and learning lots of new things.

Pakistan

South Africa

Russia

Philippines

Marshall Islands

Ethiopia

10   11

Big Book pages 10–11

To be a kid means walking home together, sharing a story, having a cool snack on a hot summer day, or marching in a parade.

Bolivia

South Africa

Ecuador

Denmark

Botswana

Bolivia

12   13

Big Book pages 12–13

To be a kid means playing ball, running races, going skating, riding a merry-go-round, or playing a board game.

Mexico

France

France

Sweden

India   Mexico

United States

14   15

Big Book pages 14–15

To be a kid means painting beautiful pictures, sharing the joy of music, or dancing your heart out.

South Africa

Poland   Peru

China

United States

United Kingdom   Ireland

16   17

Big Book pages 16–17

To be a kid means taking care of animals.

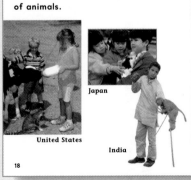

Japan

Haiti

United States   India

Ecuador   Mongolia

18   19

Big Book pages 18–19

Reading the Big Book: *To Be a Kid*   T23

Discussion Tips

- Display and review the How to Speak and How to Listen charts.

(**Reading the Big Book,** continued)

Oral Language and Comprehension

> ## ▶ Responding

Retelling Remind children of the things they wanted to find out from the story, and discuss whether or not their questions were answered. Next, display pages 14–15 and read aloud the text: "To be a kid means playing ball..." Point out that the photos show different ways of playing ball. Have children use the details provided by the photos to identify how kids in different countries play ball.

As you page through the story from beginning to end, have children use the photos to retell the story.

Literature Discussion Circle Review *How to Speak* and *How to Listen* before posing the questions below.

- *What do you think it means to be a kid?*

- *How are the kids in this book alike? How are they different?*

- *The book says, "To be a kid means goofing off and acting silly." Do you agree? Do you think it's okay to act silly sometimes?*

Reading the Little Big Book For children who are ready to read independently, there is a five-day lesson plan on pages T34–T35 for using the **Little Big Book,** *To Be a Kid.*

Reaching All Students
Extra Support

Responding Reinforce that *To Be a Kid* is about things kids like to do and about things they need—such as love. Have children take turns completing this sentence: "I'm a kid and I like to ___."

Reaching All Students
Challenge

Help children locate on a globe some of the countries mentioned in the selection.

Reaching All Students
English Language Learners

Beginning/Preproduction Ask English language learners to say what the people in the photos are doing.
Early Production and Speech Emergence Ask children to find the names of their parents', friends', or classmates' home countries.
Intermediate and Advanced Ask children whose parents' home countries are represented in the photos to add any information they can about those countries, or help children compile a list of all the home countries represented in your class.

DAY 1

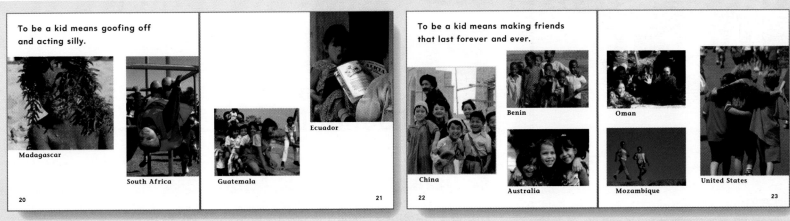

To be a kid means goofing off and acting silly.

Madagascar

South Africa

Guatemala

Ecuador

20

21

To be a kid means making friends that last forever and ever.

China

Benin

Australia

Oman

Mozambique

United States

22

23

Big Book pages 20–21

Big Book pages 22–23

Reading the Big Book: *To Be a Kid*

Phonics

✓ Consonants d, w, l, x

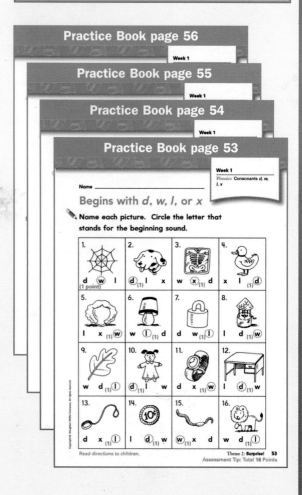

Practice Book page 56

Practice Book page 55

Practice Book page 54

Practice Book page 53

▶ Develop Phonemic Awareness

Blend Phonemes Read the poem aloud. Say: *I have a word from the poem. Listen:* /f//ŏ//x/. Have children say the individual sounds, blend them, and then say the word *fox*. Repeat with: /d//ŏ//t/ *(dot)*, /b//ŏ//x/ *(box)*, /l//ŏ//t/ *(lot)*, /r//ŏ//d/ *(rod)*, /w//ă//g/ *(wag)*, /t//ŏ//t/ *(tot)*.

> Willy was a little fox;
> His fur was soft and red.
> Danny was a little tot
> Who took that fox to bed.

▶ Connect Sounds to Letters

Introduce the Sound/Spelling Cards Display **Large Sound/Spelling Card** *duck* and have children name the picture. Point to the letters *Dd*. Tell children that a *d* stands for the /d/ sound at the beginning of *duck*. Have children chant /d/, /d/, /d/ as you point to the letter. Repeat with the *worm, lion*, and *fox* cards, explaining that *x* stands for the /ks/ sounds at the end of *fox*.

Dd

Distribute the punchout sound/spelling cards. Explain that the sounds for *d* and *l* can come at the beginning or at the end of words, but that the /w/ sound for *w* comes at the beginning of a word and the /ks/ sounds for *x* come at the end of a word. Say *dŏt*, emphasizing the /d/. Have children say the beginning sound in *dot* and hold up the letter that stands for that sound. Repeat for final *d* with *nod*. Continue, asking children what sound they hear at the beginning or end of a word and what letter stands for that sound. Say these words without emphasizing the sounds: *win, tail, dog, six, late, walk, den, box, bed, lap*.

Check Understanding Hold up each **Large Sound/Spelling Card** and call on individuals to say a word that begins or ends with that letter's sound.

▶ Connect Sounds to Spelling and Writing

Say: *Listen as I say* dig. *What sound do you hear at the beginning of* dig? *What letter should I write to spell that sound?* (*d*) Model writing the letter *d*. Have several children write *d* on the board as they say /d/. Repeat for *w, l*, using *we, like*. Then have children tell you what letter to write for the last sound in *sad, seal, wax*.

Practice Book pages 53–56 support this skill.

Phonics

✓ Short o

▶ Connect Sounds to Letters

Introduce the Sound/Spelling Card Display **Large Sound/Spelling Card** *ostrich.* Have children name the picture. Point to the letters *Oo.* Tell children that *o* is a vowel that stands for the /ŏ/ sound at the beginning of *ostrich.* Have them chant /ŏ/,/ŏ/,/ŏ/ as you point to the letter. Explain that /ŏ/ can be at the beginning of a word, as in *ostrich,* or in the middle of a word, as in *box.*

Write the letter *o* on the board. Then display **Picture Card** *box.* Say *bŏŏŏx,* elongating the /ŏ/ sound. Ask children what sound they hear in the middle of the word. Explain that *o* stands for the /ŏ/ sound in the middle of *box.*

Check Understanding Ask children to hold up punchout sound/spelling card *ostrich* when they hear a word that has the /ŏ/ sound. Then say *ostrich, shop, egg, job, on, lamp, cot, moth, ox, cut, hill, top, Bob, lock, map.*

▶ Connect Sounds to Spelling and Writing

Tell children that you want to write *on.* Together, say each sound in *on* and blend to say the word: /ŏ//n/, *on.* Then, draw two boxes on the chalkboard. As children say the first sound in *on,* model writing *o* in the first box. Then ask what sound comes after /ŏ/ in *on* and what letter stands for the /n/ sound. Model writing *n* in the second box. Then draw three boxes.

- Say *fox.* Ask: **What sound do you hear at the beginning of fox? What letter should I write in the first box?** Write *f.*

- Ask: **What sound do you hear next in fox?** Call on a child to write *o* in the second box.

- Ask: **What sounds do you hear at the end of fox? What letter should I write in the last box?** Write *x.*

Follow the same steps with the words *dot, dog, box, nod, mop, pot.*

Practice Book Page 57 supports this skill.

MATERIALS

- punchout sound/spelling card *ostrich*
- **Picture Card** *box*

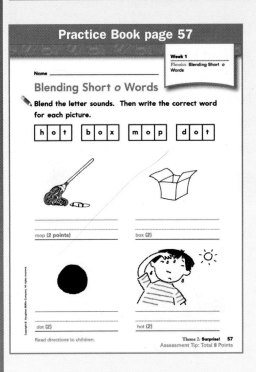

Practice Book page 57

Teacher's Note

Children may pronounce words such as *dog* with either the /ô/ sound or the /ŏ/ sound. Both pronunciations are acceptable.

UNIVERSAL ACCESS

Reaching All Students

English Language Learners

Make sure English language learners understand the meanings of the words you are writing. To help ensure understanding, have volunteers act out *nod* and *on.* Use **Picture Cards** for *pot, dog, box, mop* and *dot.* Have children make their own labeled drawings where possible.

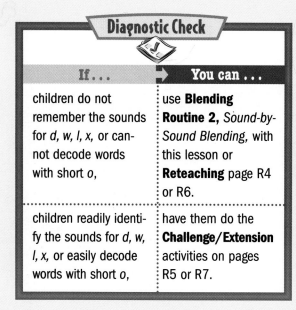

(**Phonics,** *continued*)

 Blending Short o Words (VC, CVC)

▶ **Connect Sounds to Letters**

Display **Large Letter Cards** *d, l, t,* and *x.* Have children name each letter and say its sound. Tell children that today they will read some words with these letters, but that first they need a vowel letter. Display **Large Letter Card** *o.* Remind children that *o* often stands for the /ŏ/ sound.

Blending Routine 1 Place **Large Letter Cards** *l, o,* and *t* together. Point to each letter in a sweeping motion as you model how to blend: *lllŏŏŏt, lot.* Repeat, having children blend the sounds and pronounce the word with you. Then have children blend and pronounce the word on their own. Call on volunteers to use *lot* in a sentence. Repeat this routine with the word *ox.*

Check Understanding Display **Large Letter Cards** *n, o,* and *t.* Have children blend *not* as you point to the letters.

Mixed Practice Write *got* and ask children to blend the sounds to read the word. Repeat for *ax, cot, wig, lap, dip, at, hop,* and the sentence *Bob Fox did not win.*

▶ **Connect Sounds to Spelling and Writing**

Distribute punchout trays and letter cards *f, h, n, o, p, t, x.* Say *pot* and have children repeat it. Ask: **What is the first sound? Put the letter that stands for that sound on your tray.** Continue to spell the word sound by sound. Then write the word on the board and have children check their work. Repeat for the words *fox, on, hot, top.* Then dictate this sentence for children to write: *Tom Fox got hot.*

Practice Book Pages 58–59 support this skill.

▶ **Practice/Apply**

Have children complete **Practice Book** pages 53–59 independently, with a partner, or in small groups. Then have them read **I Love Reading Books,** Books 10–14.

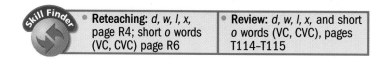

Skill Finder	• **Reteaching:** *d, w, l, x,* page R4; short *o* words (VC, CVC) page R6	• **Review:** *d, w, l, x,* and short *o* words (VC, CVC), pages T114–T115

Reading

▶ Phonics/Decoding Strategy

Distribute the **Phonics Library** story *Dot Fox*. Ask children to tell what is happening in the picture on page 5.

Teacher Modeling Use **Poster A** to review the steps of the Phonics/Decoding Strategy. Then model how to use the strategy to read the story title.

Think Aloud

I see two words in the title. I look at the first word and see the letters D, o, t. I put the sounds together: /d/ /ŏ/ /t/, Dot. That is a name I know. Then I look at the second word. I think about the sounds for the letters and blend the sounds: /f/ /ŏ/ /ks/, Fox. Fox makes sense and is a word I know. I put the two words together: Dot Fox. I think this story will be about a fox named Dot!

Phonics/Decoding Strategy

1. Look at the letters from left to right.
2. Think about the sounds for the letters.
3. Blend the sounds to read the word.
4. Ask yourself:
   Is it a word I know?
   Does it make sense in what I am reading?

HOUGHTON MIFFLIN
Reading
A Legacy of Literacy

Poster A

Tell children to look for letters that they know as they read the rest of the story independently or take turns reading with a partner.

Reading the Decodable Book If children have difficulty, remind them to look at each letter and sound out the word. Encourage them to sound out the words silently "in their heads." If necessary, coach them in applying the strategy to words such as *lot*.

- **What are the letters from left to right?** (l, o, t)
- **What sound does each letter stand for?** (/l/, /ŏ/, /t/)
- **Say each sound and hold it until you say the next sound. What is the word?** (lllŏŏŏt, lot)
- **Is** lot **a word you know? Does it make sense in the story?**

Oral Language Discuss the following questions with children. Have them speak in complete sentences.

- **What does Dot Fox's wig look like?**
- **Why does Dot Fox get hot?** (She gets hot because she runs a lot.)
- **How does the squirrel help Dot?** (The squirrel cools her off with a fan.)

Phonics Library

Purposes for decodable text
- applying phonics skills

Dot Fox
by Denise Zimmer
illustrated by Dominic Catalano

Dot Fox got a wig.

5

Dot Fox ran a lot.

6

Dot Fox got hot.

7

Dot Fox got a fan.

8

Home Connection

A **take-home version** of *Dot Fox* is available in the **Phonics Library Blackline Masters**. At the end of the day, children can take the story home to read with their families.

Word Work

Day 1

Spelling and Phonics

Letters and Sounds: d, l

Display **Large Sound/Spelling Cards** *duck* and *lion.* Review their letters and sounds. Then model how to write *d* and *l.*

■ Tell children they will practice spelling.

■ Display the **Picture Cards** one at a time in random order. Have children write the letter that stands for each beginning sound.

Have children complete **Practice Book** page 60.

Penmanship For children who need extra practice, model how to write lower case *l* and *d.* Have children practice writing the letters. Then have them practice writing the words *lot* and *dot.* Compare the words, noting the difference between the *l* and the *d.*

Two penmanship models (continuous stroke, ball and stick) are available in the **Practice Book** (pp. 198–205) and the **Teacher's Resource Blackline Masters** (pp. 143–194).

Word Pattern Board

Words with Short o Post the word *ox* on the Word Pattern Board. Point to *ox,* and have children "clap and spell" the word: *o-x, ox!*

■ Hold up word card *ox,* and pick a child to read the word. "Clap and spell" the word: *o-x, ox!* Repeat with *box* and *fox.*

■ Ask how all the words are alike. (They rhyme. They all have *ox.*) Tell children that knowing how to spell *ox* will help them spell the words *box* and *fox.* Post the word cards with *box* and *fox* on the Word Pattern Board.

Follow a similar procedure with the words *dot, lot, cot, pot, hot, got,* and *rot.*

OBJECTIVES

Children:

● **Spelling and Phonics** name and write the letters *d* and *l*

● **Word Pattern Board** review words with short *o*

MATERIALS

Phonics and Spelling

● **Large Sound/Spelling Cards** *duck, lion*

● **Picture Cards** *desk, dive, dog, doll; lamp, leaf, lip, log*

● teacher-made word cards with *ox, box, fox; dot, lot, cot, pot, hot, got, rot*

Practice Book page 60

···· **Houghton Mifflin Spelling and Vocabulary** ····
Correlated Instruction and Practice pp. 28, 31

 # Writing

Independent Journal Writing

Have children write in their journals. They may choose to

- respond to the daily writing prompt on page T21
- do some free writing

Word Pattern Board Remind children to look on the Word Pattern Board for help with spelling words.

Phonetic Spelling Encourage children to use what they know about letters and letter sounds to record their ideas.

Listening and Speaking

Sharing Information

Remind children that in *To Be a Kid,* they read about boys and girls from countries all over the world. They learned that kids from other places are very much like themselves.

- Reread the section of the book that tells what games and sports kids like to play.

- Have each child draw pictures of his or her favorite game or sport. Tell children to write their names on their pictures.

- Have a sharing time, in which children take turns holding up their pictures, telling who they are, and describing the activities they have chosen.

- Group children with similar interests. Have those children meet in small groups to talk more about their favorite games and sports.

Technology

Type to Learn™ Jr.

Children may use **Type to Learn™ Jr.** to familiarize themselves with the computer keyboard. ©*Sunburst Technology Corporation, a Houghton Mifflin Company. All Rights reserved.*

Reaching All Students
English Language Learners

Connect the concept of children from other places being very similar to the diverse cultures represented in your class. Encourage children to ask more proficient children from the same language background for help with names of favorite games and sports in English. If they have trouble, suggest that children demonstrate the game or sport. Help them come up with the name in English for the same or a similar activity.

Easy

Five Big Boxes
by Irma Singer
Illustrated by Karen Schmidt

Houghton Mifflin

Story Summary
Dot Fox fits five gifts in five boxes for her friends.

Reaching All Students
English Language Learners

During picture walks, tap children's prior knowledge by asking them to tell what they know about the topic of the story. Build background to strengthen children's understanding of what they are about to read.

Five Big Boxes
On My Way Practice Reader

▶ Preparing to Read

Building Background Read the title and author's name aloud and ask children what they think the book will be about. Have children share their own experiences of getting gifts in boxes.

▶ Supporting the Reading

Introducing the Book Page through the book with children. You may want to point out the following words: *boxes, time, everyone.* The suggestions below can help prepare children to read the story independently.

page 1:	Find the phrase *Once upon a time.* How many words are in the phrase?
page 3:	Two words rhyme with *fig.* Can you point to them? (wig, big)
page 6:	The number word on this page begins like *fill.* Can you find the word? (five)
page 8:	Can you find the word that means more than one box? (boxes)

Prompting Strategies Listen to and observe children as they read, and use prompts such as the following to help them apply strategies:

- *Look at the letters in this word from left to right.*
- *What sound does each letter stand for?*
- *Blend the sounds. What is the word?*

▶ Responding

Give children an opportunity to express their thoughts about the story. Were there any surprises in the story?

A small group of children can reread the story and act it out.

"What Is That?" Said the Cat

Theme Paperback

On Level

▶ Preparing to Read

Building Background Read the title aloud. Point out the sign on the box and read it aloud. Ask children to predict what they think might be in the box.

▶ Supporting the Reading

Introducing the Book Page through the book with children. The suggestions below can help prepare children to read the story independently.

Story Summary
Some animals are in for a surprise when they open a box labeled *Do Not Open.*

page 2: **Can you find the two rhyming words?** (fox, box)

page 5: **The words *know* and *crow* end with the letters *ow*. Can you point to each word?**

page 9: **Force begins like *fence*. Find the word *force*.**

Prompting Strategies Listen to and observe children as they read, and use prompts such as the following to help them apply strategies:

- *What sound does each letter stand for?*

- *Blend the sounds. What is the word?*

- *Does that word make sense here?*

- *What happens in this story? Can you tell it in your own words?*

▶ Responding

Ask children what they thought was the funniest part of the story. Be sure they understand that *See you later, Alligator* is an expression some people use instead of saying *Good-bye.*

Brainstorm and write a list of rhyming words, beginning with some of those from the story. Generate sentences using the rhyming words and print them on the chart. Children can choose a sentence to copy and then illustrate.

box	fox
cat	sat
frog	log
duck	stuck
bird	word

"I just sat," said the cat.

Challenge

Story Summary
This photo-essay explores the many ways in which children from all over the world are alike.

To Be a Kid
Little Big Book

Day 1 Preparing to Read

Building Background Display the Little Big Book and ask a child to identify aloud the title and author names. Remind children that you have read aloud the corresponding Big Book. Then have children page through the book.

Ask children to name things they like to do alone or with others. Point out similarities and differences in the activities children name.

Developing Story Vocabulary Print the italicized words on index cards. (Put *goofing off* on one card.) Display each card, read the word aloud, and have children repeat it. Read aloud the sentences and have children pantomime them.

Jan *carried* the book to her desk.
Tim is *sharing* his treat with me.
Ana rides on the *merry-go-round*.

Look at those *beautiful* flowers!
Al is *goofing off* because he is so tired!
You will be my friend *forever*.

Now shuffle the six cards. Display one card and have a volunteer read the word. Ask other children to find the word in the Little Big Book and raise their hand when they see it. The first child to correctly identify a page on which the word appears wins the card. Continue with the other cards.

Day 2 Reading the Little Big Book

Applying Phonics Skills Help children access the story text by using what they know about letters and letter sounds. Have them turn to these pages.

page 4:   **What letter would come first in the word *love*?** (l) **How do you know?** (*l* stands for the / l / sound.) **Point to the word *love* on the page.**

page 6:   **You know the word *go*. Which word is another form of *go*?** (going)

page 10:   **You hear the / ks / sounds in the middle of *Mexico*. Which picture label is the word *Mexico*?** (It is under the picture on the right.) **Which letter stands for that sound?** (x)

page 12:   **What letter would be first in *dancing*?** (d) **Find that word on the page. Look closely at the word. What letter stands for the / s / sound in dancing?** (c)

Day 2 continued...

Now have children turn to page 14. Model how to read an unfamiliar word, using this Think Aloud: *If I didn't know the last word in the sentence on this page, I would blend the first part: /ă//n/, that's* an. *I also know the sound for* i *and the other letters, so I can sound out the word,* an-i-mal-s. Animals. *When I reread the sentence,* animals *makes sense in it.*

Have partners read the book together and help each other identify words.

Day 3 · Rereading the Little Big Book

Applying Comprehension Skills Remind children that when they read the Little Big Book, they should look for important details to remember. Have them turn to pages 8 and 10, read each sentence, and look at the pictures. Then ask:

- **What are some ways that kids can share with one another?** (They can share a walk, a story, or a snack.)

- **What are some ways that kids can play together?** (They can play ball, run races, go skating, ride a merry-go-round, or play a board game.)

Independent Rereading Ask children to read *To Be a Kid* independently. Remind them that when they come across an unfamiliar word, they can look for letters they know to figure it out. If they read something that doesn't make sense, encourage them to reread it or to try another word before asking for help.

Day 4 · Revisiting the Little Big Book

Retelling the Story Review the main ideas from the Little Big Book. List those ideas on chart paper. Assign partners one idea from the chart and have them copy it on a sentence strip. Children can review the corresponding pictures in the Little Big Book and plan how to act out one or two examples. Then do a group retelling, asking partners to display and read aloud their strips before performing the actions.

Day 5 · Extending the Little Big Book

Moving Beyond the Story Point out that each sentence in the book began with *To be a kid means...* Discuss with children what they think it means to be a kid. Then ask each child to create a page, completing this sentence frame in a new way: *To be a kid means ____.* Have children illustrate their pages. Then bind the pages together to create a class book.

love your family,
go to school,
play together,
make art or music,
take care of animals,
act silly,
make friends

Day 2

Day at a Glance

Learning to Read

Reading Instruction, T38–T41

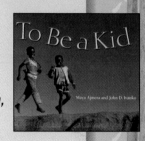

✓ **Comprehension:** Noting Details in *To Be a Kid*

✓ **High-Frequency Words:** *five, four, in, once, three, two, upon, what*

Phonics Application, T41

* **Phonics Library:** *Bob Pig and Dan Ox*
* **I Love Reading Books, Books 10–14**

Word Work

Spelling and Phonics, T42

* Matching Sounds to Letters: *w, x*
* Penmanship

Word Pattern Board, T42

Writing & Language

Shared Writing, T43

* Class Letter

✓ = Tested Skill

Opening

Daily Message

Note: Before sharing the Daily Message, put the Big Book *To Be a Kid* in a box by the door of your classroom.

Use the Daily Message for a quick review of high-frequency words, phonics, and language skills.

■ Read the message aloud, pointing to each word as it is read.

■ Have children find and circle examples of consonants *d, w, l,* and *x.*

■ Have children find and underline high-frequency words: *and, we, To, find, a, the.*

> Welcome, Boys and Girls! Today we will read <u>To Be a Kid</u> again. Can you find the book for me? Look in a box by the door.

Concepts of Print

* Point out the title of the Big Book in the first sentence.
* Have children match the words to the title of the actual book.

Daily Phonemic Awareness

Blending Phonemes: Name the Picture

- Into the box you used for the book, put the following **Picture Cards:** *bat, box, cat, cot, fan, fox.*

- Select the card for *bat* and name the picture, but hold it so the picture is hidden, segmenting the sounds: /b//ă//t/.

- Have children guess the picture name by blending the sounds together, saying the word naturally to themselves and raising their hands when they know the word.

- When all hands are up, show children the picture so that they can check their responses.

- Repeat this activity with the **Picture Cards** *box, cat, cot, fan,* and *fox.*

Daily Independent Reading

Have children share a book with a partner!

- Bibliography, pages T4–T5

  Choose books from this list for children to read, outside class, for at least twenty minutes a day.

- Books for Small-Group Reading, pages T32–T35

- Reread I Love Reading Books, Review Books 5–9

Daily Prompt for Independent Writing

Use the prompt below, or allow children to write about a topic of their choice. Encourage them to use what they know about letters and sounds to record their ideas.

I would feed flies to my frog.

- Draw and write about a pet you would like to take care of or about a friend you would like to have.

OBJECTIVES

Children

- name or describe important details in photographs
- name or describe important details in text

Big Book

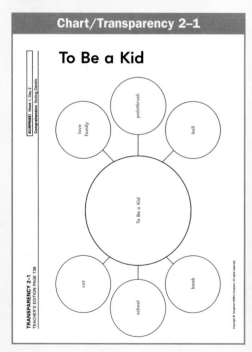

To Be a Kid

Maya Ajmera and John D. Ivanko

Chart/Transparency 2–1

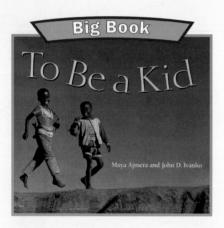

Comprehension
✓ Noting Details

▶ Rereading the Big Book

Setting a Purpose Remind children that *To Be a Kid* is about real boys and girls who live all over the world. Point out that the book tells about things the kids need and what they do. Have children look at the photos as you read the book again to learn more about these kids.

- As you reread the book, track the words on each two-page spread for children.

- Before turning to the next spread, point out the photographs and allow time for children to respond to them. You may also want to read the labels that tell what countries the people are from.

▶ Teach

Display the web shown on **Chart/Transparency 2–1**. In the center, write *To Be a Kid,* and read the title for children. If you wish, add a stick figure of a child.

- Reread the first sentence of the Big Book (page 8). Ask children what this part of the book tells us about being a kid. Draw a heart in one of the outer circles of the web. You may also want to write the words *love* and *family*, and read the words for children.

- Reread pages 10–11 and ask what this part of the book tells about being a kid. Draw a small schoolhouse in another outer circle. Ask children what label to write for this picture. (school)

- Continue through the book in this manner, adding to the web several more details from the selection. You might add pictures of a book, a ball, a paintbrush, a pet, and so on. (It's not necessary to add a picture for each and every detail; add just enough to give children something to talk about.)

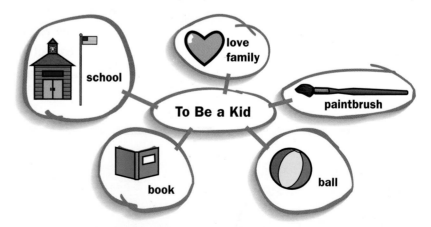

Practice

■ Have children use information from the web to tell about some of the details they noticed in *To Be a Kid*.

■ Have each child choose a photograph from the book and tell how the photograph shows what it is like to be a kid. You may wish to have children do this in small groups. Each group can then report back to the class by displaying the photo chosen and telling how it relates to the title *To Be a Kid*.

Apply

Choose one or both of the following activities:

■ Have children tell how they are like the children pictured in the book.

■ Have children work independently or with a partner to complete the activity on **Practice Book** page 61.

Themes 6, 9	**Revisiting:** pages T49, T50, T61, T62, T63, T64	**Reteaching:** page R22

Reaching All Students

Extra Support

Provide each child with a picture card.
Have the child name the card and then provide two or three details about the item pictured.

Diagnostic Check

If . . .	You can . . .
children cannot provide at least one important detail about a picture,	use the **Reteaching** lesson on page R22.
children can easily provide two or more important details about a picture,	have them do the **Challenge/Extension** activities on page R23.

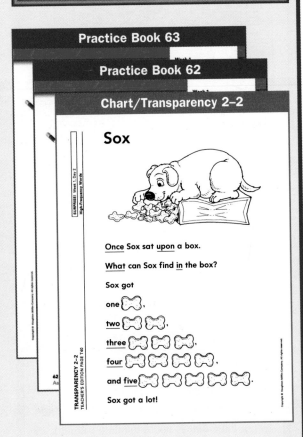

Practice Book 63

Practice Book 62

Chart/Transparency 2–2

Sox

Once Sox sat *upon* a box.

What can Sox find *in* the box?

Sox got

one,

two,

three,

four,

and *five*.

Sox got a lot!

✓ High-Frequency Words

▶ Teach

Write the high-frequency words *find, here,* and *one* on the chalkboard and review them. Ask which word tells how many of something. (*one*) Have a child write the numeral *1* on the chalkboard. Ask other children to continue writing numerals through *5*.

Tell children that they will now learn to read and spell eight new words that are used often in speaking, reading, and writing. Display **Chart/Transparency 2–2**, and have children follow along as you read the first two sentences.

- Point to the word *What*, and have children repeat it after you.

- Lead the class in a cheer in which you clap each letter as you spell and say the word: *w-h-a-t, what*.

- Repeat for the word *in*.

- Read the next set of sentences. For each number word, ask a child to count the number of dog biscuits. Then have all children clap and spell the words *once, upon, two, three, four,* and *five*.

- Have children match each number word with its corresponding numeral.

▶ Practice

- Write *one, two, three, four, five* on the chalkboard. Have children match each number word with the corresponding numeral.

- Write *in, once,* and *upon*. Call on children to read the words and use them in sentences.

- Write *Who* and *What* on the board, one word under the other. Tell children that these words often begin sentences. Point to a word, and ask a volunteer to read the word and then ask a question beginning with that word.

Word Pattern Board Post the words in the "New Words" section of the Word Pattern Board. Remind children to look on the Word Pattern Board when they are writing the new words.

▶ Apply

Have children work with partners to complete **Practice Book** pages 62 and 63.

| *Skill Finder* | Reteaching: page R16 | Review: Word Pattern Board, pages T42, T72 |

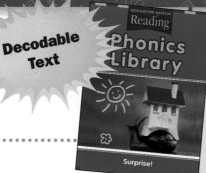

Reading

▶ Phonics/Decoding Strategy

Distribute the **Phonics Library** story *Bob Pig and Dan Ox*. Have children describe the pictures on pages 9–10.

Teacher/Student Modeling Ask children to tell how they read new words. Use **Poster A** to review the steps of the Phonics/Decoding Strategy. Choose someone to read the story title and tell how he or she read each word.

Assign children to read the story. Circulate as they read, offering support and encouragement.

Reading the Decodable Book If children have difficulty decoding words such as *lot*, help them apply the strategy.

- **What should you look at first?** (letters in the word)

- **How can you sound out the word?** (Blend the sounds /l/ /ŏ/ /t/.)

- **How can you decide if** lot *is the correct word?* (See if the word makes sense.)

Supply the words only when absolutely necessary.

Oral Language Have children respond in complete sentences to the following.

- **Where do Bob Pig and Dan Ox sit in this story?** (They sit in a big box.)

- **Do you think Bob Pig and Dan Ox are friends? Why do you think so?**

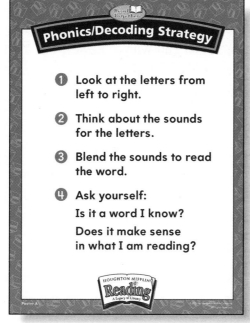

Phonics/Decoding Strategy

1. Look at the letters from left to right.
2. Think about the sounds for the letters.
3. Blend the sounds to read the word.
4. Ask yourself: Is it a word I know? Does it make sense in what I am reading?

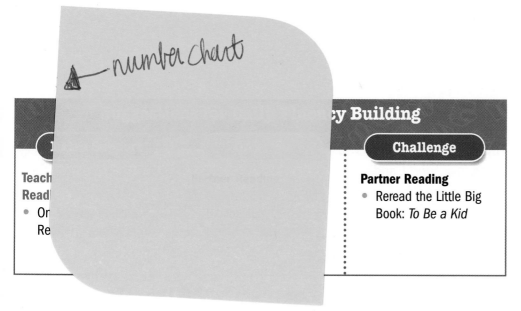

number chart

cy Building

Challenge

Partner Reading
- Reread the Little Big Book: *To Be a Kid*

Phonics Library

Purposes for decodable text
- applying phonics skills
- applying high-frequency words

Bob Pig and Dan Ox
by Virginia Houston
illustrated by Dominic Catalano

What can fit in a big, big box?

9

Bob Pig can fit.

10

Dan Ox can fit.

11

A lot can fit in a big, big box!

12

Home Connection

A take-home version of *Bob Pig and Dan Ox* is available in the **Phonics Library Blackline Masters.** At the end of the day, children can take the story home to read with their families.

DAY 2

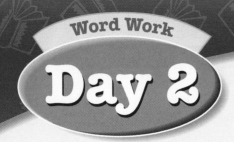
Spelling and Phonics
Matching Sounds to Letters: w, x

Display **Large Sound/Spelling Card** *worm,* and ask children to name the letter and say the sound. Model how to write the letter *w* on the board.

Next, display **Large Sound/Spelling Card** *fox.* Tell children that there are very few words that begin with *x,* but that there are some that end with *x.* Review the sounds for *x* at the end of a word, as in *six:* / ks /. Model how to write *x.*

- Tell children that they will practice some spelling.

- Display the **Picture Cards** one at a time in random order. First, have children write the letter that stands for the beginning sound in each picture name. Then have them write the letter that stands for the final sound.

Have children complete **Practice Book** page 64.

Penmanship For children who need extra practice, model how to write lowercase *w* and *x* on the board. Then have children practice writing the letters. You may also want to model how to write the word *wax,* and have children practice it.

Two penmanship models (continuous stroke, ball and stick) are available in the **Practice Book** (pp. 198–205) and the **Teacher's Resource Blackline Masters** (pp. 143–194).

Practice Book page 64

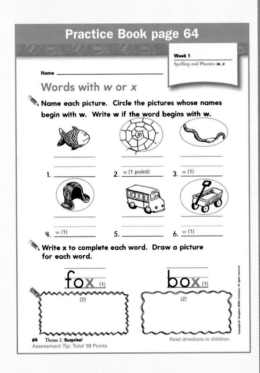

Name _____

Week 1
Spelling and Phonics w, x

Words with w or x

✎ Name each picture. Circle the pictures whose names begin with w. Write w if the word begins with w.

1.   2. w (1 point)   3. w (1)

4. w (1)   5.   6. w (1)

✎ Write x to complete each word. Draw a picture for each word.

fox (1)   box (1)
(2)   (2)

64 Theme 2: **Surprise!**
Assessment Tip: Total **10 Points**   Read directions to children.

Word Pattern Board

High Frequency Words Call attention to the "New Words" *five, four, in, once, three, two, upon,* and *what.* Clap and spell the new words. Emphasize that the words on the Word Pattern Board will help children as they read and write.

✏️ Shared Writing

A Class Letter

Ask children to tell about any letters they may have sent or received in the mail. Point out that almost everyone enjoys receiving letters—and that they will now write one together to send to their parents. In their letters, they will tell about some of the things they are doing at school.

- Brainstorm with children to make a list of some of the things they have done at school during the past few days. As each child makes a suggestion, write his or her name after the suggestion.

- On chart paper, write today's date, the greeting and (at the bottom) the closing of a letter.

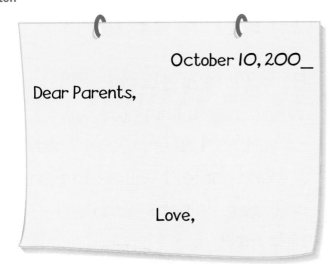

October 10, 200_

Dear Parents,

Love,

- Tell children you will begin the letter by writing a sentence. Write: *We can do a lot at school.* As you write, model how to write each word.

- Have children take turns dictating sentences to add to the letter, which may be like an extended list. Refer children to the list they helped to develop during brainstorming.

- Reread the finished letter aloud as children follow along.

- Point out the closing, and tell children that they will write their own names on a copy of the letter, which you will give them later.

Prepare copies of the letter for children to take home. Remind them to sign their names at the bottom.

OBJECTIVES ◎

Children

- dictate sentences to add to a class letter

- sign their own names to a copy of the class letter

MATERIALS

- chart paper

········· **Houghton Mifflin English** ··········
Correlated Instruction and Practice, p. 299

Reaching All Students

English Language Learners

As an alternative, write a group letter detailing how children are progressing with their English, including some of the new words they have learned.

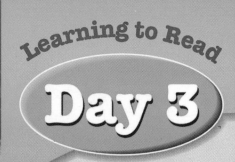

Day 3

Day at a Glance

Learning to Read

Reading the Anthology, T46–T51

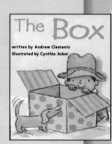

The Box
written by Andrew Clements
illustrated by Cynthia Jabar

☑ **Comprehension:** *Noting Details*

• **Reading Strategy:** *Question*

☑ **Applying Phonics and High-Frequency Words**

Phonics Review, T52–T53

☑ **Words with Short *i***

• **I Love Reading Books, Review Book 5**

Word Work

Spelling and Phonics, T54

• **Letters and Sounds:** *d, w, l, x,* Short *o*

• **Penmanship**

Vocabulary, T54

• **Number Words**

Writing & Language

Grammar, T55

• **Capitalizing Names**

 ☑ = **Tested Skill**

Opening

Daily Message

Use the Daily Message for a quick review of high-frequency words, phonics, and language skills.

■ Read the message aloud, pointing to each word as it is read.

■ Call on a few children to find and circle examples of consonants *d* and *l*. When a child circles a letter, ask where in the word it appears.

■ Call on volunteers to find and underline the words *and, What, we, a, two, three,* and *Who.*

> Hello, Girls and Boys!
> What do you think we will
> do today? Later, we will play
> a word game. I will need two
> or three helpers. Who will
> help me?

Concepts of Print

Ask children to point out any capital letters they see in the message. Review that we use a capital letter to begin a sentence. Ask if children recall any other times we use capital letters.

If necessary, write on the board the names of children who volunteer to help. Point out that you have used a capital letter to begin each person's name.

Daily Phonemic Awareness

Blending Phonemes: Riddles

Tell children that you have some word riddles. They should blend the sounds to form the word.

- Read the following clues:

  You put cocoa into it: / m // ŭ // g /. (*mug*)

  You clean the floor with it: / m // ŏ // p /. (*mop*)

  It rings: / b // ĕ // l /. (*bell*)

  It means the opposite of cold: / h // ŏ // t /. (*hot*)

  You ride it to school: / b // ŭ // s /. (*bus*)

  You use it to cool off: / f // ă // n /. (*fan*)

Daily Independent Reading

Have children reread stories from Theme 1 on their own.

- **Bibliography, pages T4–T5**

  Choose books from this list for children to read, outside class, for at least twenty minutes a day.

- **Books for Small-Group Reading, pages T32–T35**

- **Reread I Love Reading Books, Review Books 5–9**

Daily Prompt for Independent Writing

Use the prompt below, or allow children to write about a topic of their choice. Encourage them to use what they know about letters and sounds to record their ideas.

- **Draw and write about one of your favorite school activities.**

> I like it when we have plays. We tell stories.

Day 3

The Box

written by Andrew Clements
illustrated by Cynthia Jabar

Purpose • applying reading strategies, comprehension skills, phonics/decoding skills, high-frequency words, and critical thinking

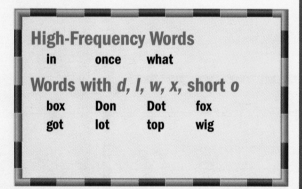

High-Frequency Words

in	once	what

Words with *d, l, w, x,* short *o*

box	Don	Dot	fox
got	lot	top	wig

Preparing to Read

▶ Building Background

Boxes Tell children to turn to Anthology page 133 and look at the picture of the boy with the box. Ask if children can guess what the boy will do with the box. Encourage children to tell about times they have used boxes to make things or to play a game.

▶ Using "Get Set to Read"

Call on individuals to read the words and sentences on Anthology pages 130–131. Ask children what things about each word helped them to read it.

- Did they recognize the letters?

- Did they blend the sounds for the letters?

- Did they recognize the word from the Word Pattern Board?

Get Set to Read

The Box

Words to Know

once	got
what	lot
box	on
Don	top
Dot	wig
fox	

Once Don and Dot got a big box. What can fit in the big box?

130

A wig can fit.
A fox can fit.
Can Don and Dot sit on top?

A lot can fit in the big box.

131

Anthology pages 130–131

Strategy & Skill Focus

▶ **Strategy Focus:**
Question

Teacher Modeling Have children turn to Anthology page 133. Read the selection title and the name of the author. To prepare children for the Question strategy, say:

Think Aloud

After I read this story, I will work with a partner. I will ask my partner a question. Then my partner will ask me a question. One question I might ask is this: "What does the boy do with the box?"

Quick Write Have children draw and write about something they want to find out about the box.

Purpose Setting Ask children to read to find out the answer to your question: *What does the boy do with the box?* Remind children also to use their other reading strategies as they read the selection.

✓ **Comprehension Skill Focus:**
Noting Details

Remind children to think about the important details of the story as they read it. Then they can use these details to ask questions and retell the story.

Strategy and Comprehension Skills Connection In order to engage in interactive questioning, children will need to note details provided by pictures and text.

Focus Questions

Have children turn to Responding on page 146. Read the questions aloud and tell children to keep them in mind as they read *The Box.*

Reaching All Students
English Language Learners

Make sure English language learners know what a wig is. If possible, show what one looks like. Have children say these words with you: *in, once, what, Dot, got, lot, box, Don, fox, top, wig.* Do a picture walk and have children find the *box, fox,* and *wig* in the story.

Preparing to Read: *The Box* (T47)

DAY 3

Learning to Read
Day 3

Reading the Anthology

Options for Reading

▶ **Universal Access** See the Classroom Management tips at the bottom of these pages for suggestions to meet individual needs during and after reading.

About the Author Andrew Clements was a teacher. He loved to read books to his class. Now he writes books and visits schools whenever he can.

About the Illustrator Cynthia Jabar is the illustrator of a number of books for children, including *Rain Song* and *Snow Dance*.

Key to Underlined Vocabulary
Words with *d, l, w, x*, short *o* ═══
High-Frequency Words ────

Meet the Author
Andrew Clements

Meet the Illustrator
Cynthia Jabar

132

Story 1

The Box
written by Andrew Clements
illustrated by Cynthia Jabar

133

Anthology pages 132–133

Once Don got a big box.

134

What can fit in the box?

135

Anthology pages 134–135

Reaching All Students
Classroom Management

On Level

Partner Reading Remind children of their purpose for reading. After reading, children should join the rest of the class to discuss: Comprehension/Critical Thinking, T49, T50; Noting Details, T50; Think About the Story, T51.

Challenge

Independent Reading Children can read the story independently and begin **Practice Book** page 65 before joining the rest of the class to discuss: Comprehension/Critical Thinking, T49, T50; Noting Details, T50; Think About the Story, T51

English Language Learners

Intermediate and Advanced Have partners alternate reading pages. After each page, children can name other objects they see in the illustrations. For English language learners at other proficiency levels, see Language Development Resources.

One tan <u>fox</u> can fit.

136

One pig in a <u>wig</u> can fit.

137

Anthology pages 136–137

One big hat can fit.

138

A <u>lot</u> can fit in the box.

139

Anthology pages 138–139

Comprehension/Critical Thinking

1 ✓ What was the box like when Don first got it? (It was empty; it was big.) **Noting Details**

2 ✓ What did Don put into the box? (one fox, one pig, one hat) **Noting Details**

3 **Strategy Focus: Teacher/Student Modeling** What question might you ask a partner about the things Don put into the box? (Possible answer: What kind of fox did Don put into the box?) **Question**

4 How are the tan fox, the pig in a wig, and the big hat all alike? (They are all things that belong to Don; they all fit into the box.) **Compare and Contrast**

Revisiting the Text

Concepts of Print

Display the word card *once*, and ask children to find this word on page 134. Point out that on page 134, *once* begins with a capital letter because it is the first word in a sentence.

DAY 3

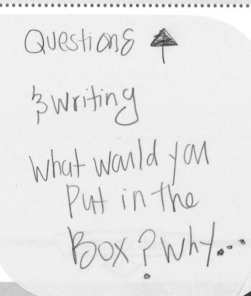

Questions ⬆

3 writing

What would you put in the Box? why...

children have difficulty noting details,	guide them in rereading the story and pointing out important details.
children have difficulty reading specific words,	coach them in using the Phonics/Decoding Strategy.

Reaching All Students
English Language Learners

Teacher-Supported Reading Take children on a picture walk of the story. Have them take turns reading in a small group. Use the Comprehension/Critical Thinking questions, as needed. After reading, they join the rest of the class to discuss: Comprehension/Critical Thinking, T49, T50; Noting Details, T50; Think About the Story, T51

Phonics/Decoding Strategy Coach children in the strategy, as needed.

Reading the Anthology: *The Box*   **T49**

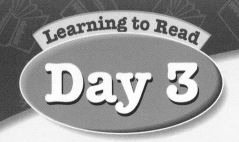

Learning to Read
Day 3

Comprehension/Critical Thinking

1.  Look at the picture on page 140. How is the box different now? (It has a bow on it.) **Noting Details**

2. Why did Don take the box to Dot's house? (He wanted to give Dot a gift.) **Cause and Effect**

3. How does Dot seem to feel about Don's gift? (very happy) **Noting Details**

4. ✓ **Strategy Focus: Student Modeling**
   What question would you ask a partner for page 145? (Children's questions will vary.) **Question**

5. How could you use what you know about letters and sounds to help you figure out this word (*fox*, page 142)? (Blend the sounds /f//ŏ//k//s/.) **Phonics/Decoding**

Revisiting the Text

Retelling the Story:
Noting Details

Have children summarize the story by telling what the box is like at the beginning of the story, how it changes during the story, and what it is like at the end of the story.

Dot got the box.
140

What can Dot find in the box?
141

Anthology pages 140–141

Dot can find a tan fox on top.
142

Dot can find a pig in a wig.
143

Anthology pages 142–143

 Reaching All Students
Extra Support

Writing Support for Responding Ask children to look around the classroom for ideas. Have each child choose one object that might fit in Don's box. Have the child take that object to his/her seat. Help children make labels for the objects, if they don't already have them. Children can use the objects and labels to draw and write.

Dot can find a big hat.

144

Don and Dot can fit!
A lot can fit in a box!

145

Anthology pages 144–145

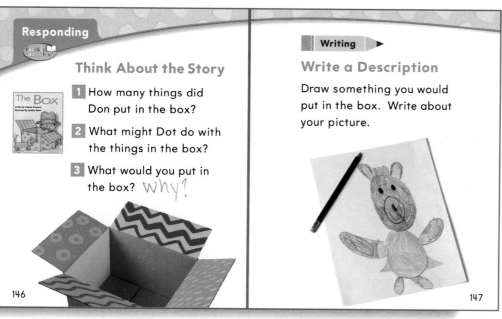

Responding

Think About the Story

The BOX

1 How many things did Don put in the box?

2 What might Dot do with the things in the box?

3 What would you put in the box? *why?*

Writing ▶

Write a Description

Draw something you would put in the box. Write about your picture.

146

147

Anthology pages 146–147

Reaching All Students

English Language Learners

Beginning/Preproduction Ask children: "What did Don put in the box for Dot?" Make a list on the board or on chart paper.

Early Production and Speech Emergence Use boxes of different sizes and ask children to decide what can and cannot fit in each box. In addition to classroom objects and people, ask about other things children have to recall the size of, such as an elephant or a television.

Intermediate and Advanced Work in two groups. Have each child in the first group take a turn and say in order what Don put in the box; have those in the second group say in order what Dot took out.

Responding

Think About the Story

Discuss the questions on Anthology page 146. Accept reasonable responses.

1 **Noting Details** Three

2 **Making Predictions** Dot may play with the things. She may pack them up and give them back to Don.

3 **Critical Thinking** Answers will vary.

★ **4** **Connecting/Comparing** What is the surprise in this story? (Don's giving the box to Dot; Dot and Dan are playing with and in the box.)

Comprehension Check

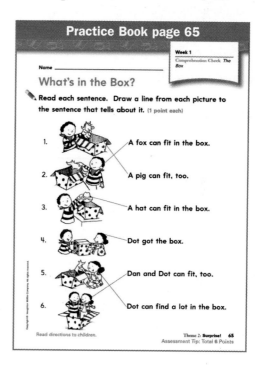

Student Self-Assessment

Help children assess by asking:

• What was easy for you as you read this story?

• Were you able to think of questions to ask about the story?

DAY 3

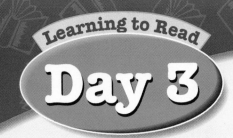

OBJECTIVES

Children

- review consonants *b, c, d, f, g, h, l, m, n, p, r, s, t, w, x*
- review short *i*
- read words with short *i* and known consonants

MATERIALS

- **Large Letter Cards** *b, c, d, f, g, h, i, l, m, n, p, r, s, t, w, x*
- punchout letters *b, c, d, f, g, h, i, l, m, n, p, r, s, t, w, x* for each pair of children
- punchout tray for each child
- teacher-made word cards *bib, big, bit, dig, fig, fin, fit, him, hit, kit, lip, lit, pin, pit, sip, sit, six, wig, win*
- **I Love Reading Books**, Review Books 5–9

Phonics Review

Words with Short i

▶ **Building Words**

Reviewing Consonants Display **Large Letter Cards** *b, c, d, f, g, h, l, m, n, p, r, s, t, w, x.* Remind children that they know the sounds for these letters. Have children name each letter and say its sound.

Reviewing Short *i* Tell children that today they will build some words with consonants they know and the vowel *i.* Display **Large Letter Card** *i* and tell children to say the short *i* sound, /ĭ/.

Playing "Make It, Read It" Invite children to play "Make It, Read It" with partners. To play:

- Place punchout letter cards for all known consonants face up on a table.

- Give each player a punchout tray and the letter card *i.*

- Players take turns choosing two cards from among those on the table and using the cards to build a consonant-vowel-consonant word with short *i.* (For example, the player chooses *h* and *m,* and makes the word *him.*) The player reads the word aloud and then keeps the two consonant cards. (If a real word is not made, or if the player cannot read the word, the consonant cards are returned, face up, to the table.)

- Play continues until as many words as possible have been formed. (To make the game more challenging, require children to use the words they have made in sentences.)

▶ Reading Short *i* Words

Playing "Hit or Miss" Invite children to play "Hit or Miss." To play:

- Randomly display the following word cards: *bib, big, bit, dig, fig, fin, fit, him, hit, kit, lip, lit, pin, pit, sip, sit, six, wig, win.*

- Arrange children in two groups, or teams.

- Team A chooses a word card and gives it to the first player on Team B. The child to whom the word is given must blend the sounds and read the word aloud. If the child is successful, his or her team "gets a hit" and scores one run.

- Team B then selects a card and gives it to the first player on Team A. Again, to score a run, the child receiving the card must blend and read the word.

- The team with the most runs wins the game.

- As children become more accurate, you might want to set a time limit for each turn.

Practice Have children read **I Love Reading Books**, Review Books 5–9.

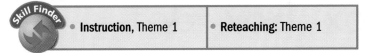

Skill Finder	
• Instruction, Theme 1	• Reteaching: Theme 1

Suggestions for Daily Fluency Building

Extra Support	On Level	Challenge
Partner Reading	**Teacher-Supported Reading**	**Independent Reading**
• Reread On My Way Practice Reader: *Five Big Boxes*	• On Level/Challenge Theme Paperback: *"What Is That?" Said the Cat*	• Check in with teacher after reading the Little Big Book: *To Be a Kid*
• Reread Anthology, Phonics Library, and I Love Reading Books selections		

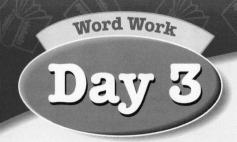

Word Work

Day 3

OBJECTIVES

Children

- **Spelling and Phonics** recognize and write the letters *d, w, l, x;* write words with short *o*

- **Vocabulary Skills** number words

MATERIALS

Spelling and Phonics

- **Large Sound/Spelling Cards** *duck, worm, lion, fox, ostrich*

- **Picture Cards** *dig, dot, fox, log, six, wig*

··· **Houghton Mifflin Spelling and Vocabulary** ···
Correlated Instruction and Practice, p.73

Spelling and Phonics

Words with: d, w, l, x; and Short o

Review the letters and sounds for *d, w, l, x,* and short *o* using **Large Sound/Spelling Cards** *duck, worm, lion, fox* and *ostrich.* Remind children how to write the letters by modeling on the chalkboard.

- Display **Picture Card** *dig,* and have children write the letter that stands for the beginning sound. Repeat for *wig* and *log.*

- Display **Picture Card** *six,* and have children write the letter that stands for the ending sounds.

- Display **Picture Cards** *fox* and *dot.* Say each word slowly, and ask a child to spell the word orally as you model how to write it. Then have children practice writing each word.

Penmanship For children who need extra practice, model how to write the word *ox.* Have children practice writing the word several times. You may also want to have children practice writing *box* and *dot.*

Two penmanship models (continuous stroke, ball and stick) are available in the **Practice Book** (pp. 198–205) and the **Teacher's Resource Blackline Masters** (pp. 143–194).

Vocabulary

Number Words

Reread pages 136–138 of *The Box.* Ask children to count the number of things that Dan put into the box.

- Write the numerals 1–3 in a column on the board. Beside each, write the number word: *one, two, three.* Have children say the numbers and read the words. Add the numerals 4–5 to the first column, and write *four* and *five.* Have children read the words with you.

- Ask each child to choose a number from one through five. Each child can write the numeral and the number word at the top of a sheet of drawing paper. Have children illustrate their numbers by drawing the corresponding number of objects (for example, five hats for the number 5).

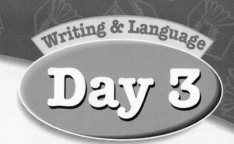

Grammar

Capitalizing Names

Ask if children recall the names of the boy and the girl in the story *The Box*. Write *Don* and *Dot* on the chalkboard. Ask what letter you have used to begin each name. (capital *D*) Then play a Name Game with children.

- Ask each child to write his or her first name on a strip of paper. Remind children to begin their names with capital letters—and to use lowercase letters for the remaining letters in their names.

- Put all the names in a box. Invite a child to come forward and draw a name from the box—without letting anyone else in the class see it.

- The child who has drawn the name then spells it, saying capital (letter name) for the first letter. If, for example, the child draws the name *Bill,* he or she would say: "Capital *B, i, l, l.*"

- Others in the class try to guess to whom the name belongs—before the owner of the name can retrieve it. Continue until all the names have been drawn and spelled.

Depending on the number of names in the box, you may want to spread the activity out over two or three days.

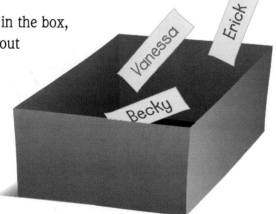

OBJECTIVES

Children

- use capital letters to begin the names of people

·········· **Houghton Mifflin English** ··········
Correlated Instruction and Practice, pp. 69–70

Reaching All Students

Extra Support

Extra Support Provide each child in the group with a capital letter card for the first letter of the child's name. Provide lowercase letters for the remaining letters in each child's name. Have children arrange the letters to spell their names. Then have each child clap and spell his/her own name and the name of a partner.

Day at a Glance

Learning to Read

Reading the Anthology, T58–T65

☑ **Comprehension:**
Noting Details

• **Reading Strategy:**
Question

☑ **Applying Phonics
and High-Frequency
Words**

Word Work

Spelling and Phonics, T66

• **Word Wheels with Short *o***

• **Penmanship**

Vocabulary, T66

• **Fun Things**

Writing & Language

Writing, T67

• **Using Alliteration**

 = **Tested Skill**

Opening

Daily Message

Use the Daily Message for a quick review of high-frequency
words, phonics, and language skills.

■ Read the message aloud, pointing to each word as it is read.

■ Call on children to find and circle examples of the consonants *d, w, l,* and
x. Have children tell where in the word each circled consonant appears.

■ Call on other children to find and underline words they can read, such as
we, a, The, too, five, in, and *One.*

> Good Morning, Children!
>
> Yesterday we read a story
> about a box. The story for
> today is about a box, too.
> The story has five animal
> characters in it. One is Pat
> Pig. Pat can really hit a ball!

Concepts of Print

Have children find the
name of a story character.
Point out that each word
in the character's name –
Pat Pig – begins with
a capital letter.

Count Them!

Have children count the sentences
in the message.

Daily Phonemic Awareness

Blending Phonemes: Seal's Words

■ Use the **Picture Card** *seal.* Say: *Remember Sammy Seal? Sammy, the talking seal, needs your help again to figure out a word he heard today. The word is / f // ĭ // n /. Blend the sounds together. Raise your hand when you know the word.* (fin)

■ Repeat this activity, segmenting the sounds for the word *lot.* Ask children to blend the sounds together and say the word.

■ Challenge a volunteer to provide a rhyming word, such as *pot*, to solve for Sammy Seal. Ask the volunteer to whisper the word to you. Segment the word. Ask the class to blend the word together. The volunteer can confirm their response.

Daily Independent Reading

Remind children to practice reading the Word Pattern Board.

■ Bibliography, pages T4–T5

 Choose books from this list for children to read, outside class, for at least twenty minutes a day.

■ Books for Small-Group Reading, pages T32–T35

■ Reread I Love Reading Books, Review Books 5–9

✎ Daily Prompt for Independent Writing

Use the prompt below, or allow children to write about a topic of their choice. Encourage them to use what they know about letters and sounds to record their ideas.

This Bigfoot Pig has 14 toes!

■ Draw a picture of a silly animal and give it a name. Write about your animal.

DAY 4

Day 4

Anthology

Wigs in a Box
by Valeria Petrone

Purpose • applying reading strategies, comprehension skills, phonics/decoding skills, high-frequency words, and critical thinking

---

High-Frequency Words

five	four	in
three	two	upon
what		

Words with *d, l, w, x,* short *o*

box	Dog	Don
Dot	Fox	got
lot	Ox	wig
win		

Preparing to Read

▶ Building Background

At the Fair Ask children who have been to a carnival or fair to tell what they did there. Talk about playing games of chance, and ask if children have ever played a game to win a prize.

▶ Developing Story Vocabulary

■ ball ■ shelf ■ thanks ■ wigs

Display **Chart/Transparency** 2–3. Tell children that there are some silly things going on in this picture, and that their job is to follow the directions to find certain things. Read the title, and then each direction. Pause after each to allow time for children to find the item(s) in the picture. Then have children read the underlined words with you as you point to them.

Practice Have children complete **Practice Book** page 66 as a class or with partners.

▶ Using "Get Set to Read"

Have children turn to Anthology pages 148-149. Explain that the words in the box are words they will read in the next story. Ask volunteers to read the words. Then have children read the sentences.

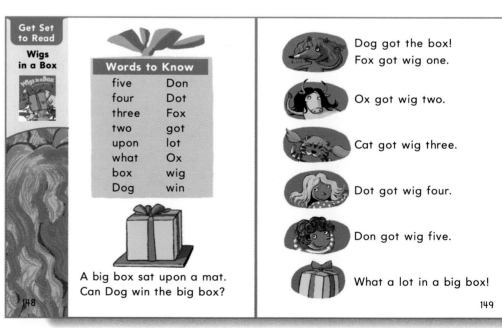

Anthology pages 148–149

Strategy & Skill Focus

▶ Strategy Focus:
Question

Have children turn to Anthology page 151. Read the selection title and the name of the author/illustrator.

Teacher Modeling Have children follow along as you read aloud pages 152–153. Model how to use the Question strategy.

 Think Aloud

After we read this story, we will ask each other questions about it. If I were to ask a question about this page, I might look at the picture and ask: "Where does this story take place?" I might think about the sentence on the page and ask: "What is the prize for winning this game?"

✏ **Quick Write** Ask children to write a question they might ask about pages 152–153.

Purpose Setting Ask children to think about questions they will want to ask later as they read this story. Remind children also to use their other reading strategies as they read the selection.

✓ Comprehension Skill Focus:
Noting Details

Tell children to look for important details as they read this story. They can use the details when it's time to make up questions to ask each other.

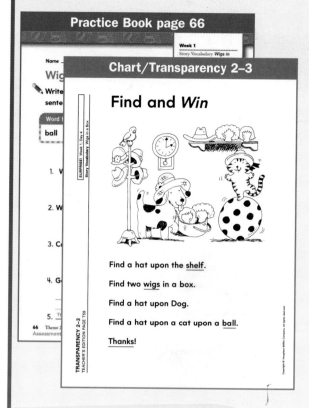

Practice Book page 66

Week 1
Story Vocabulary *Wigs*

Chart/Transparency 2–3

Find and *Win*

Find a hat upon the <u>shelf</u>.

Find two <u>wigs</u> in a box.

Find a hat upon Dog.

Find a hat upon a cat upon a <u>ball</u>.

<u>Thanks!</u>

TRANSPARENCY 2–3
TEACHER'S EDITION PAGE T59

Handwritten note:

Fin and Win

- Shelf
- Wigs
- ball
- Thanks!

DAY 4

 Reaching All Students

English Language Learners

Do a picture walk with children. Ask them to name the various animals. Most English language learners will not be familiar with the words *fair* or *carnival*. Show photos if possible and say that's where the animals are in this story. Then ask if children have ever been to a fair or carnival. Invite them to talk about the experience. Assist with vocabulary as needed.

Wigs in a Box

Reading the Anthology

Options for Reading

▶ **Universal Access** See the Classroom Management tips at the bottom of these pages for suggestions to meet individual needs during and after reading.

About the Author and Illustrator Valeria Petrone was born in Italy. She illustrates children's books for writers from many countries. She also draws pictures for Italy's most popular newspaper.

Key to Underlined Vocabulary

Words with *d, l, w, x,* short *o* ═══

High-Frequency Words _____

Story Vocabulary _____

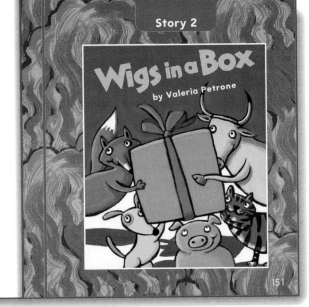

Meet the Author and Illustrator
Valeria Petrone

150

Story 2

Wigs in a Box
by Valeria Petrone

151

Anthology pages 150–151

A big box sat upon a shelf.
Can Pat Pig win the box?

152

153

Anthology pages 152–153

On Level

Partner Reading Children can ask each other questions about the pictures and/or text. After reading they join the class to discuss Comprehension/Critical Thinking, T61, T62, T63; Noting Details, T63; Think About the Story, T64.

Challenge

Independent Reading Children can read the story independently, then join the rest of the class to discuss: Comprehension/Critical Thinking, T61, T62, T63; Noting Details, T63; Think About the Story, T64.

English Language Learners

Intermediate and Advanced As children read with partners, encourage them to compare elements in *The Box* and *Wigs in a Box*. For English language learners at other proficiency levels, see **Language Development Resources**.

Pat Pig can win.
Pat Pig can hit the <u>ball</u> in.

154

Pat Pig <u>got</u> the big box!
<u>What</u> can Pat Pig find in it?

155

Anthology pages 154–155

Pat Pig can find a <u>wig</u>.

156

Pat Pig can find <u>five wigs</u>
in the big box!

157

Anthology pages 156–157

Comprehension/Critical Thinking

1 What does Pat Pig do to win the prize? (He hits the ball in; the ball hits the target.) **Cause and Effect**

2 ✓ What does Pat Pig find in the big box? (five wigs) **Noting Details**

3 **Strategy Focus: Teacher/Student Modeling** Let's reread pages 156–157. Now think of a question you might ask. (Answers will vary, but children may suggest such questions as "What does Pat Pig find in the box?" or "How many wigs are there?") **Question**

4 How could you use what you know about letters and sounds to figure out this word (*wig*, page 156)? (Blend sounds /w//ĭ//g/.) **Phonics/Decoding**

Questions↑

DAY 4

Extra Support

Audio Tape

Teacher-Supported Reading Have children describe the first few illustrations, then take turns reading in a small group. Periodically, have children stop and ask each other questions about story details. Use the Comprehension/Critical Thinking questions, as needed. After reading, they join the class to discuss: Comprehension/Critical Thinking, T61, T62, T63; Noting Details, T63; Think About the Story, T64.

Phonics/Decoding Strategy Coach children in the strategy, as needed.

Learning to Read

Day 4

Comprehension/Critical Thinking

1. How are the wigs alike? How are they different? (Children should look at the illustrations to note similarities and differences.) **Compare and Contrast**

2. ☑ How do the animals seem to feel about their wigs? (They look happy. They are having fun wearing the wigs.) **Noting Details**

Wig one can fit Pat Pig.
158

Wig <u>two</u> can fit <u>Dot</u> <u>Fox</u>.
159

Anthology pages 158–159

Wig <u>three</u> can fit <u>Don</u> <u>Dog</u>.
160

Wig <u>four</u> can fit Fat Cat.
161

Anthology pages 160–161

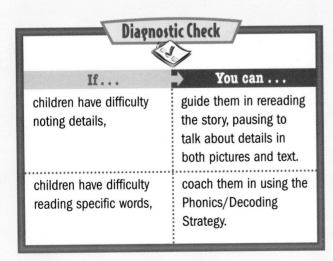

Diagnostic Check

If...	You can...
children have difficulty noting details,	guide them in rereading the story, pausing to talk about details in both pictures and text.
children have difficulty reading specific words,	coach them in using the Phonics/Decoding Strategy.

Wig five can fit Tan <u>Ox</u>.

162

Thanks a <u>lot</u>, Pat Pig!

163

Anthology pages 162–163

Comprehension/Critical Thinking

1 Which wig do you like best? Which is the funniest? (Answers will vary.) **Evaluate**

2 Why do the animals thank Pat Pig? (He won the box of wigs; there is a wig to fit each one of them.) **Cause and Effect**

3 **Strategy Focus: Student Modeling** Have children work with partners to ask each other two or three questions about the story. (Questions will vary.) **Question**

Retelling the Story: Noting Details

After discussion of the Comprehension/Critical Thinking questions, call on individuals to summarize the story. Before children begin, emphasize that a good summary includes the important details—but not the unimportant ones. Give children time to look back through the story to decide which details to include and which to leave out.

DAY 4

Reaching All Students
English Language Learners

Ask: "Is there a wig for each animal? How do you know? Are all the wigs the same or are they all different?"

Ask children what the *!* at the end of the sentence on page 163 is called and what it means. Ask children to find this same type of punctuation in another place in the story. (page 155 or 157) Then ask children to look for two other types of end punctuation in the story.

Student Self-Assessment

Help children assess by asking:

• What parts were easy to read? Which parts were hard?

• What did you do well as you read this story?

• Did you like this story? Why or why not?

Learning to Read

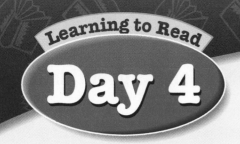

Day 4

Responding

▶ Think About the Story

Discuss the questions on Anthology page 164.
Accept reasonable responses.

1 **Noting Details** Pat Pig planned to give each of his friends a wig.

2 **Cause and Effect** The animals thanked him because they thought the wigs were fun.

3 **Critical Thinking** Answers will vary.

4 **Connecting/Comparing** What is the same in *The Box* and *Wigs in a Box*? (There is a box in both stories; each box holds a surprise.) Which story could never happen in real life? (*Wigs in a Box*)

▶ Comprehension Check

Practice Book page 67

Responding

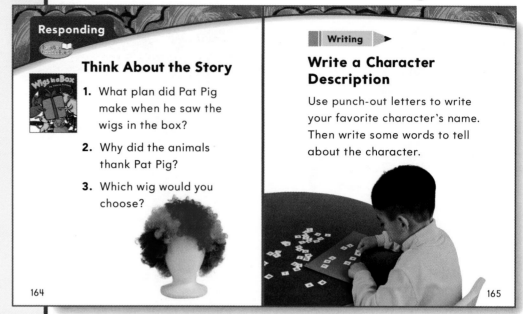

Think About the Story

1. What plan did Pat Pig make when he saw the wigs in the box?

2. Why did the animals thank Pat Pig?

3. Which wig would you choose?

Writing ▶

Write a Character Description

Use punch-out letters to write your favorite character's name. Then write some words to tell about the character.

Anthology pages 164–165

Reaching All Students

Extra Support

Writing Support for Responding List the characters' names on chart paper, and display for children's reference. Remind children to use the Word Pattern Board if they need help spelling other words.

Reaching All Students

English Language Learners

Beginning/Preproduction Ask children to draw another different animal for the story. Help them label the picture with the animal's name.

Early Production and Speech Emergence Ask each child to decide what he or she would put in the box instead of five wigs. List their ideas on chart paper. Assist with vocabulary.

Intermediate and Advanced Say: "Name the animals in the story. What parts of the story are real? What parts of the story are not real?"

Anthology pages 166–167

Poetry Link

▶ Skill: How to Read a Poem

Tell children that the poem on this page is a fingerplay. Recall with children any familiar fingerplays; then direct their attention to the pictures on pages 166–167. Explain that the pictures show the actions that go along with the poem.

Help children read the title. Point out that this fingerplay is about bees in a beehive. If necessary, explain that a beehive is a home for bees.

Read the poem aloud. Then ask children to listen for rhyming words as you read the poem again. You may want to pause to have children supply the rhyming words *sees* (rhymes with *bees*) and *five* (rhymes with *hive*).

Show children how to perform the actions for the fingerplay, then have them do the actions as you read the poem a third time.

Comprehension/Critical Thinking

1 How many bees come out of the hive in this poem? (five) **Noting Details**

2 What do the bees do at the end of the poem? (They fly away.) **Noting Details**

3 Did you enjoy the poem? Why or why not? (Answers will vary.) **Critical Thinking**

Reaching All Students
English Language Learners

Write the word *fingerplay* on the board. Ask children what two words they can find in this compound. Ask children what they think a fingerplay is. Ask them to listen for the answer as you read and do "Here Is the Beehive." Later, ask them to find another compound word in the title and the same word in the poem. (*beehive*) Analyze the compound word; explain its meaning.

Suggestions for Daily Fluency Building

Extra Support	On Level	Challenge
Teacher-Supported Reading • Phonics Library	**Independent Reading** • Reread On Level Theme Paperback: *"What Is That?" Said the Cat* • Reread Anthology selections	**Partner Reading** • Reread Anthology selections • Literature Resources

DAY 4

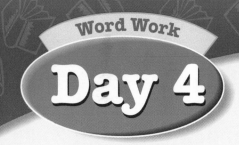
Spelling and Phonics
Word Wheels with Short o

Using **Blackline Master** 201, prepare three word wheels. In the boxes on one of the smaller circles, print the letters *o* and *t*. Print the letters *c, d, g, h, l, n, p, r,* and *t* on the lines of the larger circle of the same color. Use a paper fastener to make the word wheel as shown.

Make two more word wheels with these combinations: *o* and *p* and initial consonants *c, h, m, p, t; o* and *g* and initial consonants *d, f, h, l.* If there are extra lines on a wheel, you might repeat letters or leave them blank to fill in later as children learn new letter sounds.

Demonstrate how to turn the wheel to make words. Have partners take turns blending the sounds to read each word. Then have them write and spell the words they made.

Penmanship For children who need extra practice, model how to write this sentence: *The pot got hot.* Have children write the sentence.

Two penmanship models (continuous stroke, ball and stick) are available in the **Practice Book** (pp. 198–205) and the **Teacher's Resource Blackline Masters** (pp. 143–194).

Vocabulary
Fun Things

Review the story *The Box.* Ask children to name some of the things that Dan put into the box for Dot. Then tell children they will make a class toy box. Ask each child to name a favorite toy or plaything and to tell why he or she likes this thing. Write the name of each toy on the board. Have each child use the list to draw a picture of a favorite toy on a large index card and label the picture.

Put all the index cards into a shoebox. Have children take turns choosing a card, naming the toy, and saying a sentence about it.

OBJECTIVES

Children

- **Spelling and Phonics** build, read, write, and spell words with short *o*

- **Vocabulary** learn and recall words that name fun things

MATERIALS

- **Blackline Master** 201

··· **Houghton Mifflin Spelling and Vocabulary** ···
Correlated Instruction and Practice, p. 73

✏️ Writing

Using Alliteration

On the chalkboard, write the names of these story characters: *Pat Pig, Dot Fox, Don Dog,* and *Fat Cat.* Ask children which name is made up of two words that rhyme. (Fat Cat) Ask which two names are made up of words that begin with the same sounds. (Pat Pig, Don Dog)

Have children make a class book of animal friends with alliterative names.

- Display the **Picture Cards.**

- Each child chooses an animal and creates an alliterative name for it. Explain that each animal's name must be made up of two words—and the two words must begin with the same sound and letter. To get children started, remind them of those Alphafriends whose names alliterate, for example *Tiggy Tiger.*

- Children draw pictures of their animals and label the pictures. Remind them to use capital letters to begin each word in the name.

- Below each picture, each child writes a sentence about his or her animal, using this frame:

_____ **likes to** _____.

Tell children that the animal's name goes in the first blank, and then something the animal likes to do goes in the second blank. The activity should begin with the same sound as the animal's name. Provide examples: *Dandy Duck likes to dance. Soupy Seal likes to surf.*

- Have children share their work. Others in the class can listen for words that begin with the same sounds.

- Have children complete **Practice Book** page 69.

Practice Book page 69

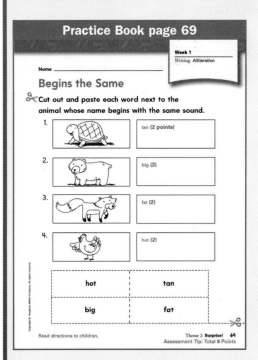

Type to Learn™ Jr.

Students may use **Type to Learn™ Jr.** to familiarize themselves with the computer keyboard. © *Sunburst Technology Corporation, a Houghton Mifflin Company. All Rights reserved.*

Portfolio Opportunity

Save a copy of each child's page as a sample of his or her writing development.

Learning to Read

Day 5

Day at a Glance

Learning to Read

Reading Instruction, *T70*

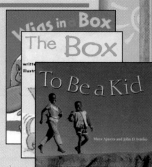

✓ Revisiting the Literature: *Noting Details*

Reading Check, *T71*

- Phonics Library: *Once Upon a Dig*
- I Love Reading Books, Books 10–14

Word Work

Spelling and Phonics, *T72*

- Spelling Words with Short *o*
- Penmanship

Word Pattern Board, *T72*

Writing & Language

Grammar Review, *T73*

- Word Order in Sentences

Viewing, *T73*

- Compare and Contrast

 ✓ **= Tested Skill**

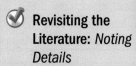

Opening

Daily Message

Note: If you have a copy of *The Three Little Pigs,* display it somewhere in the classroom before displaying the Daily Message.

Use the Daily Message for a quick skill review.

■ As you write the message, you might write each sentence in a different color.

■ Read the message aloud, pointing to each word as it is read.

■ Have children find and underline these high-frequency words: *once, upon, four, three, what.* Then have children point out other words they can read.

> Good Morning Boys and Girls!
> Once upon a time there were four pigs. One pig was big. She was the mother. Three pigs were little. Each of the three little pigs built a house. One was made of straw. Do you know what the other houses were made from?

Concepts of Print

- Have children find the sentence that asks a question. Ask if anyone can answer the question about the pigs' houses.

- Write <u>The Three Little Pigs</u> on the board, and have children frame each word. Point out that each word begins with a capital letter because the words form the title of a book.

Routines

Daily Phonemic Awareness

Blending Phonemes: Let's Cheer

Tell children that they will learn a cheer.

■ Model the first line as shown, segmenting the sounds of the last word. Then call out the word.

Teacher: *Give me a / y // ă // k /! Yak!*

■ As you read each remaining line, have children blend the sounds together and call out the word.

Teacher: *Give me a / h // ŏ // p /!* Children: *Hop!*

Teacher: *Give me a / w // ĕ // b /!* Children: *Web!*

Teacher: *Give me a / z // ĭ // p /!* Children: *Zip!*

Teacher: *Give me a / h // ĕ // n /!* Children: *Hen!*

■ After lots of practice, you might have children make up their own cheers to share with the class.

Daily Independent Reading

Have children read with partners.

■ Reread *Dot Fox* or *Bob Pig and Dan Ox* from the Phonics Library.

■ Bibliography, pages T4–T5

Choose books from this list for children to read, outside class, for at least twenty minutes a day.

■ Reread I Love Reading Books, Review Books 5–9

Daily Prompt for Independent Writing

Have children draw and write on self-selected topics or respond to the prompt below.

■ Draw and write about something interesting that comes in a box.

Chart/Transparency 2–4

Revisiting the Literature

✔ Noting Details

Comparing Texts Remind children that there were surprises in all the stories they read during the week. In two stories, the surprises came in boxes.

Think Aloud

In The Box, *Don planned a surprise for Dot by putting some of his favorite things in a box. Then he took the box to Dot's house.*

Display **Chart/Transparency** 2–4. Point out that the pictures are of some of the things in the stories for this week.

- Ask children to point out those things that Don put into his box. (a fox, a pig in a wig, a big hat)

- Point to the wigs, and ask if children recall what story these are from. (*Wigs in a Box*)

- Point out Pat Pig wearing a wig on Anthology page 158. Compare and contrast with the pig in a wig on the chart.

- Mention that there were lots of fun things in *To Be a Kid,* also. Ask children to point out what some of the kids in that book did to have fun. (They played ball; they skated.)

Additional Practice Assign children to reread other selections from the week (**On My Way Practice Reader** and **On Level/Challenge Theme Paperback, Phonics Library** selections) and think about details in those stories. To help focus their thinking, you might ask them to look for things in each story that led to a surprise.

Decodable Text

Reading Check

▶ Phonics/Decoding Strategy

Student Modeling Ask children to tell how they have used the Phonics/ Decoding Strategy to read new words. Tell them that they should use what they know about letters, sounds, and words to read the next story. Choose a child to model how to use the strategy to read the title *Once Upon a Dig*. Then have children read the story independently.

Reading the Decodable Book If children have difficulty decoding words like *dig* on their own, coach them with prompts such as these:

- *What are the letters from left to right?* (d, i, g)

- *What sound does each letter stand for?* (/d/, /ĭ/, /g/)

- *Blend the sounds. What is the word?* (dĭ ĭ ĭg, dig)

- *Does* dig *make sense in the story?*

Developing Fluency Encourage children to read aloud fluently and with expression. Model reading fluently, and coach children to read with feeling and expression as needed.

Phonics Library

Purposes for decodable text
- assessment
- applying phonics skills
- applying high-frequency words

Once Upon a Dig
by Shiyun Wong
illustrated by Dominic Catalano

Bob Pig can dig, dig, dig.

13

Dot Fox can dig, dig, dig.

14

Dot Fox can dig a lot.

15

Dot Fox can find Bob Pig!

16

Assessment Options

Oral Reading Records You may wish to take oral reading records as children read the **Phonics Library** book individually or in small groups.

Alternative Assessment Use **Blackline Master** 27 to assess individual children's phonics and high-frequency word skills.

Suggestions for Daily Fluency Building

Extra Support	On Level	Challenge
Partner Reading	**Independent Reading**	**Teacher-Supported Reading**
• Books from Bibliography	• Books from Bibliography	• Phonics Library
• Literature Resources	• Literature Resources	

Home Connection

A take-home version of *Once Upon a Dig* is available in the **Phonics Library Blackline Masters**. At the end of the day, children can take the story home to read with their families.

DAY 5

Revisiting/Reading Check **T71**

Word Work

Day 5

OBJECTIVES

Children

- **Spelling and Phonics** read, build, and write words with short *o*
- **Word Pattern Board** review the Word Pattern Board

MATERIALS

- teacher-made cards with *dot, lot, tot, cot, not, pot, hot, got, rot; fox, box, lox*

Houghton Mifflin Spelling and Vocabulary
Correlated Instruction and Practice, p. 73

Spelling and Phonics

Spelling Words with Short o

Make and display cards for short *o* words that end with *t* or *x,* as shown under Materials. Call on volunteers to read the words.

- With scissors, cut *pot* into its individual letters. Mix up the letters and put them on a table or in a pocket chart.

- Ask: **Which letter stands for the first sound in** pot? **...the second sound? ...the third sound?**

- As the letters are named, have a child arrange them to spell *pot.*

- Have children write *pot* on a sheet of paper.

- Choose other listed words and follow the same procedure.

Penmanship Model how to write *Dot got the box.* Monitor children's progress as they write the sentence.

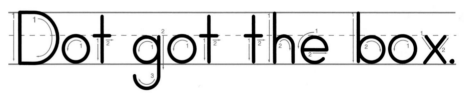

Two penmanship models (continuous stroke, ball and stick) are available in the **Practice Book** (pp. 198–205) and the **Teacher's Resource Blackline Masters** (pp. 143–194).

Word Pattern Board

High-Frequency Words Tell children that today you will move this week's high-frequency words from the "New Words" section to the permanent Word Pattern Board.

- Review the "New Words" section with clap and spell. Remove each word as it is reviewed.

- Call on volunteers to move the words to the permanent Word Pattern Board. The class can chant the words as they are moved.

- Review the entire Word Pattern Board with clap and spell.

Vocabulary Speed Drills On index cards, write this week's new words and add a few decodable words that feature the week's phonics/decoding elements. At small group time, have children take turns holding up the cards for a partner to read. After this warm-up, display the cards as a list on a table and have individuals read them to you as quickly as they can.

Diagnostic Check

If...	You can ...
children need more practice in discriminating sounds,	use **Back to School** or Daily Phonemic Awareness, page T57.

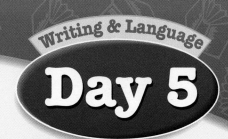
Grammar Review

Word Order in Sentences

Display **Blackline Master 28**. Tell children that the words in each row are not in order.

■ Choose children to read the group of words in each row. Have children cut out the squares in each row and order the words to make a sentence. Write the correct sentence on the board and have children compare it to their sentence.

Coached Writing Dictate the following sentence from *The Box:* **A big hat can fit.** Have children write the words in the order that you say them in the sentence. Remind them to begin the sentence with a capital letter and end it with a period.

Viewing

Compare and Contrast

Display pages 18–19 of *To Be a Kid.* Point out that the photographs on these pages show how kids from different countries take care of animals. Then use the following questions to help children focus on similarities and differences.

■ **When you look at these pictures, what do you see that is alike in all of them?** (There are kids and animals in all the pictures.)

■ **Are all the animals the same? What different animals do you see?** (As children name the animals, you may want to read aloud the captions that name the countries.)

■ **Are all the people dressed exactly the same?** (Children will probably note differences in the way the kids are dressed.)

■ **Look carefully at the expressions on the kids' faces. How do you think they feel about caring for the animals?** (Most are smiling; they look happy.)

Have children work with partners or in small groups to compare and contrast other photographs in this book or in other photo-essays.

 OBJECTIVES

Children

● **Grammar Review** order words to form sentences

● **Viewing** compare and contrast details in photographs

MATERIALS

Viewing

● Big Book *To Be a Kid*

● **Blackline Master 28**

Reaching All Students
English Language Learners

Begin by having children name all of the animals in *To Be a Kid*. Next, brainstorm words used to describe clothing. Refer to articles of clothing worn by those in class, colors, and fabrics. If children are having difficulty with the comparison and contrast, use questions to call attention to specific details of the clothing and facial expressions in the photos.

DAY 5

Literature for Week 2
Different texts for different purposes

BY Janet Morgan Stoeke

Decodable Text
What Can a Vet Do?

Decodable Text
HOT FOX SOUP

by SATOSHI KITAMURA

Big Book

Purposes

- oral language development
- reading strategies
- comprehension skills

 Also available on audiotape

Awards

★ IRA-CBC Children's Choice

★ Bank Street College Best Children's Books of the Year

Challenge

Little Big Book

Purposes

- vocabulary development
- reading fluency
- application of phonics/decoding and comprehension skills

 Also available on audiotape

Anthology: Main Selections

Purposes

- reading strategies
- comprehension skills
- phonics/decoding skills
- high-frequency words
- critical thinking

Award Winner

 ★ Books by Kitamura have been named *New York Times* Notable Children's Books of the Year, Library of Congress Children's Books of the Year, IRA Teachers' Choices, and have received Parents' Choice Awards.

Anthology: Get Set to Read *What Can a Vet Do?*

Anthology: Get Set to Read *Hot Fox Soup*

Purpose
- applying phonics skills and high-frequency words

Anthology: Music Link

Purposes
- skill: how to sing a song
- critical thinking; discussion

Decodable Text

Phonics Library

Purposes
- applying phonics skills
- applying high-frequency words

Also available in take-home version

I Love Reading Books

Purposes
- applying phonics skills
- applying high-frequency words

Books for Small-Group Reading

Use these resources to ensure that children read, outside class, for at least twenty minutes a day.

On My Way Practice Reader

Easy

The Pet
by Maria Cara
page T92

Theme Paperback

On Level

The Pet Vet
by Marcia Leonard
page T93

Technology

Education Place

www.eduplace.com
Log on to Education Place for more activities relating to *Surprise!*

Book Adventure

www.bookadventure.org
This Internet reading-incentive program provides thousands of titles for students to read.

Daily Lesson Plans

Instructional Goals

	Day 1	**Day 2**

Learning to Read

(90–110 minutes)

Strategy Focus: Monitor/Clarify

✓ **Comprehension Skill:** Fantasy and Realism

Phonemic Awareness: Blend Phonemes

✓ **Phonics Skills:** Consonants y, k, v; Short e; Blending Short e Words (CVC)

• Additional lessons for phonics skills are included in the *Extra Support Handbook* and *Handbook for English Language Learners*. (See Universal Access Plans.)

Phonics Skill Review: Words with Short o

✓ **High-Frequency Words:** *do, for, I, is, me, my, said, you*

Day 1

Opening Routines: *T80–T81*

Reading the Big Book
Minerva Louise at School, T82–T85

Phonemic Awareness
• Blend Phonemes, *T86*

Phonics Instruction, Practice, Application
• Consonants y, k, v, *T86; Practice Book, 71–72*
• Short e, *T87; Practice Book, 73*
• Blending Short e Words, *T88; Practice Book, 74–75*
• Phonics Library, *Not Yet!, T89*

Day 2

Opening Routines: *T96–T97*

Rereading the Big Book
Minerva Louise at School, T98–T99

Comprehension Skill Instruction
• Fantasy and Realism, *T98–T99*
• *Practice Book, 77*

High-Frequency Words
• Instruction, *T100*
• *Practice Book, 78–79*

Phonics Application
• Phonics Library, *Big Ben, T101*

Word Work

(30–40 minutes)

Spelling and Phonics: Words with y, v, k, and Short e

Word Pattern Board: High-Frequency Words; Words with Short e

Vocabulary: Opposites, Foods

Day 1

Spelling and Phonics
• Instruction: Letters and Sounds y, v, *T90*
• *Practice Book, 76*

[Word Pattern Board]
• Words with Short e, *T90*

Day 2

Spelling and Phonics
• Instruction: k, *T102*
• *Practice Book, 80*

[Word Pattern Board]
• High-Frequency Words, *T102*

Writing & Language

(30–40 minutes)

Grammar: Naming Words

Writing: A Class Message; Writing About Animals

Listening/Speaking/Viewing: Conflict Resolution, Main Ideas and Details

Day 1

✎ **Writing**
• Independent Journal Writing, *T91*

Viewing
• Main Idea and Details, *T91*

Day 2

✎ **Shared Writing**
• A Class Message, *T103*

Teacher's Notes

Books for Small-Group Reading, T88–T89, T92–T95, T101, T115, T135
For reading outside class and homework

Technology

Lesson Planner CD-ROM
Customize your planning for the week with the
Lesson Planner.

Day 3

Opening Routines: *T104–T105*

Preparing to Read *What Can a Vet Do?*
- Building Background, *T106*
- Get Set to Read, *T106*
- Strategy/Skill Preview, *T107*

Reading the Anthology *What Can a Vet Do?*
- Comprehension/Critical Thinking, *T109, T110, T111, T112*
- Strategy Focus, *T109, T111, T112*
- Responding, *T113*, **Practice Book**, *81*

Phonics Application/Review
- Anthology: *What Can a Vet Do?, T108–T112*
- Review/Maintain: Words with Short *o*, *T114–T115*

Spelling and Phonics
- Words with: *y, k, v,* and Short *e, T116*

Vocabulary
- Opposites, *T116*

Writing
- Response Activity, *T113*

Grammar Skill Instruction
- Naming Words, *T117*

Day 4

Opening Routines: *T118–T119*

Preparing to Read *Hot Fox Soup*
- Building Background, *T120*
- Story Vocabulary, *T120*, **Practice Book**, *82*
- Get Set to Read, *T120*
- Strategy/Skill Preview, *T121*

Reading the Anthology *Hot Fox Soup*
- Comprehension/Critical Thinking, *T123, T125, T126, T127*
- Strategy Focus, *T126, T127*
- Responding, *T128*, **Practice Book**, *83*

Reading the Music Link
- "Polly, Put the Kettle On," *T129*

Phonics Application
- Anthology: *Hot Fox Soup, T122–T127*

Spelling and Phonics
- Word Slides with Short *e, T130*

Vocabulary
- Foods, *T130*

Writing Instruction
- Writing About Animals, *T131*
- **Practice Book**, *85*

Day 5

Opening Routines: *T132–T133*

Revisiting the Literature:
Comprehension Skill Instruction
- Fantasy and Realism, *T134*

Reading Skills Check:
Phonics Application, Assessment
- Phonics Library, *Get Wet, Ken!, T135*

Spelling and Phonics
- Spelling Words with Short *e, T136*

Word Pattern Board
- High-Frequency Words, *T136*

Writing
- Independent Writing Prompt, *T133*

Grammar Review
- Naming Words, *T137*

Listening and Speaking
- Conflict Resolution, *T137*

Daily Writing: Opening Routines, T81, T97, T105, T119, T133

**See Universal Access
Planning Chart on
the following pages.**

Universal Access Plans
for Reaching All Learners

Grouping for Instruction

30–45 minutes

	Day 1	**Day 2**

With the Teacher

Extra Support
Teach—Use Extra Support Handbook

Day 1
Preteach Phonics: Consonants *y* and *v*
Preteach Phonics: Blending Short *e* Words
Preview *Not Yet!*
■ Extra Support Handbook   pp. 56–57

Day 2
Preteach Comprehension: Fantasy and Realism
Preview *Big Ben*
■ Extra Support Handbook   pp. 58–59

Working Independently

On Level
Use Classroom Management Handbook

Challenge
Use Challenge Handbook

English Language Learners
Use Classroom Management Handbook or
Challenge Handbook

Day 1
Independent Activities
For each group, assign appropriate activities—your
own or those in the handbooks listed below.
Then get students started on their independent work.

■ Classroom Management Handbook   pp. 34–41
■ Challenge Handbook   pp. 20–23

Day 2
See plan for Day 1

Monitor
Answer questions,
if necessary.

30–45 minutes

With the Teacher

English Language Learners
Teach—Use Handbook for
English Language Learners

Day 1
Preteach Outside Our Window
Preteach Big Book, *Minerva Louise at School*
Preteach Phonics: Consonants *y, k, v*
■ Handbook for ELL   pp. 60–61

Day 2
Preteach Words That Tell Where
Preteach Get Set to Read; *What Can a Vet Do?*
Preteach High-Frequency Words: *for, I, is, me, said*
■ Handbook for ELL   pp. 62–63

Working Independently

On Level
Use Classroom Management Handbook

Challenge
Use Challenge Handbook

Extra Support
Use Classroom Management Handbook

Day 1
Independent Activities
Students can continue their assigned activities,
or you can assign new activities from the
handbooks below.

■ Classroom Management Handbook   pp. 34–41
■ Challenge Handbook   pp. 20–23

Day 2
See plan for Day 1

Monitor
Partner Extra
Support students,
if needed.

Independent Activities

Classroom Management Handbook
• Daily Activities
• Grouping
• Management

Resources for Reaching All Learners

Extra Support Handbook
• Daily Lessons
• Preteaching and Reteaching
• Skill Support

Handbook for English Language Learners
• Daily Lessons
• Language Development
• Skill Support

Challenge Handbook
• Independent Activities
• Instructional Support

Day 3

Reteach High-Frequency Words
Preview *What Can a Vet Do?*
■ Extra Support Handbook   pp. 60–61

See plan for Day 1

Check in
Reinforce instruction, if needed.

Preteach City and Country
Preteach Get Set to Read; *Hot Fox Soup*
Reteach High-Frequency Words: *do, my, you*
■ Handbook for ELL   pp. 64–65

See plan for Day 1

Check in
Reinforce instruction, if needed.

Day 4

Reteach Phonics: Consonants *y, k, v*
Reteach Phonics: Blending Short *e* Words
Preview *Hot Fox Soup*
■ Extra Support Handbook   pp. 62–63

See plan for Day 1

Check in
Regroup English learners, if needed.

Preteach Going Places
Reteach *What Can a Vet Do?* and *Hot Fox Soup*
Reteach Phonics: Blending Short *e* Words
■ Handbook for ELL   pp. 66–67

See plan for Day 1

Monitor
How well are challenge projects progressing?

Day 5

Reteach Comprehension: Fantasy and Realism
Revisit *Not Yet! Big Ben, What Can a Vet Do?* and *Hot Fox Soup*
■ Extra Support Handbook   pp. 64–65

See plan for Day 1

Build confidence
Reinforce successful independent work.

Preteach Pulling It All Together
Reteach Grammar: Naming Words
■ Handbook for ELL   pp. 68–69

See plan for Day 1

Share work
Allow students time to share work.

Universal Access Plans   T77B

Managing Small Groups

Small-Group Resources

Books for Small-Group Reading

Decodable

- Phonics Library
- I Love Reading Books

Easy

- On My Way Practice Reader

On Level

- Theme Paperback

Challenge

- Little Big Book

Other Resources

- Literature Resources Grade 1
- Level 1.1–1.2 Practice Book

Center Activities

- ▶ Word Booklets
- ▶ Make a Label Book
- ▶ How Many Make 12?
- ▶ Sock Puppets

Sample Small-Group Schedule

Independent Work

- ▶ Independent Reading
- ▶ Phonics Library Stories
- ▶ Center Activities
- ▶ Practice Book pages

Teacher-Led Group

- ▶ Books for Small-Group Reading
- ▶ Vocabulary Speed Drills

Daily Fluency Building

Children need to read leveled texts fluently before moving on to higher levels of challenge. Daily Fluency Building, as supported by the Little Big Book lesson on T34–T35, facilitates the successful application of reading strategies and consolidates skills, allowing children to move toward independence in reading.

Suggestions for Daily Fluency Building

	Extra Support	On Level	Challenge
DAY 1	**Partner Reading** • Reread Anthology, Phonics Library, and I Love Reading Books	**Teacher-Supported Reading** • Phonics Library	**Independent Reading** • Books from Bibliography • Literature Resources
DAY 2	**Teacher-Supported Reading** • On My Way Practice Reader: *The Pet*	**Partner Reading** • Books from Bibliography • Literature Resources	**Partner Reading** • Reread the Little Big Book: *Minerva Louise at School*
DAY 3	**Independent Reading** • Reread On My Way Practice Reader: *The Pet* • Reread Anthology, Phonics Library, and I Love Reading Books	**Teacher-Supported Reading** • On Level Theme Paperback: *The Pet Vet*	**Independent Reading** • Check in with teacher after reading the Little Big Book: *Minerva Louise at School*
DAY 4	**Teacher-Supported Reading** • Phonics Library	**Independent Reading** • Reread On Level Theme Paperback: *The Pet Vet* • Reread Anthology selections	**Independent Reading** • Reread Anthology selections • Literature Resources
DAY 5	**Partner Reading** • Books from Bibliography • Literature Resources	**Independent Reading** • Books from Bibliography • Literature Resources	**Teacher-Supported Reading** • Phonics Library

Technology

Education Place

www.eduplace.com

Log on to Education Place for more activities relating to *Surprise!*

Book Adventure

www.bookadventure.org

This Internet reading-incentive program provides thousands of titles for students to read.

Management Routine

Monitoring Center Activities

Make a chart like the one shown here. List children's names at the left, and use icons such as those suggested to identify your centers.

	K V	✏️	✒️	=2 9×
Juan		🙂		
Sandy				
Kim				
Remi				

Explain that the pictures at the top of the chart are for the centers in your classroom. Help children match each icon with the corresponding center. (You may want to put similar icons at each center for children's reference.) Show children how to find their names on the chart and then paste a sticker in the space to the right once they have completed work in that center. You can use commercially prepared stickers or have children make their own at the Writing and Technology center.

Instructional Routine

Word Booklets Have children continue to work on the Word Booklets. (See page T19.) Use **Blackline Masters** 199–200 to create short *o* pages. Using the word *cot*, remind children what to do.

■ Write the word *cot* on the first line.

■ Draw a picture of a cot to illustrate the word.

Children can write and illustrate other short *o* words to make their own short *o* Word Booklets.

Center Activities

Phonics and Language

Word Booklets Have children work independently to make the Word Booklets. (See above.) Children can get together with partners or in small groups to share them.

Materials
- **Blackline Masters** 199–200
- safety scissors
- crayons or markers
- pencils

Math

How Many Make 12? Tell children that eggs are often sold by the dozen, which is 12. Have children put different combinations of red and blue counters in the egg-carton sections—one counter to a section—and record their combinations on a T-chart.

Materials
- egg cartons
- counters (12 red, 12 blue for each child)

Writing and Technology

Make a Label Book Point out any labels you have on objects in the classroom. (You may want to label objects now.) Children can contribute to a *Let's Teach Minerva Louise* book by drawing school objects and labeling each one. After children have made a cover, staple the pages together and add the book to the class library.

Materials
- drawing paper
- crayons/markers
- pencils
- stapler

Creative Arts

Sock Puppets Children can act out the story about Minerva Louise with sock puppets. To make the puppets, trace each child's hand (with thumb and little finger spread apart) onto a double fold of felt. Cut along the traced line. Have children sew the pieces together and decorate with yarn and scraps of felt.

Materials
- felt squares
- scraps of felt and yarn
- white glue
- needle and thread

Day at a Glance

Learning to Read

Reading the Big Book, *T82–T85*

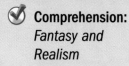 Comprehension: *Fantasy and Realism*

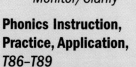

- Reading Strategy: *Monitor/Clarify*

Phonics Instruction, Practice, Application, *T86–T89*

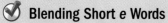 Review *y, k, v*

 Blending Short *e* Words

- Phonics Library: *Not Yet!*
- **I Love Reading Books, Books 15–18**

Word Work

Spelling and Phonics, *T90*

- Letters and Sounds: *y, v*
- Penmanship

Word Pattern Board, *T90*

Writing & Language

Independent Journal Writing, *T91*

Viewing, *T91*

- Main Idea and Details

 = **Tested Skill**

# Opening

Daily Message

Use the Daily Message for a quick review of phonics, high-frequency words, and language skills.

- Read the message aloud, pointing to each word as it is read.

- Call on a few children to find and circle examples of consonants *k, v,* and initial *y.*

- Ask volunteers to underline the high-frequency words *we, a, who, The, and,* and *too.*

> Good Day, Everyone!
> Today we will read about a
> hen named Minerva Louise,
> who is an early riser.
> The story is very funny. I like it,
> and I think you will, too.

Count them!

Have children count the number of sentences in the Daily Message.

Concepts of Print

Show through modeling:

- capital letters that begin sentences and names
- periods to end sentences
- commas to show readers where to pause

Routines

Daily Phonemic Awareness

Blending Phonemes: Categories

Play "Categories" with children to name things that are found in a home.

- Say: *Many things can be found in a home. Listen: Some people have a / d // ŏ // g / in a home. Blend the sounds quietly. Raise your hand when you know what thing I named ... What's the word?* (dog)

- Continue with the words *jam, pen, pot, pan, mop,* and *mat.*

- Challenge children to think of things in a home that rhyme with *rug* or *pan.* Segment the sounds. Have children blend them together and say the words naturally.

Daily Independent Reading

Daily independent exploration and reading of books will increase children's experiences with print.

- Bibliography, pages T4–T5

   Choose books from this list for children to read, outside class, for at least twenty minutes a day.

- Little Big Book *Minerva Louise at School*

- Reread I Love Reading Books, Review Books 10–14

✏️ Daily Prompt for Independent Writing

Use the prompt below, or allow children to write about a topic of their choice. Encourage them to use what they know about letters and sounds to record their ideas.

- Draw and write about something you see in your classroom or about something you do at school.

  We got a letter from a firefighter.

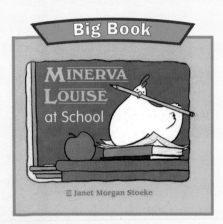

MINERVA LOUISE at School

Janet Morgan Stoeke

Purpose • oral language development • reading strategies • comprehension skills

Selection Summary
An adventuresome hen wanders into a class-room—thinking it is a barn. The consequences of her mistake are hilarious.

Key Concepts
• Farm things and school things

• Seeing things in unusual ways

Reaching All Students
English Language Learners

English language learners may experience some difficulty with the complexity of the sentences as well as the farm vocabulary in this story. As you read, pause frequently to guide children with questions such as "What is Minerva Louise doing? Is this really a barn? What is it?" Make sure all children understand that the hen mistakenly believes this is a farm. Discuss farm animals and other words, including *barn, farmer, stalls, milking stools, pen, bucket, nest(ing) boxes, hay.*

Reading the Big Book
Oral Language and Comprehension

▶ Building Background

Introduce the Big Book by reading aloud the title and the name of the author/illustrator. Introduce the hen pictured on the cover as Minerva Louise. Talk about where hens live—and whether or not they go to school.

Strategy Preview:
Monitor/Clarify

Teacher Modeling Read aloud the Strategy Focus question on Big Book page 24. Model how to use the Monitor/Clarify strategy.

> **Think Aloud**
>
> *Sometimes when I read, I don't understand what is happening. When that happens, I reread the part I don't understand. Then I look at the pictures. Sometimes the pictures in a story help readers understand what is going on.*

Comprehension Skill Preview:
Fantasy and Realism

Ask if children enjoy stories in which animals do and say silly things. Remind them of *Wigs in a Box*, and ask if what happened in that story could happen in real life. Tell children that we call a story like *Wigs in a Box* a fantasy. In a fantasy, things happen that could never happen in real life. Suggest that children think about what could—and could not—happen in real life as they listen to the story about Minerva Louise.

▶ Teacher Read Aloud

As you read the story aloud, allow children to chime in. Pause occasionally to ask: Could this really happen? Once Minerva Louise is inside the classroom, pause to talk briefly about what the hen sees—and what she thinks she sees.

Concepts of Print (pages 25–26) Demonstrate how to track print from left to right and how to make the return sweep when there is more than one line of text on a page. Monitor and guide children as necessary.

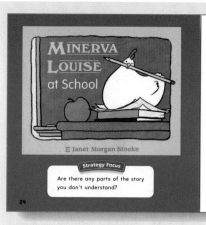

MINERVA
LOUISE
at School

≡ Janet Morgan Stoeke

Strategy Focus
Are there any parts of the story you don't understand?

24

One morning, Minerva Louise woke up before everyone else.

25

Big Book page 24–25

It was a beautiful morning, so she decided to go for a walk through the tall grass.

26

She walked on and on.

27

Big Book pages 26–27

Oh, look! A big, fancy barn, thought Minerva Louise.

28

She watched the farmer hang his laundry out to dry . . .

29

Big Book pages 28–29

. . . and she noticed that he had left the door open.

30

So many stalls! There must be all kinds of animals here.

31

Big Book pages 30–31

Here are milking stools for the cows

32

and a pen for the pigs.

33

Big Book pages 32–33

Oh, a bucket, too. It must be for feeding the chickens.

34

Nesting boxes! How wonderful!

35

Big Book pages 34–35

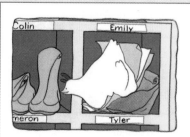

Look at them all. And each one is decorated differently.

36

This one is all done up with ribbons.

37

Big Book pages 36–37

And this one is lined with fur.

38

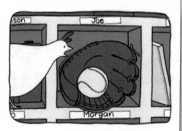

Oh my goodness, there's an EGG in this one!

39

Big Book pages 38–39

Reading the Big Book:
Minerva Louise at School

T83

(**Reading the Big Book,** continued)

Oral Language and Comprehension

▶ **Responding**

Retelling Talk with children about Minerva Louise's first mistake: thinking that the school was a fancy barn. As you page through the story again, ask:

- *What does Minerva Louise think when she sees the children's cubbies?*
  (She thinks they are nesting boxes.)

- *What does she think when she sees a baseball in a mitt?*
  (She thinks the ball is an egg.)

- *What idea does her trip to school give Minerva Louise?*
  (She redecorates her nesting box so that it looks like one of the cubbies.)

If necessary, explain that Minerva Louise mistakes the things she *sees* for things she *knows*. Point out that children should keep this in mind as they retell the story. Ask them to do that now as you display the story illustrations.

Literature Discussion Circle Review the Discussion Tips before posing these questions:

- *Do you think Minerva Louise is clever? Why or why not?*

- *What is the funniest part of this story?*

Reading the Little Big Book For children who are ready to read independently, there is a five-day lesson plan on pages T94–T95 for using the **Little Big Book,** *Minerva Louise at School.*

Discussion Tips

- Raise your hand if you want to talk.
- Wait until you are called on.
- Listen while others are talking.

Reaching All Students
Extra Support

Reread the story, pausing after each two-page spread to ask: "Could this happen in real life?" Help children understand that when Minerva Louise begins *thinking* like a real person (page 28), she stops acting like a real hen. Explain that in real life, only people can think the kind of thoughts that Minerva Louise thinks in this story.

Reaching All Students
Challenge

Responding Ask children to tell what happens at the beginning, in the middle, and at the end of the story. Also ask them to explain what makes this story a fantasy. Allow children to use the term *make-believe,* if they prefer.

Reaching All Students
English Language Learners

Beginning/Preproduction Go back through the story and ask children to name animals and objects. Assist with vocabulary. You may want to make labels for some of the words.

Early Production and Speech Emergence Ask each child to take a turn describing what is happening in the art. Assist with vocabulary.

Intermediate and Advanced Say "Imagine Minerva Louise went to your house instead of to school. How would the story be different?" Ask for ideas.

But where is his mother?
He'll get cold.

40

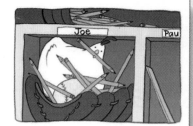

Well, this hay will keep you
warm.

41

Big Book page 40–41

I'm sure the animals are
around here somewhere.
But I have to go home now.

42

Minerva Louise hurried home
through the tall grass.

43

Big Book pages 42–43

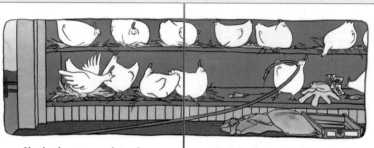

She had some work to do.

44

But she knew she'd go back
to the fancy barn some day . . .

45

Big Book pages 44–45

because it was such a
wonderful place to get
new ideas.

46

Big Book page 46

Learning to Read
Day 1

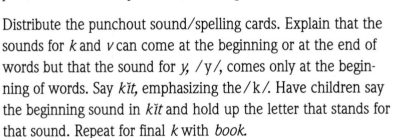

Phonics

✅ Consonants y, k, v

▶ Develop Phonemic Awareness

Blend Phonemes Read the poem aloud. Say: *I have a word from the poem. Listen: /v//ĕ//t/.* Have children say the individual sounds, blend them, and then say the word *vet.* Repeat with /k//ĕ//n/ (*Ken*), /y//ĕ//t/ (*yet*), /n//ĕ//k/ (*neck*), /w//ĕ//t/ (*wet*), /y//ĕ//s/ (*yes*), /v//ĕ//s//t/ (*vest*).

> Here we are,
> My little pet.
> You must go in
> And see the vet.

▶ Connect Sounds to Letters

Introduce the Sound/Spelling Cards Display **Large Sound/Spelling Card** *yo-yo* and have children name the picture. Point to the letters *Yy.* Tell children that a *y* stands for the /y/ sound at the beginning of *yo-yo.* Have children chant /y/, /y/, /y/ as you point to the letter. Repeat with the *kangaroo* and *volcano* cards.

Yy

Distribute the punchout sound/spelling cards. Explain that the sounds for *k* and *v* can come at the beginning or at the end of words but that the sound for *y*, /y/, comes only at the beginning of words. Say *kĭt*, emphasizing the /k/. Have children say the beginning sound in *kĭt* and hold up the letter that stands for that sound. Repeat for final *k* with *book.*

Continue, asking children what sound they hear at the beginning or end of a word and what letter stands for that sound. Say these words without emphasizing the sounds: *key, yell, cave, drink, yarn, vase, milk, yam, give, king.*

Check Understanding Hold up each **Large Sound/Spelling Card** and call on individuals to say a word that begins or ends with that letter's sound.

▶ Connect Sounds to Spelling and Writing

Say: *Listen as I say* van. *What sound do you hear at the beginning of* van? *What letter should I write to spell that sound?* (*v*) Model writing the letter *v.* Have several children write *v* on the board as they say /v/. Repeat for *y, k,* using *yet, kit.* Then have children tell you what letter to write for the last sound in *wave, sink.*

Practice Book pages 71–72 support this skill.

OBJECTIVES

Children

• blend phonemes

• recognize consonants *y, k, v* and the sounds they represent

• associate the sound /ĕ/ with the letter *e*

• blend and read words with short *e* and known consonants

MATERIALS

• **Large Sound/Spelling Cards** *yo-yo, kangaroo, volcano*

• punchout sound/spelling cards *yo-yo, kangaroo, volcano*

THEME 2: Surprise!

Phonics

✓ Short e

▶ Connect Sounds to Letters

Introduce the Sound/Spelling Card Display **Large Sound/Spelling Card** *elephant.* Have children name the picture. Point to the letters *Ee.* Tell children that *e* is a vowel that stands for the /ĕ/ sound at the beginning of *elephant.* Have them chant /ĕ/, /ĕ/, /ĕ/ as you point to the letter. Explain that /ĕ/ can be at the beginning of a word, as in *elephant,* or in the middle of a word, as in *vet.*

Write the letter *e* on the board. Then display **Picture Card** *vet.* Say *vvĕĕĕt,* elongating the /ĕ/ sound. Ask children what sound they hear in the middle of the word. Explain that *e* stands for the /ĕ/ sound in the middle of *vet.*

Check Understanding Ask children to hold up punchout sound/spelling card *elephant* when they hear a word that has the /ĕ/ sound. Then say *elephant, met, sit, hen, egg, stop, leg, mat, sled, nest, nut, shell, end, ran.*

▶ Connect Sounds to Spelling and Writing

Tell children you want to write the word *yes.* Together, say each sound in *yes* and blend to say the word: /y/ /ĕ/ /s/, *yes.* Then draw three boxes on the chalkboard.

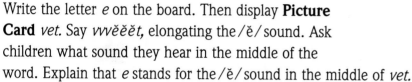

- Say the word *yes.* Ask: **What sound do you hear at the beginning of yes? What letter should I write in the first box?** Write *y.*

- Ask: **What sound do you hear next in** *yes?* Call on a child to write *e* in the second box.

- Ask: **What sound do you hear at the end of yes? What letter should I write in the last box?** Write *s.*

Follow the same steps with the words *vet, Ken, pet, red, web.*

Practice Book Page 73 supports this skill.

MATERIALS

- **Large Sound/Spelling Card** *elephant*
- punchout sound/spelling card *elephant*
- **Picture Card** *vet*

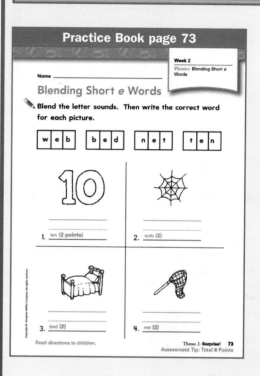

Practice Book page 73

Reaching All Students
English Language Learners

Some English language learners will have trouble with the /v/ sound. Demonstrate how to make the sound; show that your upper teeth are on your lower lip. Instruct children to put their hands on your throat to feel the vibration. Have children make the sound, putting their hands on their throats as they do it. Then explain that a *vet* is an animal doctor. Ask them to say the word *vet* after you. Also practice *very* and *vest.*

Learning to Read
Day 1

MATERIALS

- **Large Letter Cards** *b, d, e, g, l, n, p, t, y*
- **punchout trays and letter cards** *b, d, e, g, n, p, t, v, y*
- **I Love Reading Books,** Books 15–18
- **Blending Routines Card 1**

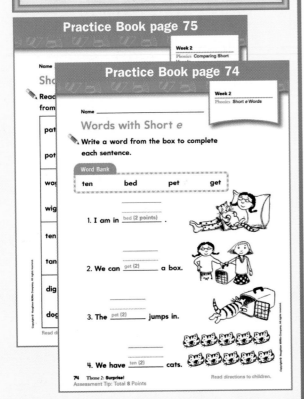

Practice Book page 75

Practice Book page 74

Words with Short e

Write a word from the box to complete each sentence.

Word Bank

| ten | bed | pet | get |

1. I am in _bed (2 points)_ .

2. We can _get (2)_ a box.

3. The _pet (2)_ jumps in.

4. We have _ten (2)_ cats.

74 Theme 2: Surprise!
Assessment Tip: Total 8 Points   Read directions to children.

Diagnostic Check

If...	You can ...
children need further instruction in the sounds for *y, k, v* or practice decoding words with short *e,*	use **Blending Routine 2,** *Sound-by-Sound Blending,* with this lesson or **Reteaching** lesson on page R8 or R10.
children readily identify the sounds for *y, k, v* or easily decode words with short *e,*	have them do the **Challenge/Extension** activities on pages R9 or R11.

(T88) THEME 2: **Surprise!**

(**Phonics,** *continued*)

✅ *Blending Short e Words (VC, CVC)*

▶ Connect Sounds to Letters

Display **Large Letter Cards** *b, d, g, l, t,* and *y.* Have children name each letter and say its sound. Tell children that today they will build some words with these letters, but that first they need a vowel letter. Display **Large Letter Card** *e.* Remind children that *e* often stands for the /ĕ/ sound.

Blending Routine 1 Place **Large Letter Cards** *y, e,* and *t* together. Point to each letter in a sweeping motion as you model how to blend: *yyy ĕĕĕt, yet.* Repeat, having children blend the sounds and pronounce the word with you. Then have children blend and pronounce the word on their own. Call on volunteers to use *yet* in a sentence. Repeat this routine with the words *leg* and *bed.*

Check Understanding Display **Large Letter Cards** *p, e,* and *n.* Have children blend *pen* as you point to the letters.

Mixed Practice Write *yes* and ask children to blend the sounds to read the word. Repeat for *net, yam, Ed, kit, van, got, fed,* and the sentence *Ken can pet the red hen.*

▶ Connect Sounds to Spelling and Writing

Distribute punchout trays and letter cards *b, d, e, g, n, p, t, v, y.* Say *den* and have children repeat it. Ask: **What is the first sound? Put the letter that stands for that sound on your tray.** Continue to spell the word sound by sound. Then write the word on the board and have children check their work. Repeat for the words *yet, beg, net, get, peg, vet.* Then dictate this sentence for children to write: *Ted met ten men.*

Practice Book Pages 74–75 support this skill.

▶ Practice/Apply

Have children complete **Practice Book** pages 71–75 independently, with a partner, or in small groups. Then have them read **I Love Reading Books,** Books 15–18.

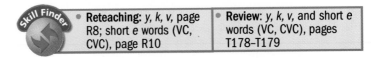

Skill Finder

| • Reteaching: *y, k, v,* page R8; short *e* words (VC, CVC), page R10 | • Review: *y, k, v,* and short *e* words (VC, CVC), pages T178-T179 |

Decodable Text

Phonics Library

Surprise!

Reading

▶ Phonics/Decoding Strategy

Distribute the **Phonics Library** story *Not Yet!* Ask children to tell what is happening in the pictures on page 17.

Teacher Modeling Use **Poster A** to review the steps of the Phonics/Decoding Strategy. Then model how to use the strategy to read the story title.

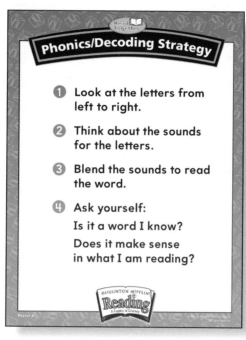

Phonics/Decoding Strategy

1. Look at the letters from left to right.
2. Think about the sounds for the letters.
3. Blend the sounds to read the word.
4. Ask yourself:
   Is it a word I know?
   Does it make sense in what I am reading?

Think Aloud

I see two words in the title. I look at the first word and see the letters N, o, t. I put the sounds together: /n//ŏ//t/, Not. That is a word I know. Then I look at the second word. I think about the sounds for the letters and blend the sounds: /y//ĕ//t/, Yet. Yet makes sense and is a word I know. I put the two words together: Not Yet!

Tell children to look for letters and words that they know as they read the rest of the story independently or take turns reading with a partner.

Reading the Decodable Book If children have difficulty, remind them to look at each letter and sound out the word. Encourage them to sound out the words silently "in their heads." If necessary, coach them in applying the strategy to words such as *ten.*

- *What are the letters from left to right?* (t, e, n)
- *What sound does each letter stand for?* (/t/, /ĕ/, /n/)
- *Say each sound and hold it until you say the next sound. What is the word?* (tĕĕĕnnn, ten)
- *Is ten a word you know? Does it make sense in the story?*

Oral Language Discuss the following questions with children. Have them speak in complete sentences.

- *What color is the van?* (The van is tan.)
- *Do ten kits fit in the van?* (No, they don't fit.)
- *Look at the last picture of Peg Hen. How is Peg feeling?*

Phonics Library

Purposes for decodable text
- applying phonics skills

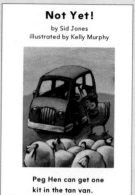

Not Yet!
by Sid Jones
illustrated by Kelly Murphy

Peg Hen can get one kit in the tan van.

17

Can two fit?

Can ten fit?

18   19

Not yet!

20

Home Connection

A **take-home version** of *Not Yet!* is available in the **Phonics Library Blackline Masters**. Children can take the story home to read with their families.

Phonics

Word Work

Day 1

Spelling and Phonics

Letters and Sounds: y, v

Display **Large Sound/Spelling Cards** *yo-yo* and *volcano.* Review their letters and sounds. Then model how to write *y* and *v.*

- Tell children they will practice spelling.

- Display the **Picture Cards** one at a time in random order. For each picture name, have children write the letter that stands for the beginning sound.

Have children complete **Practice Book** page 76.

Penmanship For children who need extra practice, model how to write lower-case *v* and *y.* Have children practice writing the letters.

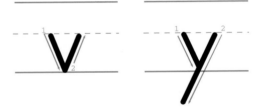

Two penmanship models (continuous stroke, ball and stick) are available in the **Practice Book** (pp. 198–205) and the **Teacher's Resource Blackline Masters** (pp. 143–194).

Word Pattern Board

Words with Short e

- Post the word card *yet* on the Word Pattern Board, and pick a child to read the word. "Clap and spell" the word: *y-e-t, yet!* Repeat with *bet, get, let, met, net, pet, set, vet,* and *wet.*

- Ask how all the words are alike. (They rhyme. They all end with *et.*)

- Follow a similar procedure with *hen.* Have children clap and spell *den, men, pen,* and *ten.*

OBJECTIVES

Children

- **Phonics and Spelling** recognize and write the letters *y* and *v*

- **Word Pattern Board** review words with short *e*

MATERIALS

Phonics and Spelling

- **Large Sound/Spelling Cards:** *yo-yo, volcano*

- **Picture Cards:** *van, vane, vase, vest, vet, vine; yam, yard, yarn, yo-yo, yolk*

- teacher-made word cards *bet, get, let, met, net, pet, set, vet, wet, yet; den, hen, men, pen, ten*

Practice Book page 76

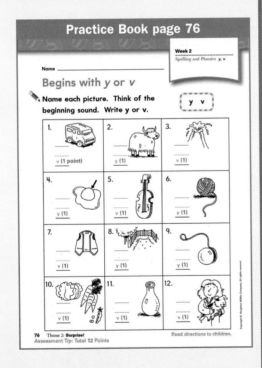

··· **Houghton Mifflin Spelling and Vocabulary** ···
Correlated Instruction and Practice, pp. 30, 32

✏ Writing

Independent Journal Writing

Have children write in their journals. They may choose to

- respond to the daily writing prompt on page T81
- write on self-selected topics

Phonetic Spelling Encourage children to use what they know about letters and letter sounds to record their ideas.

Viewing

Main Idea and Details

Remind children that when Minerva Louise looked around the classroom, she saw many things. Unfortunately, she mistook them for things usually found on a farm.

On the board, draw a web with several spokes. Ask children to take a good look all around their classroom. Write *Things in Our Room* in the center of the web, and read the title for children. Then have them tell what object they see and what it is used for. List children's suggestions on the spokes of the web.

Read the web aloud for children. Point out that all the things written on the spokes are details that tell about *Things in Our Room.*

OBJECTIVES

Children
- **Writing** write in their journals
- **Viewing** identify main idea and details while viewing

Technology

Type to Learn™ Jr.

Students may use **Type to Learn™ Jr.** to familiarize themselves with the computer keyboard. © *Sunburst Technology Corporation, a Houghton Mifflin Company. All Rights reserved.*

Reaching All Students
English Language Learners

Most English language learners will need a model to follow. For example, write: *A book is for reading.* Have children repeat after you. Emphasize the article with the noun and the *-ing* form. Then provide another sentence that follows the same pattern, such as, *A pencil is for writing.* Then present one that has the article *an* instead of *a*, as in *An apple is for eating*, and a mass noun that has no article, as in *Chalk is for writing (on the board).*

Easy

The Pet
by Maria Cara
Illustrated by Martha Weston

Houghton Mifflin

Story Summary
Ben's big brother Ken, a vet, gets him a pet turtle.

Reaching All Students
English Language Learners

Children can begin to dictate a retelling of a story. Record their ideas on a story map to demonstrate story structure.

UNIVERSAL ACCESS

The Pet

On My Way Practice Reader

▶ Preparing to Read

Building Background Read the title and author's name aloud. Discuss pets with children and ask them to predict what kind of pet the boy in the story might get.

▶ Supporting the Reading

Introducing the Book Page through the book with children. You may want to point out the following word: *brother*. The suggestions below can help prepare children to read the story independently.

page 1:	**Find Ken. Ken has a job whose name begins like *van*. Can you point to the word and read it?** (vet)
page 3:	**Can you find a rhyming word for *Ken*?** (Ben) **Can you find a rhyming word for *tan*?** (van)
page 6:	**Three words begin with *b*. Point to them and read them.** (big, big box)
page 8:	**What word begins like *yes*?** (you)

Prompting Strategies Listen to and observe children as they read, and use prompts such as the following to help them apply strategies:

■ *Look at the letters in this word. What sounds do they stand for?*

■ *Blend the sounds. What is the word?*

▶ Responding

Ask children if they were surprised by Ben's pet. Did they expect the pet to be different?

Children can make a book of pets for Ben, drawing and labeling the animals Ben imagined in the story.

The Pet Vet

Theme Paperback

On Level

> The Pet Vet
> By Marcia Leonard
> Photographs by Dorothy Handelman

....

▶ Preparing to Read

Building Background Read aloud the title and author. Point out that the two children are playing vet. Discuss what vets do.

....

▶ Supporting the Reading

Introducing the Book Page through the book with children. The suggestions below can help prepare children to read the story on their own.

pages 4–5:	**The boy's name is Bret. Point to his name in two places. Find a word that rhymes with *Bret*. What is that word?** (vet)
pages 6–7:	**The word that tells what Bret can do begins like *house*. Can you find the word?** (help)
page 10:	**Point to the word that rhymes with *hot*.** (shot)
page 16:	**The word *hurt* ends with a *t*. Point to the word.**
page 20:	**A word here means *fix*. It begins with / m /. Can you find the word?** (mend)

Prompting Strategies Listen to and observe children as they read, and use prompts such as the following to help them apply strategies:

- *Does that word make sense? What does it mean?*

- *Try rereading and see if that word is right.*

....

Story Summary
Bret pretends to be a vet just like his dad.

▶ Responding

Ask for children's opinions of the book. Discuss whether being a vet is a good job. Brainstorm a list of jobs with children and have them illustrate what they would like to be when they grow up.

Children can reread the story in pairs, taking turns on every other page. Spend some time with each pair, observing individual strengths and weaknesses.

vet
teacher
doctor
police officer
baker

Challenge

Story Summary
An adventuresome hen wanders into a classroom—thinking it is a barn. The consequences of her mistake are hilarious.

Minerva Louise at School
Little Big Book

Day 1 Preparing to Read

Building Background Display the Little Big Book and have a child identify the title and the name of the author/illustrator. Remind children that you read aloud the corresponding Big Book. Then have children browse through the book.

Get children thinking about farm things by having them quickly name some people, animals, buildings, and equipment they associate with a farm. Encourage them to think about movies, TV shows, books, or personal experiences.

Developing Story Vocabulary Print the following items in two columns on the board, or print each on an index card. Have children match the words or phrases. Then discuss in what way a pair is similar and how it is different. Use a dictionary as appropriate.

farmer	classrooms
red barn	cubby
laundry on a clothesline	flag on a flagpole
animal stalls	janitor
feeding bucket	red schoolhouse
nesting box	wastebasket

Have children find as many of the farm words in the Little Big Book as possible and read them from the page.

Day 2 Reading the Little Big Book

Applying Phonics Skills Before reading, have children look at selected words. Prompt them to use what they know about letters and letter sounds to read them. Use these words and prompts as models:

page 3: **What letter comes first in the word *woke*?** (w) **How do you know?** (*w* makes the beginning sound,/w/.) **Point to the word.**

page 8: **What letter stands for the /ĕ/ sound in *open*?** (e)

Day 2 *continued . . .*

page 34:   **You know the / k / sound. The letters *ck* can stand for the / k / sound. Where is the / k / sound in *bucket*?** (in the middle)

Now have children turn to page 15. Model how to read an unfamiliar word using this Think Aloud: *If I didn't know the last word on the page, I would blend the first part: / r // ĭ // b /, rib. I know the sounds for the next part too: / b // ŏ // n // z /, bons. I can blend the word: rib-bons. Ribbons. That's funny. Minerva thinks the jump rope is a bunch of ribbons.*

Have partners read the book together and help each other identify words.

Day 3   Rereading the Little Big Book

Applying Comprehension Skills As they read the Little Big Book, children should think about what makes it funny. Is it funny because of what Minerva is doing or because of what she is thinking? Have children turn to pages 9 and 17, read each sentence, and look at the picture. Then ask:

■ What's funny about Minerva waddling down the hall in school? (She thinks she's in a barn.)

■ What's funny about when Minerva looks at a baseball glove and ball? (She thinks it's a nest with an egg.)

Independent Reading Ask children to read *Minerva Louise at School* independently. If they are not sure of a word, they should think about the sounds for the letters, blend the sounds together, and check that the word makes sense in the sentence they are reading.

Day 4   Revisiting the Little Big Book

Retelling the Story Have children sit in a circle. Ask each child in turn to look at a page and retell it in his or her own words. The first child retells what is real and the next child tells what is fantasy, as appropriate. For example, for page 6, the first child tells what is really happening: *Minerva walks up to a school.* The next child tells what's funny because it's make-believe: *The funny thing is she thinks it's a big, fancy barn.*

Day 5   Extending the Little Big Book

Moving Beyond the Story Point out that Minerva starts out from home, has an adventure, and returns home with a new idea. Talk about other animals and a make-believe adventure that might take them from home and back. Have each child write and illustrate a short animal fantasy, either in first person or third person.

Justin Bluebird

One day I woke up.

I was a bluebird.

I flew downstairs.

I pecked at my breakfast.

I met my friend at his birdhouse.

Day at a Glance

Learning to Read

Reading Instruction, T98–T100

☑ **Comprehension:** Fantasy and Realism in *Minerva Louise at School*

☑ **High Frequency Words:** *do, for, I, is, me, my, said, you*

Phonics Application, T101

- Phonics Library: *Big Ben*
- I Love Reading Books, Books 15–18

Word Work

Spelling and Phonics, T102

- Matching Sounds to Letters: *k*
- Penmanship

Word Pattern Board, T102

Writing & Language

Shared Writing, T103

- A Class Message

☑ = Tested Skill

Opening

Daily Message

Use the Daily Message for a quick review of phonics, high-frequency words, and language skills.

■ Read the message aloud, pointing to each word as it is read.

■ Have children find and circle examples of consonants *k, v,* and initial *y.*

■ Ask children to find and underline the high-frequency words *and, we, a, the, once,* and *what.*

> Hello, Girls and Boys!
> Yesterday, we read a very funny story about a hen. Today we will read the book once again. As we read, think about what kind of story this is.

Concepts of Print

- Point out the punctuation mark used in the greeting of the message. Tell children that this is an exclamation mark.

- Ask volunteers to show you where each sentence in the body of the message begins and ends.

Routines

....

Daily Phonemic Awareness

Blending Phonemes: Secret Word

■ Whisper a different "secret word" to each child. Choose simple, single-syllable words such as *ten, hot, cat,* or *bug.*

■ Say aloud each word, segmenting the sounds. Example: /t//ĕ//n/.

■ Tell children to blend the sounds quietly and stand when they make their own "secret word." When someone stands, repeat the sounds and have the child blend them together to say the "secret word."

■ If children guess incorrectly, allow others to guess. Continue this activity until all children have guessed their words correctly.

/t/ /ĕ/ /n/

10

Daily Independent Reading

Have children share a book with a friend.

■ Bibliography, pages T4–T5

   Choose books from this list for children to read, outside class, for at least twenty minutes a day.

■ Reread Phonics Library story *Not Yet!*

■ Reread I Love Reading Books, Review Books 10–14

✏ Daily Prompt for Independent Writing

Use the prompt below, or allow children to write about a topic of their choice. Encourage them to use what they know about letters and sounds to record their ideas.

■ Write about a place you would like to visit, such as a farm, a zoo, or a park.

There are sheep at the farm.

Big Book

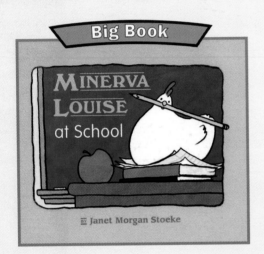

Comprehension

☑ Fantasy and Realism

▶ Rereading the Big Book

Setting a Purpose Display the cover of the Big Book. Use the illustration to focus attention on Minerva Louise. Point out that hens are real animals but they definitely do not do the things that Minerva Louise does in this story.

- Before you reread the story, tell children that they can chime in and read the words they know as you read aloud.

- Point to each word as you read, modeling left to right word tracking and the return sweep.

▶ Teach

After reading, model how to distinguish between what is real and what is make-believe in the story.

> **Think Aloud**
>
> *As I read this story, how can I tell if it is real or make-believe? The first page of the story shows a farm and some hens in a henhouse. I know that hens really do live on farms. But then the hen sees a school. She thinks the school is a barn. She sees blocks and thinks they are a pig pen. In real life, hens don't think like real people. So now I know this story is make-believe.*

Have children point out other parts of the story that are make-believe. Tell them that if any part of a story could not possibly happen in real life, then the story is called a fantasy.

▶ Practice

Have children look at the stories they have read so far in their Anthologies. Have them tell whether each story is about something real or something that could never happen. You might use these prompts:

■ *Look at the story* Nan and Fan. *Could a dog really follow a girl to school? Is there anything in this story that could never, ever happen?*

■ *Look at* We Can! *How do you know that* We Can! *is about real people?*

■ *What about* The Big Hit? *Could the events in this story possibly happen? What makes you think so?*

■ *Now look at* Wigs in a Box. *How do you know that this story is a fantasy?*

(Real pigs can't hit balls and win prizes at fairs. Real animals don't put on wigs and dance around and say "Thank you!")

▶ Apply

Choose one or both of the following activities:

■ Have children find examples of fantasy stories on the shelves of your classroom library. Even if they can't read all the words, they can probably tell from the pictures if a story is make-believe. Have children take turns holding up the books they've chosen and telling why they think the stories are fantasies, or make-believe.

■ Have children work independently or with a partner to complete the activity on **Practice Book** page 77.

Singing a Song Children may enjoy singing about another animal at school in "Mary Had a Little Lamb." Words and music are on R29.

Practice book page 77

Name _____

Could It Really Happen?

Look at each picture. If the picture shows something that could really happen, color it.

Picture should be colored. (3 points)

Picture should be colored. (3)
Read directions to children.

Theme 2: **Surprise!** 77
Assessment Tip: Total 6 Points

DAY 2

Skill Finder

| • Instruction: Theme 7 | • Revisiting: page T112 | • Reteaching: page R24 |

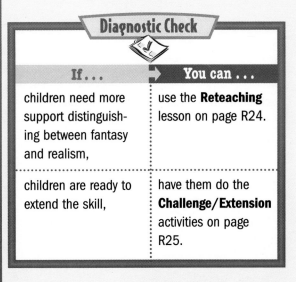

Diagnostic Check

If . . .	▶ You can . . .
children need more support distinguishing between fantasy and realism,	use the **Reteaching** lesson on page R24.
children are ready to extend the skill,	have them do the **Challenge/Extension** activities on page R25.

Comprehension T99

Learning to Read
Day 2

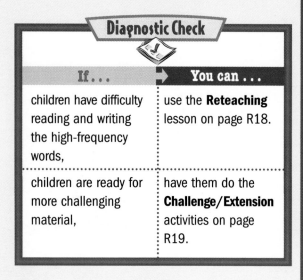

OBJECTIVES

Children

- read and write *do, for, I, is, me, my, said, you*

Practice Book page 79

Practice Book page 78

Chart/Transparency 2–5

A Pet for Ben

"Here," Nan said. "The box is for you."
"For me?" I said. "What is it?"

What can I do?
In the box is a cat.
The cat is my cat.

Diagnostic Check

If...	You can ...
children have difficulty reading and writing the high-frequency words,	use the **Reteaching** lesson on page R18.
children are ready for more challenging material,	have them do the **Challenge/Extension** activities on page R19.

(T100) THEME 2: **Surprise!**

✓ High-Frequency Words

▶ Teach

Tell children that they will learn to read and spell eight new words that are used often in speaking, reading, and writing. Display **Chart/Transparency 2–5**, and have children follow along as you read the title.

- Point to the word *for*, and have children repeat it after you.

- Lead the class in a cheer in which you clap each letter as you spell and say the word: *f-o-r, for.*

Follow a similar procedure for each set of sentences. Read the first set, and then have children clap and spell the new words *said, is, you, me,* and *I.* Read the second set, and have children clap and spell *do* and *my.*

You may want to point out the use of quotation marks to show what Nan says in the story. Tell children that the boy in the picture is Ben, and he is telling this story. Point out the quotation marks to show what Ben says.

▶ Practice

Write *said* on the chalkboard.

do, I, is, me,
my, said, you, for

- Have children read the word.

- Have children find the word on **Chart/Transparency** 2–5.

- Ask a volunteer to read aloud the sentence in which the word appears.

Repeat for each of the other high-frequency words.

Word Pattern Board Post the words in the "New Words" section of the Word Pattern Board. Remind children to look on the Word Pattern Board when they are writing *do, for, I, is, my, said,* and *you.*

▶ Apply

Have children work with partners to complete **Practice Book** pages 78–79.

| Skill Finder | Reteaching: page R18 | Review: Word Pattern Board, pages T102, T136 |

Reading

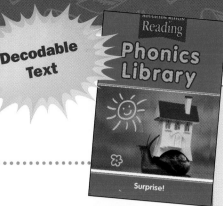
Decodable Text

Phonics Library
Surprise!

▶ Phonics/Decoding Strategy

Distribute the **Phonics Library** story *Big Ben*. Have children describe the pictures on pages 21–22.

Teacher/Student Modeling
Ask children to tell how they read new words. Use **Poster A** to review the steps of the Phonics/Decoding Strategy. Choose someone to read the story title and tell how he or she read each word.

Assign children to read the story. Circulate as they read, offering support and encouragement.

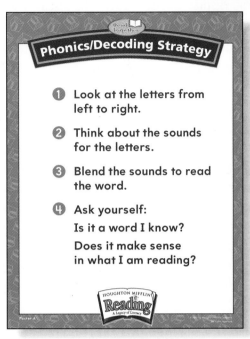

Phonics/Decoding Strategy

1. Look at the letters from left to right.
2. Think about the sounds for the letters.
3. Blend the sounds to read the word.
4. Ask yourself:
   Is it a word I know?
   Does it make sense in what I am reading?

Poster A

Reading the Decodable Book If children have difficulty decoding words like *set*, help them apply the strategy with prompts such as these:

- *What should you look at first?* (letters in the word)

- *How can you sound out the word?* (blend the sounds /s/ /ĕ/ /t/, *set*)

- *How can you decide if* set *is the correct word?* (See if the word makes sense.)

Supply the words only when absolutely necessary.

Oral Language Have children respond in complete sentences to the following.

- *What is the name of the dog in this story?* (The dog's name is Big Ben.)

- *Why do you think Big Ben was with Vet Dan?*

DAY 2

Phonics Library

Purposes for decodable text
- applying phonics skills
- applying high-frequency words

Big Ben
by Rosita Rodriguez
illustrated by Steve Cox

"Is Big Ben set yet?" said Ken.
21

Vet Dan got Big Ben for me.
22

Big Ben can sit.
23

I can pat Big Ben.
24

Suggestions for Daily Fluency Building

Extra Support	**On Level**	**Challenge**
Teacher-Supported Reading	**Partner Reading**	**Partner Reading**
• On My Way Practice Reader: *The Pet*	• Books from Bibliography • Literature Resources	• Reread the Little Big Book: *Minerva Louise at School*

Home Connection

A take-home version of *Big Ben* is available in the **Phonics Library Blackline Masters**. At the end of the day, children can take the story home to read with their families.

High-Frequency Words (T101)

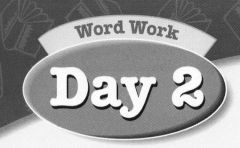

Day 2

Spelling and Phonics

Matching Sounds to Letters: k

Children

- **Spelling and Phonics** recognize and write the letter *k*
- **Word Pattern Board** read *do, for, I, is, me, my, said, you*

MATERIALS

- **Large Sound/Spelling Cards** *cat, kangaroo*
- **Picture Cards:** *can, cat, cot, kite, kit*

Practice Book page 80

Name _____

Begins with *k*

Name each picture. Color the pictures that have the same beginning sound as kit.

Picture should be colored. (1 point)   Picture should be colored. (1)   Picture should be colored. (1)

Picture should be colored. (1)   Picture should be colored. (1)

Picture should be colored. (1)   Picture should be colored. (1)

80 Theme 2: **Surprise!**
Assessment Tip: Total 6 Points   Read directions to children.

∴ **Houghton Mifflin Spelling and Vocabulary** ∴
Correlated Instruction and Practice, p. 21

First, display **Large Sound/Spelling Card** *cat.* Ask children to name the letter and say the sound: /k/. Remind children that they have already learned to spell some words in which the letter *c* spells the /k/ sound. Display the picture cards *cat, can,* and *cot.* Have children name the pictures and write the words.

Next, display **Large Sound/Spelling Card** *kangaroo,* and ask children to say the sound: /k/. Point out that the sound for *kangaroo* is the same as the sound for *cat*—but that the letters are different. Explain that some words use the letter *k* to spell /k/. Model how to write *k.*

- Write *kit* on the board, and ask children to read the word.
- Ask a volunteer to find **Picture Card** *kit.*
- Have children practice writing *kit.*
- Hold up **Picture Card** *kite,* and tell children that it begins with the same sound and letter as *kit.* Have children write that letter.

Have children complete **Practice Book** page 80.

Penmanship For children who need extra practice, model how to write lower-case *k.* Have children practice writing the letter. You may also want to have them practice writing the word *kit.*

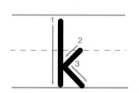

Two penmanship models (continuous stroke, ball and stick) are available in the **Practice Book** (pp. 198–205) and the **Teacher's Resource Blackline Masters** (pp. 143–194).

Word Pattern Board

High-Frequency Words Call attention to the "New Words" *do, for, I, is, me, my, said,* and *you.* Clap and spell the words. Emphasize that the words on the Word Pattern Board will help children as they read and write.

Shared Writing

A Class Message

Remind children that you have written several messages on the board. You may want to display one of these messages now for children's reference.

Suggest that children write a message to another class or to their families to tell about something they have done during the day.

■ Decide with children to whom the message should be sent.

■ Brainstorm with children ideas for the message. List their suggestions on the board, and then have the group vote to decide which idea to use.

■ Show children how to write the greeting:

Dear Family,

■ Have children dictate a few sentences for the body of the message.

■ Ask for volunteers to copy the message onto chart paper if it is to be sent to another class. If it is to be sent home, prepare copies on the computer for duplication.

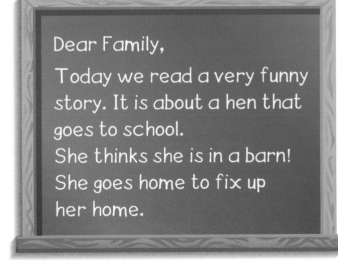

Dear Family,
Today we read a very funny story. It is about a hen that goes to school.
She thinks she is in a barn!
She goes home to fix up her home.

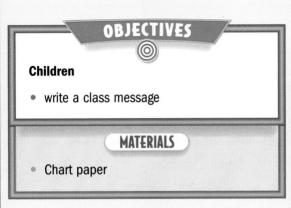

OBJECTIVES

Children
● write a class message

MATERIALS
● Chart paper

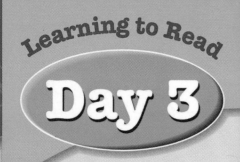

Day at a Glance

Learning to Read

Reading the Anthology, T106–T113

What Can a Vet Do?

written by Gare Thompson
illustrated by Anne Kennedy

✓ Comprehension:
Fantasy and Realism

• Reading Strategy:
Monitor/Clarify

✓ Applying Phonics
and High-Frequency
Words

Phonics Review, T114–T115

✓ Words with Short *o*

• I Love Reading Books,
Review Book 10

Word Work

Spelling and Phonics, T116

• Letters and Sounds: *y, k, v,*
Short *e*

• Penmanship

Vocabulary, T116

• Opposites

Writing & Language

Grammar, T117

• Naming Words

✓ = Tested Skill

Opening

Daily Message

Use the Daily Message for a quick review of high-frequency words, phonics, and language skills.

■ Read the message aloud, pointing to each word as it is read.

■ Call on a few children to find and circle examples of consonants *k, v,* and initial *y.* When a child circles a letter, ask where in the word it appears.

■ Call on volunteers to find and underline the words *and, We, do, a, the, you, go,* and *to.*

Good Morning, Girls and Boys!
We will do a lot of things today.
First we will read about vets
and the work that they do.
Then you will go to your centers
and do your own work.

Concepts of Print

Display word cards for each of the high-frequency words in the message. Then ask children to match the words on the cards with those same words in the message.

Daily Phonemic Awareness

Blending Phonemes: Let's Cheer

Tell children that they will learn a cheer.

- Model the first line as shown, segmenting the sounds of the last word. Then call out the word.

  Teacher: *Give me a / p / / ĭ / / t / !* *Pit!*

- As you read each remaining line, have children blend the sounds together and call out the word.

  Teacher: *Give me a / k / / ă / / n / !* Children: *Can!*

  Teacher: *Give me a / l / / ŏ / / g / !* Children: *Log!*

  Teacher: *Give me a / r / / ă / / g / !* Children: *Rag!*

  Teacher: *Give me a / l / / ĭ / / p / !* Children: *Lip!*

- After lots of practice, you might have children make up their own cheers to share with the class.

Daily Independent Reading

Have children read books with a partner and discuss their favorite parts.

- Have children reread stories from Theme 1 on their own.

- Bibliography, pages T4–T5

  Choose books from this list for children to read, outside class, for at least twenty minutes a day.

- Books for Small-Group Reading, pages T92–T95

- Reread I Love Reading Books, Review Books 10–14

Daily Prompt for Independent Writing

Use the prompt below, or allow children to write about a topic of their choice. Encourage them to use what they know about letters and sounds to record their ideas.

We have a big dog.

- Draw and write about a pet you have, a pet in your neighborhood, or a pet you have read about in a story.

DAY 3

Day 3

What Can a Vet Do?

written by Gare Thompson
illustrated by Anne Kennedy

Purpose • applying reading strategies, comprehension skills, phonics/decoding skills, high-frequency words, and critical thinking

---

High-Frequency Words

do	for	is
my		

Words with *k, v, y,* short *e*

Ben	get	kit
Ned	pen	pet
van	vet	wet
yes		

Preparing to Read

➤ Building Background

Vets Tell children to turn to Anthology page 171 and look at the picture. Ask who children think the woman is. (a vet) Ask what vets do. Tell children to use clues from the picture on page 171 to get some ideas of what vets do.

➤ Using "Get Set to Read"

Call on individuals to read the words and sentences on Anthology pages 168–169. Ask children what things about each word helped them to read it.

■ Did they recognize the letters?

■ Did they blend the sounds for the letters?

■ Did they recognize the word from the Word Pattern Board?

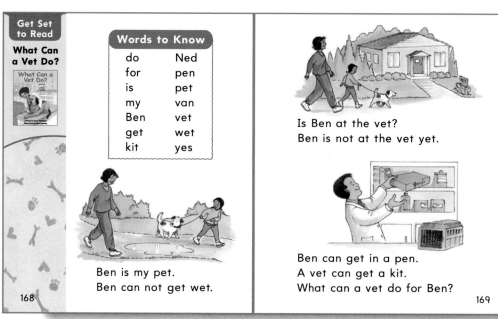

Get Set to Read

What Can a Vet Do?

Words to Know

do	Ned
for	pen
is	pet
my	van
Ben	vet
get	wet
kit	yes

Is Ben at the vet?
Ben is not at the vet yet.

Ben is my pet.
Ben can not get wet.

168

Ben can get in a pen.
A vet can get a kit.
What can a vet do for Ben?

169

Anthology pages 168–169

Strategy & Skill Focus

▶ **Strategy Focus:**
Monitor/Clarify

Teacher Modeling Have children turn to Anthology page 171. Read the selection title and the names of the author and the illustrator. Model how to use the monitor/clarify strategy.

> **Think Aloud**
>
> *If I did not know what a vet is, I might look at the picture on page 171. I see a woman bandaging a dog's paw. I see pictures of other animals on the wall. I decide that a vet cares for animals.*

Remind children to also use their other reading strategies as they read the selection.

Quick Write Ask children what they think this selection will be about. Have them draw or write predictions in their journals.

Purpose Setting Ask children to think about their predictions as they read.

✓ Comprehension Skill Focus:
Fantasy and Realism

Remind children that some stories tell about things that can happen in real life, while others are fantasy, or make-believe. As children read, they should look for clues that tell what kind of story this is.

Teacher's Note

Strategy and Comprehension Skills Connection Noting the genre of a reading selection—and identifying it as realism or fantasy—is often helpful in clarifying ideas. Events in a fantasy may be confusing to readers who do not understand that a fantasy is not about real things.

Focus Questions

Have children turn to Responding on page 186. Read the questions aloud and tell children to keep them in mind as they read *What Can a Vet Do?*

DAY 3

Reaching All Students
English Language Learners

Write *vet* on the board. Make sure children know this is a doctor who takes care of animals. Keep in mind that in many parts of the world, especially where human doctors are scarce, the idea of health care for animals is either unknown or an unjustifiable expense. Ask if anyone has ever taken a pet to the vet; encourage children to talk about the experience.

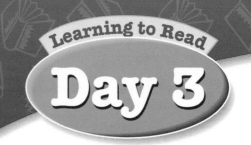

Learning to Read
Day 3

Reading the Anthology

Options for Reading

▶ **Universal Access** See the Classroom Management tips at the bottom of these pages for suggestions to meet individual needs during and after reading.

About the Author Gare Thompson knows a lot about vets. His daughter is studying to be one. Their dog, Gretchen, needs the help. She thinks she is a bird and not a dog!

About the Illustrator Before Anne Kennedy illustrated books, she was a music teacher. She likes to spend time with her dog, Brody, and her horse, Sitka. Sometimes she even rides Sitka in horse shows.

Key to Underlined Vocabulary
Words with *k, v, y,* short *e* ═══
High-Frequency Words ────

Anthology pages 170–171

Anthology pages 172–173

Can the vet fix Big Ben?
The vet can get a kit.

174

Big Ben can sit.

175

Anthology pages 174–175

Big Ben can get wet.

176

The vet can pat Big Ben.

177

Anthology pages 176–177

Comprehension/Critical Thinking

1 Why did the girl take her cat to the vet?
(Something bit her cat. Vets know how to help sick or injured pets.) **Cause and Effect**

2 Look at the picture on page 174. What is in the vet's kit? (scissors, grooming comb, thermometer, syringes) **Noting Details**

3 **Strategy Focus: Teacher/Student Modeling** I wonder why the vet gets the cat wet. Maybe the cat got an insect bite, and the vet is giving the cat a special bath to stop the itching. What do you think? If we look back at the picture on page 172, we see that the cat is scratching himself. What does that tell you? (Children will probably suggest that the cat did need a special bath to help get rid of the itch.) **Monitor/Clarify**

4 **Strategy Focus: Teacher/Student Modeling** How could you use what you know about letters and sounds to help you figure out this word (*get*, page 173)? (Blend the sounds /g/ /ĕ/ /t/.) **Phonics/Decoding**

DAY 3

Revisiting the Text

Concepts of Print

Ask children to use their index fingers to show the direction in which to read each line of text.

Reading the Anthology: *What Can a*

Comprehension/Critical Thinking

1. ✓ Is Chapter 1 of this story about something that could happen in real life, or is it a fantasy? How do you know? (It's about something that could happen in real life. Animals do get sick or injured, and vets can help them get well.) **Fantasy and Realism**

2. Do you think the vet has helped Big Ben feel better? (Yes, the cat looks much happier in the picture on page 178.) **Noting Details**

Yes, the vet can do a lot for Big Ben!
178

Chapter 2

Ned is my big pet.
Ned is in a big pen.
179

Anthology pages 178–179

Mom, get the vet!
180

Ned can not jump.
181

Anthology pages 180–181

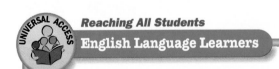

Reaching All Students
English Language Learners

More Uses of *get* Pause after reading page 180. Ask children which of the verbs discussed earlier could be used instead of *get* in this sentence: *take, bring,* or *become.* (bring) Ask children to think of other expressions they have heard with *get.* These might include *get sick, get out of school, get lost, get tired.* Discuss as needed.

Here is the vet in a tan van.

182

The vet can get a big kit.
Can the vet fix Ned?

183

Anthology pages 182–183

Comprehension/Critical Thinking

1 Look at the picture on page 179. Where does Chapter 2 of the story take place? (on a farm) **Noting Details**

2 **Strategy Focus: Student Modeling** What does the sentence on page 179 tell you about the boy's pet? (It is big, and it is in the pen.) Does it tell you what kind of pet the boy has? (no) What do you need to do to figure that out? (Look at the picture, which shows a horse in the pen) **Monitor/Clarify**

3 Why does the boy's pet need a vet? (It cannot jump.) Why do you think the horse cannot jump? (Possible answer: Maybe it is sick. Maybe it hurt its leg. The picture on page 181 shows the horse lying down and looking ill.) **Making Inferences**

DAY 3

Learning to Read
Day 3

Yes, the vet can fix Ned!

184

A vet can do a lot.

185

Anthology pages 184–185

Comprehension/Critical Thinking

1 **Strategy Focus: Student Modeling**
Have children look just at the illustrations on pages 184–185. Ask volunteers to explain how they know the horse is better. (It shows the horse standing up. The boy and mom look happy.)
Monitor/Clarify

2 Is Chapter 2 of the story about real-life things, or is it a fantasy? (It is about real-life things. Animals can get sick or hurt, and vets can help.)
Fantasy and Realism

Revisiting the Text

Retelling the Story:
Fantasy and Realism

As children retell the story, have them explain why it is a realistic story rather than a fantasy. You may want to have some children retell Chapter 1 and others retell Chapter 2.

Diagnostic Check

If . . .	You can . . .
children have difficulty distinguishing between fantasy and realism,	guide them in rereading the text and telling which things could really happen.
children have difficulty reading specific words,	coach them in using the Phonics/Decoding Strategy.

Reaching All Students
English Language Learners

Making Inferences Ask children why they think the vet went to the farm to take care of the horse. As needed, remind children that the cat went to the vet's office. Encourage children to talk about how easy or difficult it is to take a cat or dog to the vet compared to a horse. Ask children for names of other big animals that the vet might go to.

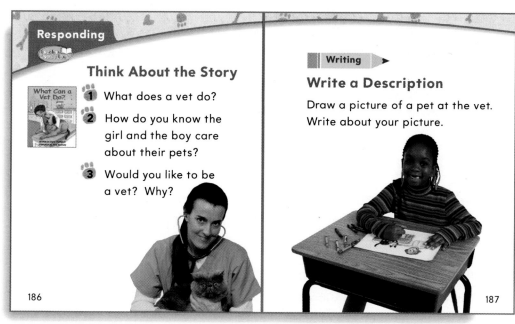

Think About the Story

1 What does a vet do?

2 How do you know the girl and the boy care about their pets?

3 Would you like to be a vet? Why?

186

Writing ▶

Write a Description

Draw a picture of a pet at the vet. Write about your picture.

187

Anthology pages 186–187

Responding

▶ Think About the Story

Discuss the questions on Anthology page 186. Accept reasonable responses.

1 **Main Idea** A vet takes care of animals that are sick, injured, or need special care.

2 **Drawing Conclusions** Each gets the help of a vet when the pet needs that help.

3 **Making a Personal Response** Answers will vary.

4 **Connecting/Comparing** What surprised you in this story? (Possible answers: A vet can take care of big and little pets. Animals can get sick like people do.)

▶ Comprehension Check

Practice Book page 81

DAY 3

Reaching All Students
Extra Support

Writing Support for Responding Ask children to name some kinds of pets. List their suggestions on the board, and suggest that children refer to the list as they draw their pictures and label them.

Reaching All Students
English Language Learners

Beginning/Preproduction Ask children to draw a picture of a vet helping an animal. Then help children describe thier drawings.

Early Production and Speech Emergence Have the children work in two groups. One group should make a list of small animals; the other should make a list of big animals. Encourage children to use their picture dictionaries.

Intermediate and Advanced Ask children to talk about how they think a vet and a medical doctor might be the same.

Student Self-Assessment

Help children assess by asking:

• What did you do well while reading this story?

• Were any parts of the story hard to understand?

• What did you do to help yourself?

Learning to Read
Day 3

Phonics Review

Words with Short o

OBJECTIVES

Children

- review consonants *b, c, d, f, g, h, k, l, m, n, p, r, s, t, v, w, x, y*
- review short *o*
- read words with short *o* and known consonants

MATERIALS

- **Large Letter Cards** *b, c, d, f, g, h, k, l, m, n, o, p, r, s, t, v, w, x, y*
- punchout letters *b, c, d, f, g, h, k, l, m, n, o, p, r, s, t, v, w, x, y*
- **Blackline Master** 198
- **Word Cards** *box, cot, dot, fox, hop, log, mop, pot, top*
- **I Love Reading Books,** Review Books 10–14

▶ Building Words

Reviewing Consonants Display **Large Letter Cards** *b, c, d, f, g, h, k, l, m, n, p, r, s, t, v, w, x, y.* Remind children that they know the sounds for these letters. Have children name each letter and say its sound.

Reviewing Short o Tell children that today they will build some words with consonants they know and the vowel *o.* Display **Large Letter Card** *Oo* and tell children to say the short *o* sound, /ŏ/.

Playing "Hot Pot" Invite children to play "Hot Pot" with partners or in small groups. To play:

- Write *Hot Pot* on a container into which punchout letter cards can fit.
- Display the punchout consonant letter cards face up.
- Give each player a letter card *o.*
- Players take turns choosing two letter cards from among those on display. If the letter can be used with *o* to make a real word, such as *box,* the player says the word and then puts the cards into the pot.
- Play continues until as many words as possible have been formed.

Making Flip Books Copy the pattern on **Blackline Master** 198. Write the letters *d, g, h, o, t, p,* one letter on each square. Copy the page for each child. Have children cut out the big rectangle and the squares. Show children how to stack *d, g,* and *h* on the left side of the rectangle, *o* in the middle, and *t* and *p* on the right. Staple the squares at the top. Have children flip the pages to make short *o* words. Tell children to write a list of the words they make. Have them read the words to you or to a partner. (Children can make four words: *dot, got, hot, hop.*)

You may want to have children make other flip books with these letters:

- *b, f,* and *r* on the left side, *o* in the middle, and *d* and *x* on the right. (*box, fox, rod*)
- *f, h,* and *l* on the left side, *o* in the middle, and *g* and *t* on the right. (*fog, hog, log, hot, lot*)

▶ Reading Short *o* Words

Playing "Hot—Not Hot" Invite children to play "Hot—Not Hot." To play:

■ Hide (but not too well) **Word Cards** *box, cot, dot, fox, hop, log, mop, pot, top.*

■ Ask for a volunteer to begin the search for a **Word Card**. Have the searcher hide his or her eyes while you point out to the class the whereabouts of one card. Show the card to the class so everyone knows what word needs to be found.

■ Tell the searcher what word he or she must find. The searcher walks around the room, looking for the word card. If the searcher moves away from the card, the class chants "Not Hot." As the searcher moves toward it, the class chants "Hot!"

■ Once the searcher finds the card, another child takes a turn to search.

Word Pairs Write the following word pairs on the board. Have children read the words aloud, saying them faster and faster each time.

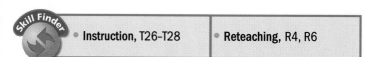

lot–lit	net–not	cot–cat
pit–pot	log–leg	pat–pot
hop–hip	pot–pet	hot–hat

Practice Have children read **I Love Reading Books,** Review Books 10–14.

Skill Finder
• Instruction, T26–T28	• Reteaching, R4, R6

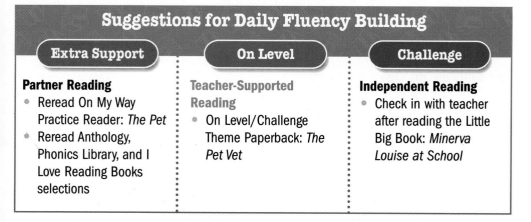

Suggestions for Daily Fluency Building

Extra Support	**On Level**	**Challenge**
Partner Reading	**Teacher-Supported Reading**	**Independent Reading**
• Reread On My Way Practice Reader: *The Pet*	• On Level/Challenge Theme Paperback: *The Pet Vet*	• Check in with teacher after reading the Little Big Book: *Minerva Louise at School*
• Reread Anthology, Phonics Library, and I Love Reading Books selections		

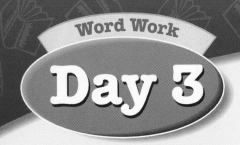

OBJECTIVES

Children

- **Spelling and Phonics** recognize and write the letters *y, k, v;* write words with short *e*
- **Vocabulary Skills** opposites

MATERIALS

Spelling and Phonics

- **Large Sound/Spelling Cards** *yo-yo, kangaroo, volcano, elephant*
- **Picture Cards** *king, kiss, kite, kit; van, vase, vest, vet; yam, yard, yarn, yolk*

Vocabulary

- Anthology Selection *What Can a Vet Do?*
- drawing paper, crayons or markers
- old magazines, scissors, paste

· · · Houghton Mifflin Spelling and Vocabulary · · ·
Correlated Instruction and Practice, p. 79

Spelling and Phonics
Words with y, k, v, and Short e

Review the letters and sounds for *y, k, v,* and short *e* using **Large Sound/Spelling Cards** *yo-yo, kangaroo, volcano* and *elephant*. Remind children how to write the letters by modeling on the chalkboard.

■ Display the **Picture Cards** in random order one at a time, and have children write the letter that stands for the beginning sound.

■ Display the **Picture Card** *vet*. Say the word slowly, and ask a child to spell the word orally as you model how to write it. Then have children write the word on their own.

Penmanship For children who need extra practice, model how to write the word *yes*. Have children practice writing the word several times. You may also want to have children practice writing *vet* and *pen.*

Two penmanship models (continuous stroke, ball and stick) are available in the **Practice Book** (pp. 198–205) and the **Teacher's Resource Blackline Masters** (pp. 143–194).

Vocabulary
Opposites

Have children turn to page 183 of *What Can a Vet Do?* Ask them to find a word that tells the size of this vet's kit. (*big*) Compare the kit with the one pictured on page 174. Ask for a word that means the opposite of big. (*little, small*)

Tell children that words like *big* and *little* are opposites. Provide other examples, such as *on/off, hot/cold, wet/dry, up/down, rough/smooth*. For each pair, say a sentence and ask children to provide a second sentence that means the opposite:

The lights are on. (*The lights are off.*)

The weather is hot. (*The weather is cold.*)

The dog is wet. (*The dog is dry.*)

The window shades are up. (*The window shades are down.*)

This cloth feels rough. (*This cloth feels smooth.*)

Grammar
Naming Words

An excellent way to introduce the concept of noun is to read aloud the book *Incredible Ned* by Bill Maynard (G. P. Putnam's Sons, 1997). Whenever Ned says a naming word, like *bananas*, the object named appears.

> If a word that Ned said was the name of a "thing,"
>
> Then that "thing" might float by on the end of a string!
>
> He could say "and" or "the" and have nothing to fear,
>
> It was words like "baboons" that made baboons appear.

Distribute the **Picture Cards** to children. Pretending to be Ned, they can take turns saying the naming word and holding up the picture.

Place the **Picture Cards** *nurse, store, kite,* and *horse* along the chalkboard ledge. Ask children to find the picture that names:

■ a person ■ an animal ■ a place ■ a thing

Then hold up the remaining cards, one at a time. Have children name the picture and then tell whether the word names a person, an animal, a place, or a thing.

■ Children can use all the **Picture Cards** to play a sorting game in which they group picture cards according to whether they name people, animals, places, or things.

 • **Review, page T137**

OBJECTIVES

Children
• identify naming words

MATERIALS

• **Picture Cards** *bike, boat, boy, doll, girl, horse, kite, nurse, store, train, vet, yard, zebra, zoo*

·········· **Houghton Mifflin English** ··········
Correlated Instruction and Practice, pp. 61–66

DAY 3

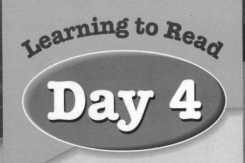

Day 4

Day at a Glance

Learning to Read

Reading the Anthology, *T120–T129*

✓ **Comprehension:**
Fantasy and Realism

• **Reading Strategy:**
Monitor/Clarify

✓ **Applying Phonics and High-Frequency Words**

Word Work

Spelling and Phonics, *T130*

• **Word Slides with Short *e***

• **Penmanship**

Vocabulary, *T130*

• **Foods**

Writing & Language

Writing, *T131*

• **Writing About Animals**

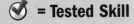

✓ = **Tested Skill**

Opening

....

Daily Message

Use the Daily Message for a quick review of high-frequency words, phonics, and language skills.

■ Read the message aloud, pointing to each word as it is read.

■ Call on children to find and circle examples of the consonants *k, v,* and initial *y.*

■ Call on other children to find the high-frequency words *you, for, is, The, and, my, I, Do,* and *too.*

Hello, All of You!

Our story for today is very funny. The story is <u>Hot Fox Soup</u>, and it is my favorite. I love soup! Do you like soup too?

Concepts of Print

Ask a volunteer to point out where the first sentence begins and ends.

Count Them!

Have children count the sentences in the message.

Routines

Daily Phonemic Awareness

Blending Phonemes: Blend the Rhyme

- Say: *I'm going to say a rhyme. Listen carefully to the last word of the rhyme! I will say the sounds in it. You blend the sounds together and say the word.*

- Say: <u>Fun</u> in the / s / / ŭ / / n /. *Blend the sounds. Raise your hand when you know the word.* (sun)

- Continue with the following rhymes:

  <u>Pat</u> wears a / h / / ă / / t /. (hat)

  <u>Pack</u> a fat / s / / ă / / k /. (sack)

  <u>Bob</u> got a / j / / ŏ / / b /. (job)

  <u>Get</u> the / v / / ĕ / / t /. (vet)

Daily Independent Reading

Encourage children to illustrate favorite scenes from some of the books they read during independent reading time.

- Remind children to practice reading the Word Pattern Board.

- Bibliography, pages T4–T5

  Choose books from this list for children to read, outside class, for at least twenty minutes a day.

- Books for Small-Group Reading, pages T92–T95

- Reread I Love Reading Books, Review Books 10–14

Daily Prompt for Independent Writing

Use the prompt below, or allow children to write about a topic of their choice. Encourage them to use what they know about letters and sounds to record their ideas.

- Draw and write about your favorite food.

I love grapes.

Anthology

HOT FOX SOUP

by
SATOSHI KITAMURA

Purpose • applying reading strategies, comprehension skills, phonics/decoding skills, high-frequency words, and critical thinking

---

High-Frequency Words

I	is
me	my
said	you

Words with y, k, v, short e

get	Hen	kit
let	met	vat
wet	yes	yet

Preparing to Read

▶ Building Background

Making Soup Ask if children have ever helped make soup at home. Ask if the soup came from a can or a kit—or if it was made "from scratch." Ask children to name their favorite kinds of soup.

▶ Developing Story Vocabulary

■ fire ■ noodle ■ soup ■ vat ■ wanted

Display **Chart/Transparency 2–6.** Read the title and the first sentence for children. Then have them read the underlined words *fire, noodle, soup, vat,* and *wanted* as you point to them. Ask children to take turns reading the remaining sentences.

Practice Have children complete **Practice Book** page 82 as a class or with partners.

▶ Using "Get Set to Read"

Have children turn to Anthology pages 188–189. Explain that the words in the box are words they will read in the next story. Ask volunteers to read the words. Then have children read the sentences.

Anthology pages 188–189

Strategy & Skill Focus

▶ Strategy Focus:
Monitor/Clarify

Have children turn to Anthology page 191. Read the selection title and the name of the author/illustrator.

Teacher Modeling Have children follow along as you read aloud pages 192–193. Model how to use the monitor/clarify strategy.

Think Aloud

> *If I didn't know what a vat was, I might look for clues in the pictures. On page 193, I see a very large pot, or tub, over a fire. I might think that a vat is a kind of container.*

Tell children that as they read *Hot Fox Soup*, they should look at the pictures and/or reread the text if they don't understand something. Remind children also to use their other reading strategies as they read the selection.

✏️ **Quick Write** Ask children what they think Fox will do next. Have them record their predictions by drawing or writing in their journals.

Purpose Setting Ask children to check their predictions and change them as needed while they read.

✓ Comprehension Skill Focus:
Fantasy and Realism

Ask children how they can tell right away that this story is a fantasy, or is make-believe. (The illustration on page 191 shows animals sitting at a table that has been set with such things as dishes and spoons and napkins. Pages 192–193 show Fox wearing an apron and starting to cook over a fire. Real animals don't do these things.)

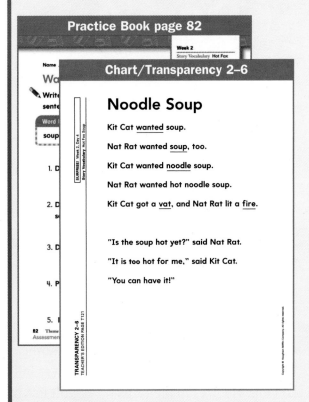

Practice Book page 82

Chart/Transparency 2–6

Noodle Soup

Kit Cat <u>wanted</u> soup.

Nat Rat wanted <u>soup</u>, too.

Kit Cat wanted <u>noodle</u> soup.

Nat Rat wanted hot noodle soup.

Kit Cat got a <u>vat</u>, and Nat Rat lit a <u>fire</u>.

"Is the soup hot yet?" said Nat Rat.

"It is too hot for me," said Kit Cat.

"You can have it!"

Focus Questions

Have children turn to Responding on page 210. Read the questions aloud and tell children to keep them in mind as they read *Hot Fox Soup*.

Teacher's Note

Strategy and Comprehension Skills Connection Knowing that a story is a fantasy prepares readers to expect the unexpected. Things can—and do—happen that would cause consternation in any other kind of story.

Reaching All Students

English Language Learners

Make sure children know what *soup* is and how it is made. Ask children what their favorite type of soup is. Ask volunteers to explain how their parents make soup at home. Assist with vocabulary as needed, or ask more proficient English speakers from the same language background to help.

DAY 4

Learning to Read

Day 4

Reading the Anthology

Options for Reading

▶ **Universal Access** See the Classroom Management tips at the bottom of these pages for suggestions to meet individual needs during and after reading.

About the Author and Illustrator Satoshi Kitamura was born in Japan. Now he lives in London. He likes to fill his pictures with lots of details and color. He hopes you will see the details in *Hot Fox Soup*.

Key to Underlined Vocabulary
Words with *k, v, y,* short *e* ═══
High-Frequency Words ───
Story Vocabulary ───

Meet the Author and Illustrator
Satoshi Kitamura

Story 4

HOT FOX SOUP

by
SATOSHI KITAMURA

191

Anthology pages 190–191

Fox wanted hot hen soup.

192

Fox got a big, big vat.
Fox lit a hot, hot fire.

193

Anthology pages 192–193

Reaching All Students

Classroom Management

On Level

Partner Reading Have partners point out elements of fantasy as they read and then join the class to discuss: Comprehension/Critical Thinking, T123, T125, T126, T127; Fantasy and Realism, T127; Think About the Story, T128.

Challenge

Independent Reading Children can read the story independently and join the class to discuss: Comprehension/Critical Thinking, T123, T125, T126, T127; Fantasy and Realism, T127; Think About the Story, T128.

English Language Learners

Intermediate and Advanced
Have partners read this story. Have children look at the art for clues to the meaning of unfamiliar words. For English Language learners at other proficiency levels, see Language Development Resources.

Fox got a noodle soup kit in a box.

194

Fox met Hen.
"What can I get?" said Hen.

195

Anthology pages 194–195

"Get wet in my vat, Hen," said Fox.

196

"Not me!"
Hen ran.

197

Anthology pages 196–197

Comprehension/Critical Thinking

1 What *kind* of soup did Fox want? (hot *hen* soup) **Noting Details**

2 Why didn't Hen want to get wet in Fox's vat? (The noodle soup was very hot. Hen would have gotten cooked in such hot soup.) **Cause and Effect**

3 Is that what Fox wanted—for Hen to get cooked? (Yes. He said on page 192 that he wanted hot *hen* soup.) **Cause and Effect**

4 ✓ What did Fox do in this part of the story that real foxes do not do? (Fox wore an apron, lit a fire, prepared soup, talked with a hen.) **Fantasy and Realism**

5 How could you use what you know about letters and sounds to figure out this word (*met*, page 195)? (Blend the sounds /m/ /ĕ/ /t/.) **Phonics/Decoding**

Revisiting the Text

Concepts of Print

Point out the use of quotation marks on page 195 to show the exact words that Hen said. Tell children to use index fingers to point to where the quotation marks open and close. Then have them read aloud just the words between their index fingers.

DAY 4

Reaching All Students
Extra Support

Teacher-Supported Reading Have children take turns reading in a small group. Periodically, have them stop and point out things in the story that could never happen in real life. Use the Comprehension/Critical Thinking questions, as needed. Then have them join the class to discuss: Comprehension/Critical Thinking, T123, T125, T126, T127; Fantasy and Realism, T127; Think About the Story, T128.

Phonics Decoding Strategy Coach children in the strategy, as needed.

Revisiting the Text

Concepts of Print

Have children read aloud the question that Pig asked on page 199. Remind them to read only the words inside the quotation marks.

For pages 200–201, ask children how they can tell who said "Get wet in my vat, Pig" and who said "Not me!"

Fox met Pig.
Fox wanted hot pig soup.

198

"What can I get?" said Pig.

199

Anthology pages 198–199

"Get wet in my vat, Pig," said Fox.

200

"Not me!"
Pig ran.

201

Anthology pages 200–201

Reaching All Students

English Language Learners

Predicting After reading page 199, pause and ask children what they think will happen next. As needed, guide the children with questions such as: "What do you think Fox will say? Do you think Pig will go in the vat?"

Fox met Ox.
Fox wanted hot ox soup.

202

"What can I get?" said Ox.

203

Anthology pages 202–203

Comprehension/Critical Thinking

1 Why did Fox keep changing his mind about the kind of soup he wanted? (Hen wouldn't get into the vat, so Fox asked Pig to get in. When Pig wouldn't, he asked Ox.) **Cause and Effect**

2 What kind of story is this—a fantasy or a realistic story? (a fantasy) How do you know? (Things happen that could never happen in real life.) **Fantasy and Realism**

3 What excuse did Ox give for not getting into the vat? (He said he could not fit.) **Noting Details**

"Get wet in my vat, Ox," said Fox.

204

"Not me!
I can not fit in a vat."

205

Anthology pages 204–205

Reaching All Students

English Language Learners

Pause after reading page 203 and help the children review what has happened up to this point. Guide the children with questions such as: "What was the first kind of soup that Fox wanted? What did Fox ask Hen to do? What was the second kind of soup that Fox wanted?"

Reading the Anthology: *Hot Fox Soup*

T125

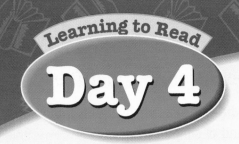

Learning to Read
Day 4

"Fox, you get in," said Ox.
"We can fix hot, hot fox soup!"
206

"Not hot fox soup!" said Fox.
"Let me fix hot, hot noodle soup."
207

Anthology pages 206–207

Comprehension/Critical Thinking

1 **Strategy Focus: Teacher/Student Modeling** Were you puzzled about anything on pages 206–207? Why do you think Fox suggested that they have hot *noodle* soup? (He didn't want to be in the soup!)

Monitor/Clarify

Cross-Curricular Connection

Science If children wonder what a real fox eats, tell them that foxes eat many kinds of fruit as well as small animals they can catch. These animals may include mice, frogs, insects, and rabbits. Because they kill mice, foxes are helpful to farmers, even though they sometimes do raid henhouses.

Diagnostic Check

If . . .	You can . . .
children have difficulty distinguishing between fantasy and realism,	guide them in rereading the story, pausing to talk about what could and could not possibly happen in real life.
children have difficulty summarizing the story,	have them retell it with partners or in small groups, using stick puppets for the characters.
children have difficulty reading specific words,	coach them in using the Phonics/Decoding Strategy.

"Is it hot yet, Fox?"

208

"Yes, it is hot, hot, hot," said Fox. "Dig in!"

209

Anthology pages 208–209

Comprehension/Critical Thinking

1 **Strategy Focus: Student Modeling**
Have children identify any parts of the story they did not understand and tell what they did to help themselves figure things out. (Answers will vary.) **Monitor/Clarify**

2 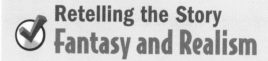 Look again at page 209. What are the animals doing here that only people do in real life? (They are sitting in chairs, eating at a table that has been set, and talking about food.) **Fantasy and Realism**

Revisiting the Text

Retelling the Story
Fantasy and Realism

After discussion of the Comprehension/ Critical Thinking questions, call on individuals to summarize the story. Before children begin, remind them that the story is a fantasy. After each retelling, the class might chant, "That's fantastic!"

DAY 4

Student Self-Assessment

Help children assess by asking:

- What parts were easy to read? Which parts were hard?

- What did you do well as you read this story?

- Did you think this story was funny? What part was the funniest?

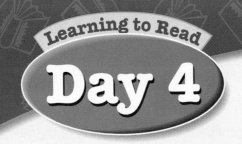

Responding

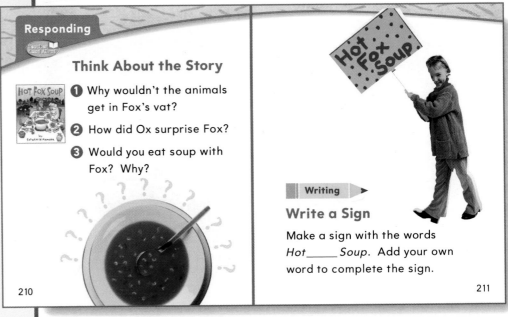

Responding

Think About the Story

❶ Why wouldn't the animals get in Fox's vat?

❷ How did Ox surprise Fox?

❸ Would you eat soup with Fox? Why?

210

Writing ▶

Write a Sign

Make a sign with the words *Hot_____ Soup*. Add your own word to complete the sign.

211

Anthology pages 210–211

▶ **Think About the Story**

Discuss the questions on Anthology page 210. Accept reasonable responses.

❶ **Cause and Effect** They wouldn't get into the vat because they didn't want to be cooked.

❷ **Drawing Conclusions** Ox said that he was going to put Fox into the vat and make fox soup.

❸ **Making a Personal Response** Answers will vary but should be supported.

⭐ **Connecting/Comparing** Think about both stories, *What Can a Vet Do?* and *Hot Fox Soup*. Which story surprised you more? Why? (Answers will vary.)

▶ **Comprehension Check**

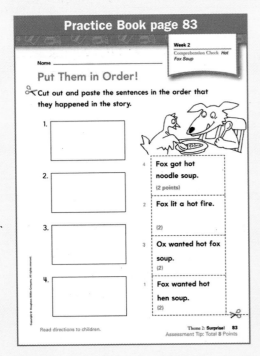

Practice Book page 83

Week 2
Comprehension Check *Hot Fox Soup*

Name _____

Put Them in Order!

✂ Cut out and paste the sentences in the order that they happened in the story.

1. _____
2. _____
3. _____
4. _____

4 | Fox got hot noodle soup. (2 points)

2 | Fox lit a hot fire. (2)

3 | Ox wanted hot fox soup. (2)

1 | Fox wanted hot hen soup. (2)

Read directions to children.

Theme 2: Surprise! **83**
Assessment Tip: Total 8 Points

Reaching All Students
Extra Support

Writing Support Ask children to name some different kinds of soup. List their suggestions on chart paper. Tell children to refer to the list as they make their signs.

Reaching All Students
English Language Learners

Beginning/Preproduction Ask children to go back through the selection naming the various animals. Help children write and say the words for these animals.

Early Production and Speech Emergence Have children take the parts of the animals in a Reader's Theater. Ask a more proficient speaker to read the narrator's part. Help children understand that they are to read the parts in quotes.

Intermediate and Advanced Have children retell the story, using time words such as *first, second, next, then after that.*

Polly, Put the Kettle On

Polly, put the kettle on,
Polly, put the kettle on,
Polly, put the kettle on,
We'll all have tea.

English Traditional Song

212   213

Anthology pages 212–213

Music Link

▶ Skill: How to Sing a Song

Ask if children know the nursery rhyme "Polly, Put the Kettle On." Ask those who do to recite the rhyme. Tell children that this rhyme is also a song. Sing it for children. (The music appears on page R30.)

Have children turn to Anthology pages 212–213. Read aloud the title. Point out that the title is the same as the first line of the song. Ask if children can find other lines that are also the same. Have them compare the words in the first three lines, word by word.

Have children read the first three lines of the song with you. Read the last line for them. Then have children read the entire song along with you. Once children are familiar with the words, have them sing the song.

Comprehension/Critical Thinking

1 Look at the picture on pages 212–213. What are these animals doing that real animals cannot do? (They are sitting at a table and having tea and cookies.) **Fantasy and Realism**

2 How is this song like the ending of the story Hot Fox Soup? (In the story, the animals sit at a table and eat, just as these animals are doing.) **Compare and Contrast**

3 How is a kettle like a vat? (Both are containers; both can be used for cooking liquids.) How is soup like tea? (Both are liquids and usually enjoyed hot.) **Vocabulary Development**

DAY 4

Suggestions for Daily Fluency Building

Extra Support	On Level	Challenge
Teacher-Supported Reading • Phonics Library	**Independent Reading** • Reread On Level Theme Paperback: *The Pet Vet* • Reread Anthology selections	**Partner Reading** • Reread Anthology selections • Literature Resources

OBJECTIVES

Children

- **Spelling and Phonics** build, read, write, and spell words with short e
- **Vocabulary Expansion** learn and recall words that name foods

MATERIALS

Vocabulary

- old magazines, scissors, paste
- **Blackline Master** 197

··· **Houghton Mifflin Spelling and Vocabulary** ···
Correlated Instruction and Practice, p. 79

Spelling and Phonics
Word Slides with Short e

Using **Blackline Master** 197, prepare two sets of word slides. One set will have the letters *m, p, v, w,* and *y* on the letter strip and *e* and *t* in the small boxes on the slide. The other set will have the letters *d, h, m, p,* and *t* on the letter strip and *e* and *n* in the small boxes on the slide.

Have children work with partners. Each child in the pair takes a different word slide. Have partners take turns forming three-letter words and blending the sounds to read them. After one child reads the word, the other child can write it and practice spelling.

Extension/Challenge Have children add more three-letter words with short *e* to their lists.

Penmanship For children who need extra practice, model how to write this sentence: *Ken is a vet.* Have children write the sentence.

Two penmanship models (continuous stroke, ball and stick) are available in the **Practice Book** (pp. 198–205) and the **Teacher's Resource Blackline Masters** (pp. 143–194).

Vocabulary
Foods

Review that at the end of *Hot Fox Soup,* all the animals shared Fox's noodle soup. Ask children to name other foods that they like a lot. Prepare a chart like the one shown, and have children tell for which meal they eat each food mentioned.

Breakfast	Lunch	Supper
orange juice	sandwich	chicken
cereal	apple	string beans
milk	milk	noodles

Have children look through magazines to find food pictures. Suggest that they cut out the pictures, paste each on a separate sheet of paper, and write or dictate labels. Staple the pages together to make a *Favorite Foods* book.

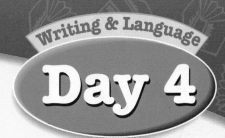
✏️ Writing

Writing About Animals

Remind children that *Hot Fox Soup* is a fantasy; the characters are animals who do things that only humans can do.

Ask each child to choose a wild animal, such as a fox. Arrange a trip to the school library so that children can find nonfiction books about the animals they have chosen. Or, display several nonfiction books and allow children to browse through them to select animals.

Have children draw and write about their animals—as the animals really are. Prompt by asking these questions:

- *Why did you choose this animal?*
- *What color is the animal?*
- *Is it big or little?*
- *Does the animal have legs? How many?*
- *Does the animal have a tail?*
- *Where does the animal live?*

Children can use the books to try to find answers to their questions. Allow them to dictate sentences that answer the questions, if they wish to.

Have children complete **Practice Book** page 85.

Reaching All Students
English Language Learners

Have children work in small mixed groups. Provide photos or drawings of wild animals from which children can choose. After children choose the animal they want to write about, work with each group to describe the animal. Help them label the various parts of the animal. Brainstorm describing words for size, color, type of hair, and so on. Then still as a group, help the children generate sentences; record their ideas on chart paper.

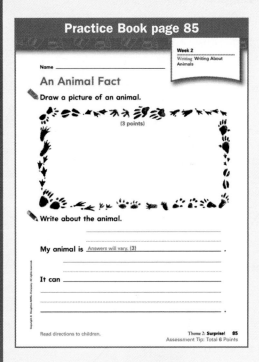

Practice Book page 85

Technology

Type to Learn™ Jr.

Students may use **Type to Learn™ Jr.** to familiarize themselves with the computer keyboard. © *Sunburst Technology Corporation, a Houghton Mifflin Company. All rights reserved.*

Portfolio Opportunity

Save a copy of each child's work as a sample of his or her writing development.

·········· **Houghton Mifflin English** ··········
Correlated Instruction and Practice, p. 197

DAY 4

Day at a Glance

Learning to Read

Reading Instruction, T134

☑ Revisiting the Literature: Fantasy and Realism

Reading Check, T135

- **Phonics Library:** *Get Wet, Ken*
- **I Love Reading Books, Books 15–18**

Word Work

Spelling and Phonics, T136

- Spelling Words with Short *e*
- Penmanship

Word Pattern Board, T136

Writing & Language

Grammar Review, T137

- Naming Words

Listening and Speaking, T137

- Conflict Resolution

☑ = Tested Skill

Opening

Daily Message

Use the Daily Message for a quick skill review.

■ Read the message aloud, pointing to each word as it is read.

■ Have children find and underline any words they can read.

> Good Morning, Everyone!
>
> If I asked you to tell me a story, what story would you tell? Today we will talk about the stories we have read this week.

Concepts of Print

Have children find a sentence that asks a question. Ask children to answer the question by naming some of their favorite stories.

Routines

Daily Phonemic Awareness

Blending Phonemes: Seal's Words

■ Use the **Picture Card** *seal.* Say: *Sammy, the talking seal, needs your help once again to figure out an unfamiliar word he heard today. The word is /w//ĕ//l/. Blend the sounds together. Raise your hand when you know the word.* (well)

■ Repeat this activity, segmenting the sounds for the word *fuzz.* Ask children to blend the sounds together and say the word.

■ Challenge a volunteer to provide a rhyming word, such as *buzz,* to solve for Sammy Seal. Ask the volunteer to whisper the word to you. Segment the word. Ask the class to blend the word together. The volunteer can confirm their response.

Daily Independent Reading

Have children read with partners.

■ Reread *Not Yet!* or *Big Ben* from the Phonics Library.

■ Bibliography, pages T4–T5

Choose books from this list for children to read, outside class, for at least twenty minutes a day.

■ Reread **I** Love Reading Books, Review Books 10–14

✎ Daily Prompt for Independent Writing

Use the prompt below, or allow children to write about a topic of their choice. Encourage them to use what they know about letters and sounds to record their ideas.

Charles Tiger saw a spider.

■ Draw and write about a favorite story.

Children

- review fantasy and realism in the week's selections

MATERIALS

- **Blackline Masters** 29–31

Revisiting the Literature

☑ *Fantasy and Realism*

Comparing Texts Review the difference between fantasy and reality.

> ### Think Aloud
>
> *Sometimes a story tells about things that could really happen. Sometimes a story is a fantasy. A fantasy story has something in it that can't happen in real life. A fantasy may have animal characters that do things only people can do in real life.*

Review the week's selections, *Minerva Louise, What Can a Vet Do?,* and *Hot Fox Soup.* Have children identify:

- an animal character from a fantasy story

- an animal from a realistic story

- a person from a realistic story

Have children explain which books are fantasy and which could be real. Help children identify the differences between the texts.

Additional Practice

- Assign children to reread other selections from the week (**On My Way Practice Reader, On Level/Challenge Theme Paperback, Phonics Library** selections) and think about fantasy and realism in those stories.

- Children can demonstrate their understanding of the comprehension skill, Fantasy and Realism, through a retelling of the story, *Hot Fox Soup* using the story characters on **Blackline Masters** 29–30.

Reading Check

▶ Phonics-Decoding Strategy

Student Modeling Ask children to tell how they have used the Phonics/Decoding Strategy to read new words. Tell them that they should use what they know about letters, sounds, and words to read the next story. Choose a child to model how to use the strategy to read the title. Then have children read the story independently.

Reading the Decodable Book If children have difficulty decoding words like *van* on their own, coach them with prompts such as these:

■ *What are the letters from left to right?* (v, a, n)

■ *What sound does each letter stand for?* (/v/, /ă/, /n/)

■ *Blend the sounds. What is the word?* (vvvăăănnn, van)

■ *Does* van *make sense in the story?*

Developing Fluency Encourage children to read aloud fluently and with expression. Model reading fluently, and coach children to read with feeling and expression as needed.

Phonics Library

Purposes for decodable text

• assessment
• applying phonics skills
• applying high-frequency words

Get Wet, Ken!
by Mark Dempsey
illustrated by Pedro Martin

Can you get wet, Ken?
25

I can not get wet yet.
26

My big tan van got wet.
27

I can do it.
I can get wet, wet, wet!
28

Assessment Options

Oral Reading Records You may wish to take an oral reading record as children read the **Phonics Library** book individually or in small groups.

Alternative Assessment Use **Blackline Master** 31 to assess individual children's phonics and high-frequency word skills.

Suggestions for Daily Fluency Building

Extra Support	**On Level**	**Challenge**
Partner Reading	**Independent Reading**	**Teacher-Supported Reading**
• Books from Bibliography	• Books from Bibliography	• Phonics Library
• Literature Resources	• Literature Resources	

DAY 5

Home Connection

A **take-home version** of *Get Wet, Ken* is available in the **Phonics Library Blackline Masters.** Children can take the story home to read with their families.

Spelling and Phonics

Spelling Words with Short e

Make and display cards with short *e* words that end with *t* or *n,* as shown under Materials. Call on volunteers to read the words.

- With scissors, cut *pet* into its individual letters. Mix up the letters and display them on a table or in a pocket chart.

- Ask: **Which letter stands for the first sound in** pet? **... the second sound? ... the third sound?**

- Choose a child to arrange the letters to spell *pet.*

- Then have children write *pet* on a sheet of paper.

- Choose other listed words and follow the same procedure.

Penmanship Model how to write *I can get my pen.* Monitor children's progress as they write the sentence.

I can get my pen.

Two penmanship models (continuous stroke, ball and stick) are available in the **Practice Book** (pp. 198–205) and the **Teacher's Resource Blackline Masters** (pp. 143–194).

Word Pattern Board

High-Frequency Words Tell children that today you will move this week's high-frequency words from the "New Words" section to the permanent Word Pattern Board.

- Review the "New Words" section with clap and spell. Remove each word as it is reviewed.

- Call on volunteers to move the words to the permanent Word Pattern Board. The class can chant the words are they are moved.

- Review the entire Word Pattern Board with clap and spell.

OBJECTIVES

Children

- **Phonics and Spelling** read, build, and write words with short *e*

- **Word Pattern Board** review the Word Pattern Board.

MATERIALS

- teacher-made cards with *bet, get, let, met, net, pet, set, vet, wet, yet; Ben, den, hen, men, pen, ten, Len, Ken*

···· **Houghton Mifflin Spelling and Vocabulary** ····
Correlated Instruction and Practice, p. 79

Diagnostic Check

If...	You can...
children need more practice in discriminating beginning sounds,	use **Back to School** or Daily Phonemic Awareness, pages T81, T97, T133.

Grammar Review

Naming Words

Display **Chart/Transparency 2–7.** Tell children that these sentences are missing naming words, or nouns.

■ Display **Word Cards** *vet, cut,* and *hop.*

■ Choose a child to read the first incomplete sentence. Ask the child to choose a noun from among the words on display to complete the sentence.

■ Write the suggested noun on the line. Have children as a group read the sentence and decide if it makes sense. Point out that the noun *vet* names a person.

■ Follow a similar procedure with the remaining sentences, using the other groups of **Word Cards.** Point out that the noun in the second sentence names an animal, while the noun in the third sentence names a thing.

Coached Writing Dictate the following sentence from *What Can a Vet Do?*: *A vet can get a kit.* Have children write the sentence. Then ask them to find the two naming words in the sentence, one that names a person (*vet*) and one that names a thing (*kit*).

Speaking and Listening

Conflict Resolution

Review the story *Hot Fox Soup.* Remind children that in the end, Fox thought of a solution to the soup problem. He suggested that they all have hot, hot noodle soup. Ask why this was a good solution. (It meant that none of the animals would end up in the vat.)

Ask if children can think of other ways to solve the soup problem. Point out that talking about ways to solve problems is a good idea. Talk often leads to a solution that pleases everyone.

Encourage children to think of a classroom problem they would like to solve. It may have to do with sharing or with using the centers in cooperative ways. Write the problem on the board, and then have several children suggest ways to solve the problem. List the suggestions.

Reread all the suggestions for children. Talk about those that have possibilities— and might even please everyone. Have the class vote to decide on the best solution. Put the class vote to work!

OBJECTIVES

Children

● **Grammar Review** use nouns to complete sentences

● **Speaking and Listening** suggest ways to resolve a conflict

MATERIALS

Grammar Review

● Word cards with *cut, hop, vet; fox, sit, mix; box, sad, smell*

Chart/Transparency 2–7

Naming Words

The ___ vet ___ can do a lot for a pet.

The ___ fox ___ ran to the den.

The ___ box ___ is for the hat.

SURPRISE! Week 2, Day 5
Grammar Naming Words

TRANSPARENCY 2–7
TEACHER'S EDITION PAGE T137

······**Houghton Mifflin English**··········
Correlated Instruction and Practice, pp. 61–66

DAY 5

Literature for Week 3

Different texts for different purposes

Nick Butterworth and Mick Inkpen

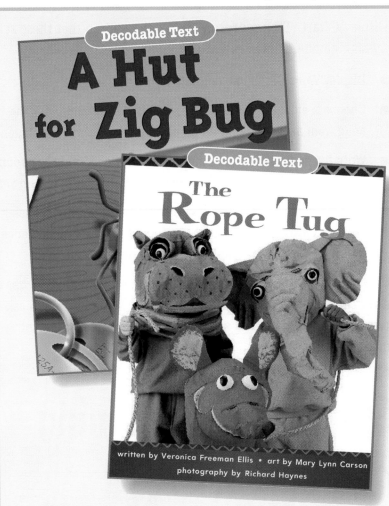

Decodable Text

Decodable Text

The Rope Tug

written by Veronica Freeman Ellis • art by Mary Lynn Carson
photography by Richard Haynes

Big Book

Purposes

- oral language development
- reading strategies
- comprehension skills

 Awards

- ★ Best Books for Children
- ★ United Kingdom Children's Book Award

 Also available on audiotape

Challenge

Little Big Book

Purposes

- vocabulary development
- reading fluency
- application of phonics/decoding and comprehension skills

Nick Butterworth and Mick Inkpen

 Also available on audiotape

Anthology: Main Selections

Purposes

- reading strategies
- comprehension skills
- phonics/decoding skills
- high-frequency words
- critical thinking

 Award Winner

- ★ A book by Ellis was given the Multicultural Publishers Exchange Book Award of Excellence.

Anthology: Get Set to Read *A Hut for Zig Bug*

Anthology: Get Set to Read *The Rope Tug*

Purpose
- applying phonics skills and high-frequency words

Anthology: Poetry Link

Purposes
- skill: how to read a poem
- critical thinking; discussion

Decodable Text

Phonics Library

Purposes
- applying phonics skills
- applying high-frequency words

Also available in take-home version

I ♥ READING BOOKS

Purposes
- applying phonics skills
- applying high-frequency words

Books for Small-Group Reading

Use these resources to ensure that children read, outside class, for at least twenty minutes a day.

On My Way Practice Reader

Easy

Where Is Tug Bug?
by Oscar Gake
page T156

Theme Paperback

On Level

Spots
by Marcia Leonard
page T157

Technology

Education Place

www.eduplace.com
Log on to Education Place for more activities relating to *Surprise!*

Book Adventure

www.bookadventure.org
This Internet reading-incentive program provides thousands of titles for students to read.

Daily Lesson Plans

Instructional Goals

| | **Day 1** | **Day 2** |

Learning to Read

☑ *Strategy Focus:* Summarize

☑ *Comprehension:* Story Structure

Phonemic Awareness: Blend Phonemes

☑ *Phonics:* Consonants *q, j, z,* Short *u;* Blending Short *u* Words (CVC) *Review:* Words with Short *e*
- Additional lessons for phonics skills are included in the *Extra Support Handbook* and *Handbook for English Language Learners.* (See Universal Access Plans.)

☑ *High-Frequency Words: are, away, does, he, live, pull, they, where*

90–110 minutes

Day 1

Opening Routines: *T144–T145*

Reading the Big Book
Jasper's Beanstalk, T146–T149

Phonemic Awareness
- Blend Phonemes, *T150*

Phonics Instruction, Practice, Application
- Consonants *q, j, z, T150; Practice Book,* 86
- Short *u, T151; Practice Book,* 87
- Blending Short *u* Words, *T152; Practice Book,* 88–89
- Phonics Library, *The Bug Kit, T153*

Day 2

Opening Routines: *T160–T161*

Rereading the Big Book
Jasper's Beanstalk, T162–T163

Comprehension Skill Instruction
- Story Structure, *T162–T163*
- *Practice Book,* 91

High-Frequency Words
- Instruction, *T164*
- *Practice Book,* 92–93

Phonics Application
- Phonics Library, *Quit It, Zig!, T165*

Word Work

Spelling and Phonics: Words with *j, z, q,* and Short *u*

Word Pattern Board: High-Frequency Words; Words with Short *u*

Vocabulary: Days of the Week, Homographs

30–40 minutes

Day 1

Spelling and Phonics
- Instruction: Letters and Sounds *j, z, T154*
- *Practice Book,* 90

[Word Pattern Board]
- Words with Short *u, T154*

Day 2

Spelling and Phonics
- Instruction: *qu, T166*
- *Practice Book,* 95

[Word Pattern Board]
- High-Frequency Words, *T166*

Writing & Language

Grammar: Action Words

Shared Writing: A Diary

Writing: Writing About Bugs

Listening/Speaking/Viewing: Retell/ Summarize, Reader's Theater

30–40 minutes

Day 1

✎ **Writing**
- Independent Journal Writing, *T155*

Listening/Speaking
- Retell/Summarize, *T155*

Day 2

✎ **Shared Writing**
- A Diary, *T167*

Teacher's Notes

Books for Small-Group Reading, T152–T153, T156–T159, T165, T179, T197
For reading outside class and homework

Technology

Lesson Planner CD-ROM
Customize your planning for the week with the Lesson Planner.

Day 3

Opening Routines: *T168–T169*

Preparing to Read *A Hut for Zig Bug*
- Building Background, *T170*
- Get Set to Read, *T170*
- Strategy/Skill Preview, *T171*

Reading the Anthology *A Hut for Zig Bug*
- Comprehension/Critical Thinking, *T173, T175, T176*
- Strategy Focus, *T173, T175, T176*
- Responding, *T177,* **Practice Book,** *96*

Phonics Application/Review
- Anthology: *A Hut for Zig Bug, T172–T176*
- Review/Maintain: Words with Short *e,* *T178–T179*

Spelling and Phonics
- Words with *qu, j, z,* and Short *u, T180*

Vocabulary
- Days of the Week, *T180*

✎ **Writing**
- Response Activity, *T177*

Grammar Skill Instruction
- Action Words, *T181*

Day 4

Opening Routines: *T182–T183*

Preparing to Read *The Rope Tug*
- Building Background, *T184*
- Story Vocabulary, *T184,* **Practice Book,** *97*
- Get Set to Read, *T184*
- Strategy/Skill Preview, *T185*

Reading the Anthology *The Rope Tug*
- Comprehension/Critical Thinking, *T187, T188, T189*
- Strategy Focus, *T187, T189*
- Responding, *T190,* **Practice Book,** *98*

Reading the Poetry Link
- "Way Down South," *T191*

Phonics Application
- Anthology: *The Rope Tug, T186–T189*

Spelling and Phonics
- Word Slides with Short *u, T192*

Vocabulary
- Homographs, *T192*

✎ **Writing Instruction**
- Writing About Bugs, *T193*
- **Practice Book,** *99*

Day 5

Opening Routines: *T194–T195*

**Revisiting the Literature:
Comprehension Skill Instruction**
- Story Structure, *T196*

Reading Skills Check:
Phonics Application, Assessment
- Phonics Library, *Rug Tug, T197*

Spelling and Phonics
- Spelling Words with Short *u, T198*

Word Pattern Board
- High-Frequency Words, *T198*

✎ **Writing**
- Independent Writing Prompt, *T195*

Grammar Review
- Action Words, *T199*

Listening/Speaking
- Reader's Theater, *T199*

✎ **Daily Writing: Opening Routines, T145, T161, T169, T183, T195**

UNIVERSAL ACCESS See Universal Access Planning Chart on the following pages.

T141

Week 3

 Universal Access Plans
for Reaching All Learners

Grouping for Instruction

	Day 1	**Day 2**
30–45 minutes		
With the Teacher	**Preteach** Phonics: Consonants *j* and *z*	**Preteach** Comprehension: Story Structure
Extra Support **Teach**—Use Extra Support Handbook	**Preteach** Phonics: Blending Short *u* Words **Preview** *The Bug Kit* ■ Extra Support Handbook pp. 66–67	**Preview** *Quit It, Zig!* ■ Extra Support Handbook pp. 68–69
Working Independently	**Independent Activities**	**See plan for Day 1**
On Level Use Classroom Management Handbook	For each group, assign appropriate activities—your own or those in the handbooks listed below.	
Challenge Use Challenge Handbook	Then get students started on their independent work.	
English Language Learners Use Classroom Management Handbook or Challenge Handbook	■ Classroom Management Handbook pp. 42–49 ■ Challenge Handbook pp. 24–27	**Monitor** Answer questions, if necessary.
30–45 minutes		
With the Teacher	**Preteach** What We Do for Fun	**Preteach** Sequence Words
English Language Learners **Teach**—Use Handbook for English Language Learners	**Preteach** Big Book *Jasper's Beanstalk* **Preteach** Phonics: Consonants *q, j, z* ■ Handbook for ELL pp. 70–71	**Preteach** Get Set to Read; *A Hut for Zig Bug* **Preteach** High-Frequency Words: *are, away, they, where* ■ Handbook for ELL pp. 72–73
Working Independently	**Independent Activities**	**See plan for Day 1**
On Level Use Classroom Management Handbook	Students can continue their assigned activities, or you can assign new activities from the handbooks below.	
Challenge Use Challenge Handbook	■ Classroom Management Handbook pp. 42–49 ■ Challenge Handbook pp. 24–27	**Monitor** Partner Extra Support students, if needed.
Extra Support Use Classroom Management Handbook		

Independent Activities

Classroom Management Handbook
- Daily Activities
- Grouping
- Management

Resources for Reaching All Learners

Extra Support Handbook
- Daily Lessons
- Preteaching and Reteaching
- Skill Support

Handbook for English Language Learners
- Daily Lessons
- Language Development
- Skill Support

Challenge Handbook
- Independent Activities
- Instructional Support

Day 3

Reteach High-Frequency Words
Preview *A Hut for Zig Bug*
- Extra Support Handbook   pp. 70–71

See plan for Day 1

Check in
Reinforce instruction, if needed.

Preteach Shapes
Preteach Get Set to Read; *The Rope Tug*
Reteach High-Frequency Words: *does, he, live, pull*
- Handbook for ELL   pp. 74–75

See plan for Day 1

Check in
Reinforce instruction, if needed.

Day 4

Reteach Phonics: Consonants *qu, j, z*
Reteach Phonics: Blending Short *u* Words
Preview *The Rope Tug*
- Extra Support Handbook   pp. 72–73

See plan for Day 1

Check in
Regroup English learners, if needed.

Preteach Game Rules
Reteach *A Hut for Zig Bug* and *The Rope Tug*
Reteach Phonics: Blending Short *u* Words
- Handbook for ELL   pp. 76–77

See plan for Day 1

Monitor
How well are challenge projects progressing?

Day 5

Reteach Comprehension: Story Structure
Revisit *The Bug Kit, Quit It, Zig!, A Hut for Zig Bug,* and *The Rope Tug*
- Extra Support Handbook   pp. 74–75

See plan for Day 1

Build confidence
Reinforce successful independent work.

Preteach Pulling It All Together
Reteach Grammar: Action Words
- Handbook for ELL   pp. 78–79

See plan for Day 1

Share work
Allow students time to share work.

Managing Small Groups

Books for Small-Group Reading

Decodable

- Phonics Library
- I Love Reading Books

Easy

- On My Way Practice Reader

On Level

- Theme Paperback

Challenge

- Little Big Book

Other Resources

- Literature Resources Grade 1
- Level 1.1–1.2 Practice Book

Center Activities

- ▶ Word Booklets
- ▶ Make a Story Sequel
- ▶ Make a Beanstalk
- ▶ Watching Things Grow

Sample Small-Group Schedule

Independent Work

- ▶ Independent Reading
- ▶ Phonics Library Stories
- ▶ Center Activities
- ▶ Practice Book pages

Teacher-Led Group

- ▶ Books for Small-Group Reading
- ▶ Vocabulary Speed Drills

Daily Fluency Building

Children need to read leveled texts fluently before moving on to higher levels of challenge. Daily Fluency Building, as supported by the Little Big Book lesson on T158–T159, facilitates the successful application of reading strategies and consolidates skills, allowing children to move toward independence in reading.

Suggestions for Daily Fluency Building

	Extra Support	On Level	Challenge
DAY 1	**Partner Reading** • Reread Anthology, Phonics Library, and I Love Reading Books selections	**Teacher-Supported Reading** • Phonics Library	**Independent Reading** • Books from Bibliography • Literature Resources
DAY 2	**Teacher-Supported Reading** • On My Way Practice Reader: *Where Is Tug Bug?*	**Partner Reading** • Books from Bibliography • Literature Resources	**Partner Reading** • Reread the Little Big Book: *Jasper's Beanstalk*
DAY 3	**Independent Reading** • Reread On My Way Practice Reader: *Where Is Tug Bug?* • Reread Anthology, Phonics Library, and I Love Reading Books selections	**Teacher-Supported Reading** • On Level Theme Paperback: *Spots*	**Independent Reading** • Check in with teacher after reading the Little Big Book: *Jasper's Beanstalk*
DAY 4	**Teacher-Supported Reading** • Phonics Library	**Independent Reading** • Reread On Level Theme Paperback: *Spots* • Reread Anthology selections	**Independent Reading** • Reread Anthology selections • Literature Resources
DAY 5	**Partner Reading** • Books from Bibliography • Literature Resources	**Independent Reading** • Books from Bibliography • Literature Resources	**Teacher-Supported Reading** • Phonics Library

Technology

Education Place

www.eduplace.com
Log on to Education Place for more activities relating to *Surprise!*

Book Adventure

www.bookadventure.org
This Internet reading-incentive program provides thousands of titles for students to read.

Management Routine

Working at the Centers Discuss with children any problems they may have encountered while working at the centers. Remind them that one way to solve a problem is to talk about it and then agree on an action plan.

Focus on one center, such as one for Creative Arts. Identify the materials in the center, and ask how they should be used. Discuss sharing and how to work carefully to avoid spills and accidents. Then have children help you develop a set of guidelines for working at the center. Display the chart in the center.

Before	Put on a smock.
	Use newspaper.
During	Share materials.
	Work carefully.
After	Clean brushes.
	Put lids on jars.

Instructional Routine

Word Booklets Have children continue to work on the Word Booklets. (See page T19.) Use **Blackline Masters** 199–200 to create new pages. Use the word *bug* to remind children what to do.

- Write the word *bug* on the first line.

- Draw a picture of a bug to illustrate the word.

Center Activities

Phonics and Language

Word Booklets Have children continue work on their Word Booklets. They can use **Blackline Masters** 199–200 to create their own pages. Children can share completed booklets with partners or in small groups.

Materials
- **Blackline Masters** 199–200
- safety scissors
- crayons
- markers
- pencils

Writing and Technology

Make a Story Sequel Display the last two pages of *Jasper's Beanstalk*. Ask children to imagine what might be at the top of the beanstalk. Giants? Something else? Children can draw and write about what Jasper might see—if he had decided to climb the beanstalk.

Materials
- drawing paper
- crayons
- markers

Creative Arts

Make a Beanstalk Suggest that children make a beanstalk for the classroom wall. They can cut a stalk and leaves from construction paper. Each day, add several more leaves to show growth. Write high-frequency words on the leaves for more practice.

Materials
- brown and green construction paper
- scissors
- tacks or tape

Science

Watching Things Grow Stick toothpicks into the seed at three or four points, and suspend it in a cup of water. Have children change the water, as needed. Have them note changes in the seed and record their observations.

Materials
- avocado seed (pit)
- markers/crayons
- pencils
- plastic glass
- toothpicks
- water

Day at a Glance

Learning to Read

Reading the Big Book, *T146–T149*

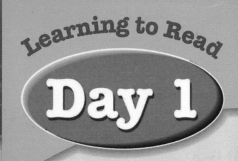

☑ **Comprehension:**
Story Structure

☑ **Reading Strategy:**
Summarize

**Phonics Instruction,
Practice, Application**
T150–T153

☑ **Review** *q, j, z*

☑ **Blending Short** *u* **Words**

• **Phonics Library:** *The Bug Kit*

• **I Love Reading Books, Books
19–22**

Word Work

Spelling and Phonics, *T154*

• **Letters and Sounds:** *j, z*

• **Penmanship**

Word Pattern Board, *T154*

Writing & Language

Independent Journal Writing, *T159*

Listening and Speaking, *T155*

• **Retell / Summarize**

☑ = **Tested Skill**

Opening

···

Daily Message

Use the Daily Message for a quick review of phonics, high-frequency words, and language skills.

■ Read the message aloud, pointing to each word as it is read.

■ Call on a few children to find and circle examples of *j*, *z*, and *q*.

■ Ask volunteers to underline the high-frequency words *and, for, is, a,* and *to.*

Hi, Boys and Girls!
Our story for today is about a cat named Jasper. Jasper is quite a cat. He likes to plant flowers and vegetables and watch them grow. Do you think Jasper will plant zinnias or zucchini?

Count Them!

Have children count the number of sentences in the Daily Message.

Concepts of Print

Ask children to point out:
• capital letters to begin sentences
• capital letters to begin names

Routines

- -

Daily Phonemic Awareness

Blending Phonemes: Sing Along

■ Sing with children the following song to the tune of "If You're Happy and You Know It":

If you're happy and you know it, blend with me.

If you're happy and you know it, blend with me.

If you're happy and you know it, then your ears will truly know it.

If you're happy and you know it, blend with me.

Chorus: *Blend / t // ă // g /. Raise your hand when you know the word.* (tag)

■ Repeat the chorus, having children blend the sounds for *sit* and *hog*.

Daily Independent Reading

Daily independent exploration and reading of books will increase children's experiences with print.

■ Bibliography, pages T4–T5

 Choose books from this list for children to read, outside class, for at least twenty minutes a day.

■ Little Big Book, *Jasper's Beanstalk*

■ Reread I Love Reading Books, Review Books 15–18

✎ Daily Prompt for Independent Writing

Use the prompts below, or allow children to write about a topic of their choice. Encourage them to use what they have been learning about letters and sounds to record their ideas.

We grew peas and corn.

■ Draw and write about something that grows in a yard or a garden.

Big Book

JASPER'S BEANSTALK

Nick Butterworth and Mick Inkpen

Purpose • oral language development
• reading strategies • comprehension skills

Selection Summary

Jasper tends the bean seed he has planted—but he loses patience when it doesn't grow. Jasper learns that some things, like growing a beanstalk, take time.

Key Concepts

• What plants need in order to grow

• The need for patience

Reaching All Students

English Language Learners

Write *beanstalk* on the board. Say the word and have children repeat after you. Make sure children understand that the *l* is silent. Draw a beanstalk or have an English-speaking volunteer find a picture of a beanstalk in the story. Have children continue with a picture walk. Find out if anyone knows of another story about a giant beanstalk.

Reading the Big Book
Oral Language and Comprehension

▶ Building Background

Introduce the Big Book by reading aloud the title and the names of the author and the illustrator. Introduce the cat pictured on the cover as Jasper.

 ### ✓ Strategy Preview:
Summarize

Teacher Modeling Read aloud the Strategy Focus question on Big Book page 49. Model how to use the Summarize strategy.

> **Think Aloud**

> *When I retell this story, I'll want to tell who the story is about. I'll also want to tell what happens at the beginning, in the middle, and at the end of the story. I'll think about these things as I read.*

 ### ✓ Comprehension Skill Preview:
Story Structure

Tell children that a story has characters, as well as a setting. The setting is when and where the story takes place. The beginning of a story usually introduces the characters and the setting. Often in a story, one character has a problem. The middle of the story tells how the character tries to solve the problem. The end tells whether or not the character solves the problem.

▶ Teacher Read Aloud

Read the story aloud, pausing after page 53 to help children identify the main character and the setting. Then, as you read the rest of the story, ask children to listen for the problem. Allow children to chime in as you read.

Concepts of Print (page 50) Demonstrate how to make the return sweep when there is more than one line of text on a page.

Big Book page 49

On Monday
Jasper found
a bean.

Big Book pages 50–51

On Tuesday
he planted it.

identify main character

Big Book pages 52–53

On Wednesday
he watered it.

Big Book pages 54–55

On Thursday
he dug and raked
and sprayed and
hoed it.

Big Book pages 56–57

On Friday night he picked up

all the slugs and snails.

Big Book pages 58–59

On Saturday
he even mowed it!

Big Book pages 60–61

On Sunday
Jasper waited
and waited
and waited . . .

Big Book pages 62–63

(Reading the Big Book, continued)

Oral Language and Comprehension

▶ Responding

Retelling Remind children that thinking about the beginning, the middle, and the end of the story will help them retell it. As you page through the story again, ask children to tell:

- What character is introduced at the beginning of the story? (Jasper, the cat)

- Where was Jasper at the beginning of the story? (outdoors, in a yard) **What did he find there?** (a bean)

- What did Jasper do with the bean? (He planted it and took care of it.)

- What problem did Jasper face in the middle of the story? (His bean wasn't growing.)

- What did Jasper do to solve this problem? (He dug the bean up and tossed it away.)

- What happened at the end of the story? (The bean grew—and finally became a beanstalk.)

Literature Discussion Circle Review the Discussion Tips before posing these questions:

- *Why do you think Jasper wanted to grow a beanstalk?*

- *Do you think Jasper will see any giants? Why or why not?*

Reading the Little Big Book For children who are ready to read independently, there is a five-day lesson plan on pages T158–T159 for using the **Little Big Book**, *Jasper's Beanstalk.*

Discussion Tips

- Think about what you want to say.
- Raise your hand before talking, and wait your turn.
- Listen politely when other people are talking.

Reaching All Students
Extra Support

To verify that children understand the concept of characters and setting, have them draw pictures of the main character (Jasper) and the story setting (a yard). Also have them draw pictures of the bean at the beginning of the story and what it becomes at the end of the story.

Reaching All Students
Challenge

Responding Call attention to the book Jasper is reading in the picture on page 71. Ask children to find a copy of *Jack and the Beanstalk* in your school or classroom library. Children who know the story can use the illustrations in the book to share the story with classmates.

Reaching All Students
English Language Learners

Beginning/Preproduction Have children draw the beanstalk to show how it grows. Suggest that they make four frames.
Early Production and Speech Emergence Have children go through the story, taking turns describing what is happening on each page.
Intermediate and Advanced Ask partners to describe how Jasper plants the bean and how it grows. Help with comparatives and superlatives as needed.

When Monday came around again he dug it up.

Big Book pages 64–65

"That bean will never make a (beanstalk)," said Jasper.

Big Book pages 66–67

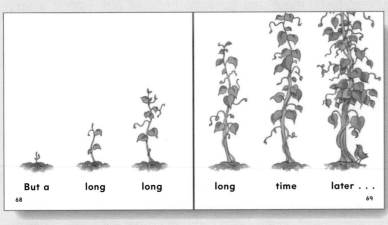

But a   long   long   long   time   later . . .

Big Book pages 68–69

It did! (It was on a Thursday, I think.)

Big Book pages 70–71

Now Jasper is looking for (giants)!

Big Book pages 72–73

Big Book page 74

Learning to Read
Day 1

Phonics

☑ Consonants q, j, z

▶ Develop Phonemic Awareness

Blend Phonemes Say: *I have a word. Listen: /b//ŭ//g/.* Have children say the individual sounds, blend them, and then say the word *bug*. Repeat with: /kw//ĭ//z/ *(quiz)*, /j//ŭ//g/ *(jug)*, /b//ŭ//z/ *(buzz)*, /j//ŏ//b/ *(job)*, /j//ă//z/ *(jazz)*, /kw//ĭ//t/ *(quit)*.

▶ Connect Sounds to Letters

Introduce the Sound/Spelling Cards Display **Large Sound/ Spelling Card** *queen* and have children name the picture. Point to the letters *qu* on the back of the card. Explain that in English, *q* is always followed by *u*, and that *qu* together stand for the /k/ and /w/ sounds at the beginning of *queen*. Have children chant /kw/, /kw/, /kw/ as you point to the letters. Then, display the *jumping Jill* card. Have children name the picture and chant /j/, /j/, /j/ as you point to the letters *Jj*. Repeat with the *zebra* card.

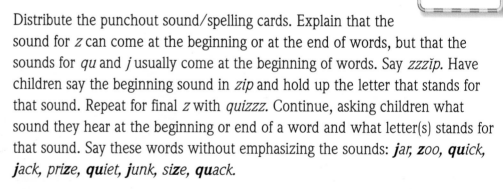

Distribute the punchout sound/spelling cards. Explain that the sound for *z* can come at the beginning or at the end of words, but that the sounds for *qu* and *j* usually come at the beginning of words. Say *zzzip*. Have children say the beginning sound in *zip* and hold up the letter that stands for that sound. Repeat for final *z* with *quizzz*. Continue, asking children what sound they hear at the beginning or end of a word and what letter(s) stands for that sound. Say these words without emphasizing the sounds: *jar, zoo, quick, jack, prize, quiet, junk, size, quack.*

Check Understanding Hold up each **Large Sound/Spelling Card** and call on individuals to say a word that begins with that letter's sound. For the *queen* card, display the back of the card and point to the letters *qu*.

▶ Connect Sounds to Spelling and Writing

Say: *Listen as I say* quit. *What sound do you hear at the beginning of* quit? *What letters should I write to spell that sound?* (qu) Model writing the letters *qu*. Have several children write *qu* on the board as they say /kw/. Repeat for *j, z*, using *jet, zero*. Then have children tell you what letter to write for the last sound in *size*.

Practice Book Page 86 supports this skill.

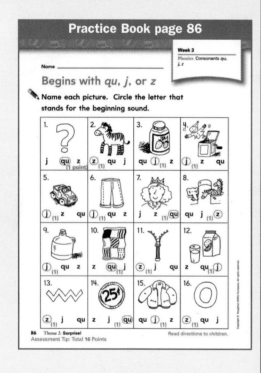

Practice Book page 86

Phonics

✓ Short u

MATERIALS

- **Large Sound/Spelling Card** *umbrella*
- punchout sound/spelling card *umbrella*
- magnetic or punchout letters *b, c, e, g, j, n, o, p, r, s, t, u*
- **Picture Card** *jug*

▶ **Connect Sounds to Letters**

Introduce the Sound/Spelling Card Display **Large Sound/Spelling Card** *umbrella.* Have children name the picture. Point to the letters *Uu.* Tell children that *u* is a vowel that stands for the /ŭ/ sound at the beginning of *umbrella.* Have them chant /ŭ/, /ŭ/, /ŭ/ as you point to the letter. Explain that /ŭ/ can be at the beginning of a word, as in *umbrella,* or in the middle of a word, as in *jug.*

Write the letter *u* on the board. Then display **Picture Card** *jug.* Say *jŭŭŭg,* elongating the /ŭ/ sound. Ask children what sound they hear in the middle of the word. Explain that *u* stands for the /ŭ/ sound in the middle of *jug.*

Check Understanding Ask children to hold up punchout sound/spelling card *umbrella* when they hear a word that has the /ŭ/ sound. Then say *umbrella, fun, pin, mud, up, tug, hut, hat, us, rub, chop, gum, rest, dust.*

(handwritten:) play po-pā cben stand up when short u word

Practice Book page 87

Week 3
Phonemic Awareness
Short u

Name _____

Short u

✎ Name each picture. Color the pictures whose names have the same vowel sound as 🍵 .

Picture should be colored. **(1 point)** Picture should be colored. **(1)**

Picture should be colored. **(1)**

Picture should be colored. **(1)** Picture should be colored. **(1)**

Read directions to children.

Theme 2: **Surprise!** **87**
Assessment Tip: Total 5 Points

▶ **Connect Sounds to Spelling and Writing**

Display the magnetic letters. Tell children that you want to make the word *up.* Together say each sound in *up* and blend to say the word: /ŭ/ /p/, *up.* As children say the first sound in *up,* position the letter *u* on the board. Ask what sound comes after /ŭ/ in *up* and what letter spells that sound. Position the *p* after the *u* on the board.

- Say that you want to make the word *jut.* Ask: **What is the beginning sound in jut? What letter should I put first to spell jut?** Position the *j* on the board.

- Ask: **What sound do you hear next in jut?** Call on a volunteer to choose the letter that has the /ŭ/ sound. Have the child place the *u* to the right of the *j.*

- Ask: **What sound do you hear at the end of jut? What letter should I put last?** Place *t* after the *u.*

Follow the same steps with the words *nut, bug, sun, rug, cup.*

Practice Book Page 87 supports this skill.

Reaching All Students
English Language Learners

English language learners may have trouble producing and differentiating between /j/ and /z/. Help them learn sentences such as *I just filled the jug* and *We saw a zebra at the zoo.* Say the sentences. Have children repeat them after you, emphasizing the underlined words.

- **Large Letter Cards** *b, g, h, j, r, t, u*
- punchout trays and letter cards *b, c, f, g, h, n, s, t, u*
- **I Love Reading Books,** Books 19–22
- **Blending Routines Card 1**

Practice Book page 89

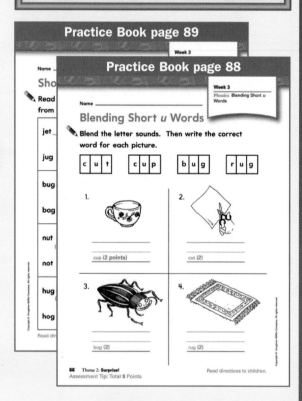

Practice Book page 88

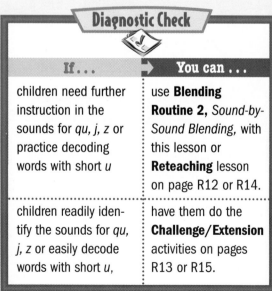

Diagnostic Check

If...	You can...
children need further instruction in the sounds for *qu, j, z* or practice decoding words with short *u*	use **Blending Routine 2,** Sound-by-Sound Blending, with this lesson or **Reteaching** lesson on page R12 or R14.
children readily identify the sounds for *qu, j, z* or easily decode words with short *u*,	have them do the **Challenge/Extension** activities on pages R13 or R15.

(Phonics, continued)

 Blending Short u *Words (VC, CVC)*

▶ **Connect Sounds to Letters**

Display **Large Letter Cards** *j, g, h,* and *t.* Have children name each letter and say its sound. Tell children that today they will read some words with these letters, but that first they need a vowel letter. Display **Large Letter Card** *u.* Remind children that *u* often stands for the /ŭ/ sound.

Blending Routine 1 Place **Large Letter Cards** *j, u,* and *g* together. Point to each letter in a sweeping motion as you model how to blend: *j ŭ ŭ ŭ g, jug.* Repeat, having children blend the sounds and pronounce the word with you. Then have children blend and pronounce the word on their own. Call on volunteers to use *jug* in a sentence. Repeat this routine with the words *hut* and *tug.*

Check Understanding Display **Large Letter Cards** *r, u,* and *b.* Have children blend *rub* as you point to the letters.

Mixed Practice Write *mug* and ask children to blend the sounds to read the word. Repeat for *tub, zip, jam, run, quiz, jog, gum,* and the sentence *Bud let us quit.*

▶ **Connect Sounds to Spelling and Writing**

Distribute punchout trays and letter cards *b, c, f, g, h, n, s, t, u.* Say *fun* and have children repeat it. Ask: **What is the first sound? Put the letter that stands for that sound on your tray.** Continue to spell the word sound by sound. Then write the word on the board and have children check their work. Repeat for *bus, cub, hut, us, bug.* Then dictate this sentence for children to write: *Gus dug up mud.*

Practice Book Pages 88–89 support this skill.

▶ **Practice**

Have children complete **Practice Book** pages 86–89 independently, with a partner, or in small groups. Then have them read **I Love Reading Books,** Books 19–22.

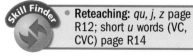

• **Reteaching:** *qu, j, z* page R12; short *u* words (VC, CVC) page R14	• **Review:** *qu, j, z,* and short *u* words (VC, CVC), Theme 3

Reading

Decodable Text

Phonics Library

Surprise!

▶ Phonics/Decoding Strategy

Distribute the **Phonics Library** story *The Bug Kit*. Ask children to tell what is happening in the pictures on page 29.

Teacher Modeling Use **Poster A** to review the steps of the Phonics/Decoding Strategy. Then model how to use the strategy to read the story title.

Think Aloud

I see three words in the title. I know that the first word is The. I look at the second word and see the letters B, u, g. I put the sounds together: /b//ŭ//g/, Bug. That is a word I know. Then I look at the last word. I think about the sounds for the letters and blend the sounds: /k//ĭ//t/, Kit. Kit makes sense and is a word I know.

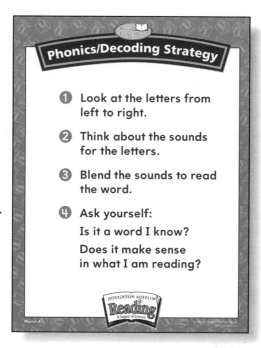

Phonics/Decoding Strategy

① Look at the letters from left to right.

② Think about the sounds for the letters.

③ Blend the sounds to read the word.

④ Ask yourself:
Is it a word I know?
Does it make sense in what I am reading?

Poster A

Tell children to look for letters and words that they know as they read the rest of the story independently or take turns reading with a partner.

Reading the Decodable Book If children have difficulty, remind them to look at each letter and sound out the word. Encourage them to sound out the words silently "in their heads." If necessary, coach them in applying the strategy to words such as *but*.

- ■ *What are the letters from left to right?* (b, u, t)

- ■ *What sound does each letter stand for?* (/b/, /ŭ/, /t/)

- ■ *Say each sound and hold it until you say the next sound. What is the word?* (bŭŭŭt, but)

- ■ *Is but a word you know? Does it make sense in the story?*

Oral Language Discuss the following questions with children. Have them speak in complete sentences.

- ■ *What is Jen trying to catch?* (She is trying to catch a big bug.)

- ■ *What does the bug do?* (It runs away.)

- ■ *What does the big bug look like?*

Phonics Library

Purposes for decodable text
- ● applying phonics skills

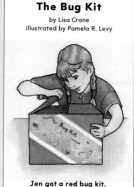

The Bug Kit
by Lisa Crane
illustrated by Pamela R. Levy

Jen got a red bug kit.

29

But can Jen get a big bug?

30

Zig, zag, zig.
The bug ran.

31

"Quit it!" said Jen.

32

Home Connection

A take-home version of *The Bug Kit* is available in the **Phonics Library Blackline Masters.** Children can take the story home to read with their families.

Phonics (T153)

Spelling and Phonics

Letters and Sounds: j, z

Children

- **Spelling and Phonics** recognize and write the letters *j* and *z*
- **Word Pattern Board** review words with short *u*

MATERIALS

Phonics and Spelling

- **Large Sound/Spelling Cards** *jumping Jill, zebra*
- **Picture Cards** *jam, jar, jeans, jeep, jet, jug; zip, zoo*

Word Pattern Board

- teacher-made word cards *bug, dug, hug, jug, lug, mug, rug, tug; but, cut, hut, jut, nut, rut*

Practice Book page 90

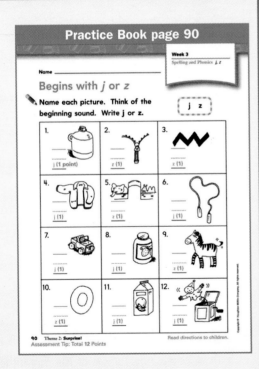

⋯ **Houghton Mifflin Spelling and Vocabulary** ⋯
Correlated Instruction and Practice, pp. 24, 33

Display **Large Sound/Spelling Cards** *jumping Jill* and *zebra.* Review their letters and sounds. Then model how to write *j* and *z*.

- Tell children they will practice spelling.

- Display the **Picture Cards** in random order one at a time. For each picture name, have children write the letter that stands for the beginning sound.

Have children complete **Practice Book** page 90.

Penmanship For children who need extra practice, model how to write lower-case *j* and *z*. Have children practice writing the letters.

Two penmanship models (continuous stroke, ball and stick) are available in the **Practice Book** (pp. 198–205) and the **Teacher's Resource Blackline Masters** (pp. 143–194).

Word Pattern Board

Words with Short *u*

- Post the word *jug* on the Word Pattern Board, and pick a child to read the word. "Clap and spell" the word: *j-u-g, jug!* Repeat with *bug, dug, hug, lug, mug, rug,* and *tug.*

- Ask how all the words are alike. (They rhyme. They all end with *ug.*)

- Follow a similar procedure with *jut.* Have children clap and spell *but, cut, hut, nut,* and *rut.*

 # Writing

Independent Journal Writing

Have children write in their journals. They may choose to

■ respond to the daily writing prompt on page T145

■ write on self-selected topics

Phonetic Spelling Encourage children to use what they know about letters and letter sounds to record their ideas.

Listening and Speaking

Retell/Summarize

Review *Charles Tiger* or another familiar story. Have children name the characters and tell where the story takes place. Record this information on the chalkboard. Then have children tell what the problem is in the story, how the characters try to solve the problem, and what happens in the end. Record this information. Call on volunteers to use what you've written on the board to retell the story in their own words.

OBJECTIVES

Children

• **Writing** write in their journals

• **Listening and Speaking** retell a story by summarizing it

Where Is Tug Bug?
by Oscar Gake
illustrated by Alfred Schrier

Houghton Mifflin

Story Summary
Two friends look for their friend, Tug Bug, who is sitting under a rug.

Reaching All Students
English Language Learners

Children who are reluctant to participate in discussions may be more comfortable assuming the role of a story character. Provide opportunities for them to pantomime story scenes or to improvise actions and dialogue.

UNIVERSAL ACCESS

Where Is Tug Bug?
On My Way Practice Reader

▶ Preparing to Read

Building Background Read aloud the title and author's name. Discuss with children where they might look for a friend. Ask them to predict where Tug Bug might be.

▶ Supporting the Reading

Introducing the Book Page through the book with children. You may want to point out the word: *glad*. The suggestions below can help prepare children to read the story independently.

page 1:	Find the words *Big Zig Pig*. Do these words rhyme?
page 4:	Tug Bug is not in the hot mug. The word *mug* begins like *man*. Point to the word *mug*.
page 6:	Which word begins like *quick*? (quit)
page 7:	The word *glad* rhymes with *dad*. Can you find the word *glad*?

Prompting Strategies Listen to and observe children as they read, and use prompts such as the following to help them apply strategies:

- *What can you try if a word doesn't sound right?*
- *Blend the sounds. What is the word?*
- *Did you understand what you just read?*

▶ Responding

Discuss the ending of the story with children. Was Tug Bug where they expected him to be?

Call on individuals to read aloud a page or two from the book in order to assess their reading fluency.

Spots

Theme Paperback

▶ Preparing to Read

Building Background Read aloud the title and the author's name. Talk about the things on the cover that have spots.

Story Summary
A girl loves spots on everything while her twin sister has other ideas.

▶ Supporting the Reading

Introducing the Book Page through the book with children. The suggestions below can help prepare children to read the story independently.

page 4:	The word *spots* begins like *spin*. **Find the word *spots*.**
page 8:	*Blots* are spots with funny shapes. *Blots* begins with *bl*. **Point to the word *blots*.**
page 14:	**Three words begin with *m*. What are they?** (my, milk, mug)
page 16:	**The word *ball* ends with the sound /l/. Can you find the word *ball*?**
page 28:	**The exclamation point after the words *Oh, yes!* means the girl said them with excitement. Read the words *Oh, yes!* with me.**

Prompting Strategies Listen to and observe children as they read, and use prompts such as the following to help them apply strategies:

- ■ *Does that word make sense in the sentence you are reading?*

- ■ *What else could you try?*

- ■ *What happens at the end of the story?*

▶ Responding

Ask children what they thought of the story. Do they have any favorite patterns or colors that they like? Children can draw pictures featuring spots or their own favorite patterns.

Have partners reread the story and observe each pair for individual strengths and weaknesses. Ask children to retell the story in their own words.

Challenge

JASPER'S BEANSTALK

Nick Butterworth and Mick Inkpen

Story Summary

Jasper tends the bean seed he has planted—but he loses patience when it doesn't grow. Jasper learns that some things, like growing a beanstalk, take time.

Jasper's Beanstalk
Little Big Book

Day 1 · Preparing to Read

Building Background Display the Little Big Book and have a child identify the title and the author and illustrator names. Remind children that you read aloud the corresponding Big Book earlier. Have children browse through the book.

Ask children what it's like to wait for an important day or occasion. Have children tell something they looked forward to, how many days they had to wait, and how they felt when the day finally arrived.

Developing Story Vocabulary Print each day of the week on an index card. Display each card, read the word aloud clapping the syllables, and have children clap the syllables as they repeat each word: *Monday, Tuesday, Wednesday, Thursday, Friday, Saturday, Sunday.*

Display the cards face up in random order. Have each child in turn arrange the cards in correct order and read them. Then use the cards as flashcards; as a child reads a word, he or she finds it on a page of *Jasper's Beanstalk.*

Day 2 · Reading the Little Big Book

Applying Phonics Skills Before reading, have children look at selected words. Prompt them to use what they know about letters and letter sounds to read them. Use these words and prompts as models:

page 4:	What letter stands for the / j / sound in *Jasper*? (j)
page 6:	The letters *ed* can stand for the syllable / ed /. What word has the final syllable / ed /? (planted)
page 13:	In what word do you hear / ŭ / in the middle (slugs)
page 20:	What compound word is made from the two shorter words *bean* and *stalk*? (beanstalk)

Day 2 *continued...*

Now have children turn to page 14. Model how to read an unfamiliar word: *If I didn't know the word beginning with* m, *I would first sound out the letter* m, */ m /. Now comes* ow, */ ō /. The last letters are* ed. *I can say / ed / for* ed. *I blend the parts:* mow-ed. *But that doesn't sound right. Maybe the word is* mowed. *That's a word I know and it makes sense on the page.*

Have partners read the book together and help each other identify words.

Day 3 Rereading the Little Big Book

Applying Comprehension Skills Jasper has a problem: he tries everything but his bean doesn't grow. As they read, tell children to think about what is causing Jasper's problem. Have children turn to pages 10–11 and pages 18–19, read each sentence, and look at the picture. Then ask:

- **Jasper thinks he is helping the bean to grow. Is he?** (No, Jasper is doing too much and trying too hard. The bean just needs time.)

- **Why didn't the bean grow into a beanstalk?** (Jasper only waited a week; that's not enough time.)

Independent Reading Ask children to read the book independently. Then have them team up with a partner. One partner reads the introductory phrase, *On (Monday),* and the other partner finishes the sentence.

Day 4 Revisiting the Little Big Book

Retelling the Story Have children fold a sheet of paper into eighths and label each block with a day of the week from Monday to Monday. Have them refer back to the story and in each block write what Jasper did that day, for example, *found a bean, planted a bean, watered a bean,* and so on. Then do a round-robin retelling, asking children to refer to the outline and perform the action. The last storyteller can sum up the ending of the story.

Day 5 Extending the Little Big Book

Moving Beyond the Story Ask children how they could make this story into a song with many verses. Remind them of the repetitive pattern of the nursery rhyme "This Is the Way We Wash Our Clothes." Have children review the story and the retelling outlines they created. Ask each child to create a sentence strip using the sentence frame, *This is the way _____.* They can use the strips to sing the song and act it out.

This is the way we pick up slugs.

This is the way a beanstalk grows.

Day at a Glance

Learning to Read

Reading Instruction, *T162–T165*

☑ **Comprehension:**
Story Structure in
Jasper's Beanstalk

☑ **High Frequency
Words:** *are, away,
does, he, live, pull,
they, where*

Phonics Application,
T165

• Phonics Library: *Quit it, Zig!*

• I Love Reading Books,
Books 19–22

Word Work

Spelling and Phonics, *T166*

• **Matching Sounds to Letters:** *qu*

• **Penmanship**

Word Pattern Board, *T166*

Writing & Language

Shared Writing, *T167*

• A Diary

☑ = **Tested Skill**

Opening

Daily Message

Use the Daily Message for a quick review of phonics, high-frequency words, and language skills.

■ Read the message aloud, pointing to each word as it is read.

■ Have children find and circle examples of consonants *q, j,* and *z*.

■ Ask children to find and underline the high-frequency words *What, is, the, too, Do, you, a,* and *have.*

> Good Morning, Class!
> What is the weather like today? Is it too hot, or is it quite cold? Do you need a jacket today? Do you have to zipper it up?

Concepts of Print

Point out that all sentences in the body of the message are questions. Have children identify the mark that ends each question.

Count Them!

Count all the sentences that are questions.

Routines

Daily Phonemic Awareness

Blending Phonemes: Riddles

Tell children you have some word riddles. They should blend the sounds to form the word.

- Read the following clues:

  It's something you read: / b // o͞o // k /. (*book*)

  You can live in this: / h // ŭ // t /. (*hut*)

  This means to talk: / ch // ă // t /. (*chat*)

  This is the opposite of out: / ĭ // n /. (*in*)

  This rhymes with Liz: / h // ĭ // z /. (*his*)

Concepts of Print

Remind children that names begin with capital letters. Have them find a name and underline the capital letters.

Daily Independent Reading

Have children share a book with a friend.

- Bibliography, pages T4–T5

  Choose books from this list for children to read, outside class, for at least twenty minutes a day.

- Reread Phonics Library story *The Bug Kit.*

- Reread I Love Reading Books, Review Books 15–18

✏ Daily Prompt for Independent Writing

Use the prompt below, or allow children to write about a topic of their choice. Encourage them to use what they know about letters and sounds to record their ideas.

- Draw and write about a book you have read and enjoyed. Include the title of the book and, if possible, the author's name.

I read Jasper's Beanstalk. It was funny.

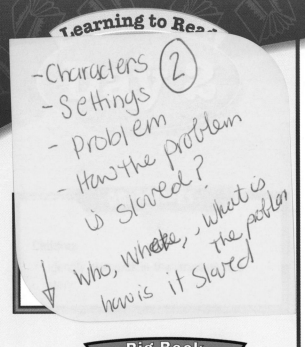

Big Book

JASPER'S BEANSTALK

Nick Butterworth and Mick Inkpen

Chart/Transparency 2–8

A Story Map

Story title	Jasper's Beanstalk
Who?	Jasper
Where?	outdoors in a yard or garden
What is the problem?	Jasper doesn't see his beanstalk growing.
How is the problem solved?	Jasper waited, and the beanstalk grew.

Comprehension

✓ Story Structure

▶ Rereading the Big Book

Setting a Purpose Display the cover and reread the title of the Big Book. Point out that Jasper is a character in this story.

- Before you reread the story, tell children that they can chime in and read the words they know as you read aloud.

- Point to each word as you read, modeling left to right word tracking and the return sweep.

▶ Teach

Tell children that when authors write stories, they follow a plan.

Think Aloud

A story has characters—the people or animals the story is about. The setting is where the story takes place. One of the characters usually wants to do something but has a problem. The events of the story tell how the problem is solved.

Display *Jasper's Beanstalk*, together with **Chart/Transparency 2–8**. Read the first two questions: *Who?* and *Where?* Review the first few pages of the story, and have children identify:

- who the story is about (Jasper)

- where the story takes place (outdoors, in a yard or garden)

Fill in the corresponding parts of the chart. Tell children that they have found two important parts of a story: the characters and the setting. Explain that these are usually introduced at the beginning of the story.

Read the third question: *What is the problem?* Review how Jasper cares for the bean he's planted. Pause on page 62 ("On Sunday Jasper waited …"), and ask how Jasper feels now. Discuss that he is disappointed because he doesn't see anything growing. Point out that this is Jasper's problem, and fill in the chart accordingly.

Finally, ask children to turn to the part of the story that shows how Jasper's problem is solved (pages 68–70, "But a long long …"). Ask children to tell you what to write for the last question: *How is the problem solved?*

DAY 2

▶ Practice

Review **Chart/Transparency 2–8** with children. Have them use the information on the chart to identify:

- the character in the story
- the setting
- the problem
- the solution

Who?	Fox, Hen, Pig, Ox
Where?	In the woods where Fox lived
What is the problem?	Fox wants hot hen soup, but hen won't get in the vat. Neither will the other animals.
How is the problem solved?	Fox decides they should all have hot noodle soup.

Recall with children another story they have read recently. Have them identify these same story elements. You might use *Hot Fox Soup* from Week 2. If so, help children complete the Chart/Transparency for that story.

▶ Apply

Choose one or both of the following activities:

- Have children work with partners to choose a familiar story and draw pictures to show the characters, the setting, and the problem and its solution. Provide them with copies of **Chart/Transparency 2–8**, if you wish.

- Have children work independently or with a partner to complete the activity on **Practice Book** page 91.

Skill Finder

• Themes 6, 9	• Revisiting, pages T176, T187, T189	• Reteaching, page R26

Practice Book page 91

Think of the Story

Think about Chapter 2 from the story **What Can a Vet Do?** Answer the questions.

1. Who is in the story?
   a boy, his pet, the vet (2 points)

2. Where do they live?
   on a farm (2)

3. What is the problem? _The boy's pet is sick. (3)_

4. How is the problem solved? _The vet helps the sick pet get better. (3)_

Assessment Tip: Total **10 Points**

Reaching All Students

English Language Learners

Write and review the words *problem, solve,* and *solution*. Ask children for examples of problems discussed in class and some of the solutions they thought of. Guide the discussion with questions. Then review problems and solutions characters have faced in the stories. Use a two-column chart to record ideas.

Diagnostic Check

If...	You can...
children need more help with story structure,	use the **Reteaching** lesson on page R26.
children are ready to extend the skill,	have them do the **Challenge/Extension** activities on page R27.

Comprehension (T163)

OBJECTIVES

Children
- read and write *are, away, does, he, live, pull, they, where*

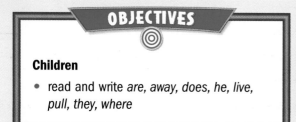

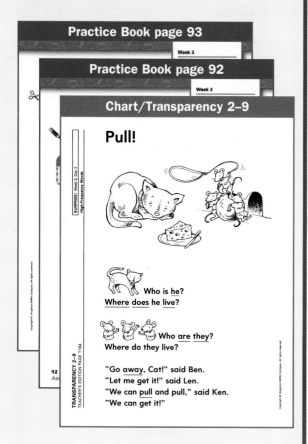

Practice Book page 93
Week 3

Practice Book page 92
Week 3

Chart/Transparency 2–9

Pull!

Who is he?
Where does he live?

Who are they?
Where do they live?

"Go away, Cat!" said Ben.
"Let me get it!" said Len.
"We can pull and pull," said Ken.
"We can get it!"

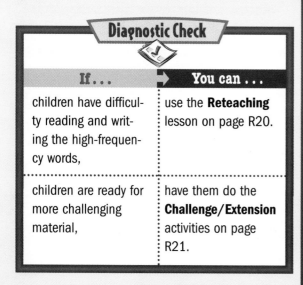

Diagnostic Check

If . . .	You can . . .
children have difficulty reading and writing the high-frequency words,	use the **Reteaching** lesson on page R20.
children are ready for more challenging material,	have them do the **Challenge/Extension** activities on page R21.

✓ High-Frequency Words

▶ Teach

Tell children that they will learn to read and spell eight new words that are used often in speaking, reading, and writing. Display **Chart/Transparency** 2–9, and have children follow along as you read the first sentence.

- Point to the word *he*, and have children repeat it after you.

- Lead the class in a cheer in which you clap each letter as you spell and say the word: *h-e, he.*

Follow a similar procedure for each sentence. Then have children read the story together.

▶ Practice

Write *they* on the chalkboard.

- Have children read the word.

- Have them find the same word on **Chart/Transparency** 2–9.

- Ask a volunteer to read aloud the sentence in which the word appears.

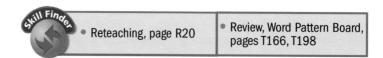

are away does he
live pull they where

Repeat for each of the other high-frequency words.

Word Pattern Board Post the words in the "New Words" section of the Word Pattern Board. Remind children to look on the Word Pattern Board when they are writing *are, away, does, he, live, pull, they,* and *where.*

▶ Apply

Have children work with partners to complete **Practice Book** pages 92–93.

Skill Finder	• Reteaching, page R20	• Review, Word Pattern Board, pages T166, T198

Decodable Text

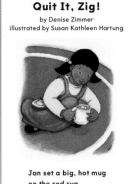
Reading
Phonics Library
Surprise!

Reading

▶ **Phonics/Decoding Strategy**

Distribute the **Phonics Library** story *Quit it, Zig!* Have children describe the pictures on pages 34–35.

Teacher/Student Modeling Ask children to tell how they read new words. Use **Poster A** to review the steps of the Phonics/Decoding Strategy. Choose someone to read the story title and tell how they read each word.

Assign children to read the story. Circulate as they read, offering support and encouragement.

Reading the Decodable Book If children have difficulty decoding the word *mug*, help them apply the strategy.

Phonics/Decoding Strategy

❶ Look at the letters from left to right.

❷ Think about the sounds for the letters.

❸ Blend the sounds to read the word.

❹ Ask yourself:
   Is it a word I know?
   Does it make sense in what I am reading?

HOUGHTON MIFFLIN
Reading
A Legacy of Literacy

Poster A

- ■ *What should you look at first?* (letters in the word)

- ■ *How can you sound out the word?* (Blend the sounds /m/ /ŭ/ /g/.)

- ■ *How can you decide if mug is the correct word?* (See if the word makes sense.)

Supply the words only when absolutely necessary.

Oral Language Have children respond in complete sentences to the following.

- ■ *What does the girl tell her dog Zig to do?* (She tells the dog to get away.)

- ■ *How do you think the girl feels when Zig spills the cocoa? How do you think Zig feels?*

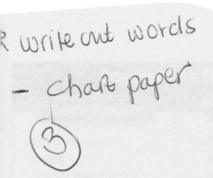
...ily Fluency Building

...Level	Challenge
...ding	**Partner Reading**
...m	• Reread the Little Big
...hy	book: *Jasper's*
...Resources	*Beanstalk*

Phonics Library

Purposes for decodable text

- applying phonics skills
- applying high-frequency words

Quit It, Zig!
by Denise Zimmer
illustrated by Susan Kathleen Hartung

Jan set a big, hot mug on the red rug.

33

Quit it, Zig!
Get away, Zig!

34

But Zig sat.
Tut, tut, Zig!

35

They are wet, wet, wet!

36

DAY 2

Home Connection

A **take-home version** of *Quit it, Zig!* is available in the **Phonics Library Blackline Masters.** At the end of the day, children can take the story home to read with their families.

High-Frequency Words (T165)

Day 2

Spelling and Phonics

Matching Sounds to Letters: qu

Children

- **Spelling and Phonics** recognize and write *qu*
- **Word Pattern Board** read *are, away, does, he, live, pull, they, where*

MATERIALS

- **Large Sound/Spelling Cards** *queen*
- **Picture Cards** *queen, quill, quilt*

Practice Book page 95

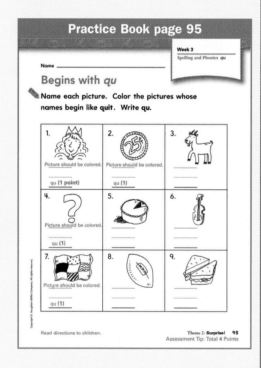

Houghton Mifflin Spelling and Vocabulary
Correlated Instruction and Practice, p. 34

First, display **Large Sound/Spelling Card** *queen*. Ask children to name the letters and say the sounds for the character: /kw/. Model how to write the letters *qu* on the board.

- Tell children they will practice some spelling.

- Display the **Picture Cards**, one at a time, and have children write the two letters that stand for the beginning sounds.

Have children complete **Practice Book** page 95.

Penmanship For children who need extra practice, model how to write lowercase *qu*. Have children practice writing the letters. You may also want to have them practice writing the word *quit*.

Two penmanship models (continuous stroke, ball and stick) are available in the **Practice Book** (pp. 198–205) and the **Teacher's Resource Blackline Masters** (pp. 143–194).

Word Pattern Board

High-Frequency Words Call attention to the "New Words" *are, away, does, he, live, pull, they,* and *where*. Clap and spell the words. Emphasize that the words on the Word Pattern Board will help children as they read and write.

Shared Writing

A Diary

Tell children that many people like to keep diaries, in which they write about things that happen during the day. Explain that a diary is a place to record what happens—and how the writer feels about what happened.

Ask children to imagine that Jasper is keeping a diary. Model what he might have written, engaging children's help as you proceed through Jasper's week.

Monday
Today I found a bean. I'd like to have a beanstalk.
That would be fun!

Tuesday
I planted the bean today. I dug a hole and put the bean into it.

Wednesday
I watered the bean so it will grow. I want it to grow tall, tall, tall.

Thursday
I dug and I raked. It was hard work!

As you near the end of Jasper's week, ask children to supply more and more of the writing. Remind them to look at the pictures in Jasper's Beanstalk to determine how Jasper feels about the events of the day.

Suggest that children keep a class diary for the rest of the week. They can write about something they did together as a class—and how they felt about what they did.

OBJECTIVES

Children
- write diary entries

MATERIALS
- chart paper

 Reaching All Students
English Language Learners

Show at least one type of diary. Ask if anyone's older sister or brother keeps a diary or journal. Mention that many people keep diaries and journals. Ask partners to talk about what they did yesterday and the day before or over the past week, depending on proficiency level. Have partners work together to write sentences describing their activities.

Day at a Glance

Learning to Read

Reading the Anthology, *T170–T177*

A Hut for Zig Bug
by Bernard Adnet

☑ **Comprehension:** *Story Structure*

☑ **Reading Strategy:** *Summarize*

☑ **Applying Phonics and High-Frequency Words**

Phonics Review, *T178–T179*

☑ **Blending Short e Words**

• **Making Words**

• **I Love Reading Books, Book 15**

Word Work

Spelling and Phonics, *T180*

• **Letters and Sounds:** *qu, j, z, Short u*

• **Penmanship**

Vocabulary, *T180*

• **Days of the Week**

Writing & Language

Grammar, *T181*

• **Action Words**

☑ **= Tested Skill**

Opening

Daily Message

Use the Daily Message for a quick review of high-frequency words, phonics, and language skills.

■ Read the message aloud, pointing to each word as it is read.

■ Call on a few children to find and circle examples of the consonant *j*.

■ Call on volunteers to find and underline the high-frequency words *and, The, is, a, where, you, to, do, My, What,* and *are.*

> Hello, Boys and Girls!
> The name of our school is (insert name). School is a place where you learn to do new things. My job is to help you learn. What are your jobs?

Concepts of Print

• Point out that each word in the name of your school begins with a capital letter. Explain that it is the name of a special place.

• Ask children to find the sentence that is a question. Call on a few volunteers to answer the question.

Routines

Daily Phonemic Awareness

Blending Phonemes: Let's Cheer!

Tell children that they will learn a cheer.

■ Model the first line as shown, segmenting the sounds of the last word. Then call out the word.

Teacher: *Give me a / b // ŭ // g /! Bug!*

■ As you read each remaining line, have children blend the sounds together and call out the word.

Teacher: *Give me a / s // ă // k /!* Children: *Sack!*

Teacher: *Give me a / b // ĕ // d /!* Children: *Bed!*

Teacher: *Give me a / m // ĭ // t /!* Children: *Mitt!*

Teacher: *Give me a / d // ŏ // t /!* Children: *Dot!*

■ After lots of practice, you might have children make up their own cheers to share with the class.

Daily Independent Reading

You may want children to choose a book from their book boxes. Or you can:

■ Have children reread *Hot Fox Soup* on their own.

■ Bibliography, pages T4–T5

Choose books from this list for children to read, outside class, for at least twenty minutes a day.

■ Books for Small-Group Reading, pages T156–T159

■ Reread I Love Reading Books, Review Books 15–18

Daily Prompt for Independent Writing

Use the prompt below, or allow children to write about a topic of their choice. Encourage them to use what they know about letters and sounds to record their ideas.

■ Draw and write about a place that is special to you.

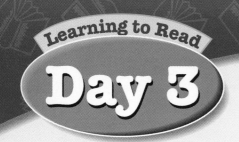

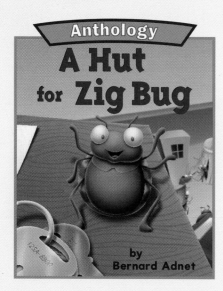

Anthology

A Hut for Zig Bug

by
Bernard Adnet

Purpose • applying reading strategies, comprehension skills, phonics/decoding skills, high-frequency words, and critical thinking

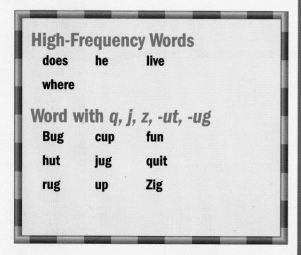

High-Frequency Words

does	he	live
where		

Word with *q, j, z, -ut, -ug*

Bug	cup	fun
hut	jug	quit
rug	up	Zig

Preparing to Read

▷ Building Background

Shelters Tell children that people and animals need shelter—a place to live and be safe. Ask children to name some different kinds of shelters. Mention a few animal shelters, such as dens and nests, if children do not.

▷ Using "Get Set to Read"

Call on individuals to read the words and sentences on Anthology pages 214–215. Ask children what things about each word helped them to read it.

■ Did they recognize the letters?

■ Did they blend the sounds for the letters?

■ Did they recognize the word from the Word Pattern Board?

Get Set to Read

A Hut for Zig Bug

Words to Know

does	fun
he	hut
live	jug
where	quit
Bug	rug
but	up
cup	Zig

Zig Bug can get a jug.
Zig Bug can get a rug.

Where does Zig Bug live?
Does he live in a hut?

Do not quit!
Can Zig Bug fix up a fun hut?

214

215

Anthology pages 214–215

Strategy & Skill Focus

 **Strategy Focus:**
Summarize

Teacher Modeling Have children turn to Anthology page 217. Read the selection title and the name of the author/illustrator. Then say:

Think Aloud

When we finish reading this story, we will summarize it. A summary includes only the most important parts of a story. When I summarize a story, I name the characters and the setting. I say what the problem is, and how the main character tries to solve it.

Quick Write Ask children whom they think the main character is in this story and where the story takes place. Have them draw and write their ideas in their journals.

Purpose Setting Ask children to think about the parts of a story—the characters, the setting, the problem and how it is solved—as they read. Remind children also to use their other reading strategies as they read the selection.

 **Comprehension Skill Focus:**
Story Structure

Quickly review the following before children read the story.

- Characters: Who is the story about?
- Setting: Where does the story take place?
- The Problem: What does the main character want to do?
- Solving the Problem: How does the main character do it?

Focus Questions

Have children turn to Responding on page 232. Read the questions aloud and tell children to keep them in mind as they read *A Hut for Zig Bug*.

 **Teacher's Note**

Strategy and Comprehension Skills Connection A good summary of a fiction story includes the following story-structure elements: characters, setting, problem and solution.

 Reaching All Students
English Language Learners

Write the word *bug* on the board. Make sure everyone knows what a bug is. Ask children to draw examples of bugs. Say that *bug* is another word for *insect,* but it is more general and more informal. Ask: "Who likes bugs?"

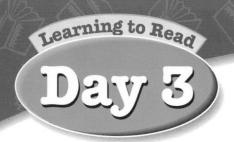

Learning to Read
Day 3

Reading the Anthology

Options for Reading

▶ **Universal Access** See the Classroom Management tips at the bottom of these pages for suggestions to meet individual needs during and after reading.

Revisiting the Text

Concepts of Print

Have children count the questions on pages 218–219. Ask them to point to the question mark that ends each sentence that asks something.

Key to Underlined Vocabulary

Words with *q, j, z,* short *u* ═══
High-Frequency Words ─────

A Hut for Zig Bug

Meet the Author and Illustrator
Bernard Adnet

Story 5

A Hut for Zig Bug

by
Bernard Adnet

216

217

Anthology pages 216–217

Does Zig Bug have a hut?
He does not have a hut yet.
218

Where can Zig Bug live?
Can he live in here?
219

Anthology pages 218–219

Reaching All Students

Classroom Management

On Level

Partner Reading Remind children of their purpose for reading. After reading, children join the class to discuss Comprehension/Critical Thinking, T173, T175, T176; Story Structure, T176; Think About the Story, T177.

Challenge

Independent Reading Children can read the story independently before joining the class to discuss Comprehension/Critical Thinking, T173, T175, T176; Story Structure, T176; Think About the Story, T177.

English Language Learners

Intermediate and Advanced
Read the selection as a group. Discuss the usual meanings of words for things found in a human home, not a bug's home. For English language learners at other proficiency levels, see Language Development Resources.

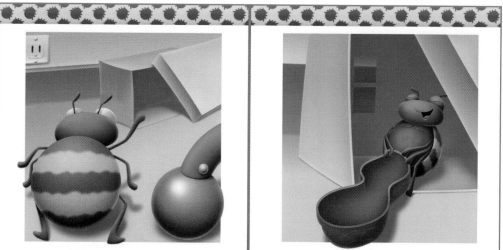

Can Zig Bug fix a box for a hut?
Yes, he can fix up a fun hut.
220

Can Zig Bug get a cot in the hut?
221

Anthology pages 220–221

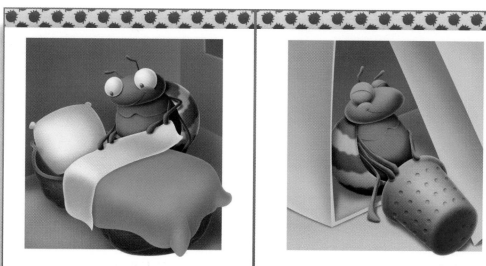

Yes, a cot can fit in the hut.
222

Can Zig Bug get a jug in the hut?
223

Anthology pages 222–223

Comprehension/Critical Thinking

1️⃣ ✅ Who is the main character in this story? (Zig Bug) **Story Structure**

2️⃣ ✅ What is the setting of the story? (a room, perhaps the kitchen, in a real person's house) **Story Structure**

3️⃣ ✅ **Strategy Focus: Teacher/Student Modeling** The problem in a story is what the main character wants to do. What does Zig Bug want to do in this story? (find a place to live and put things in it) So far, we know the characters, the setting, and the problem. Who can summarize the story so far? (Zig Bug is in a room of someone's house. He needs a place to live. He uses a box for a hut. Then he finds things to put in the hut.) **Summarize**

4️⃣ Look at pages 222–223. What tells you that this story is a fantasy? (Real bugs don't sleep on cots made from nutshells and covered with pillows and blankets.) **Fantasy and Realism**

DAY 3

Extra Support

Teacher-Supported Reading Have children tell what they see in the pictures. Then have them take turns reading in a small group. Use the Comprehension/Critical Thinking questions, as needed. After reading, they join the rest of the class to discuss Comprehension/Critical Thinking, T173, T175, T176; Story Structure, T176; Think About the Story, T177.

Phonics/Decoding Strategy Coach children in the strategy, as needed.

Learning to Read

Day 3

Yes, a jug can fit in the hut.
A cot and a jug can fit.

224

Can Zig Bug get a rug in the hut?

225

Anthology pages 224–225

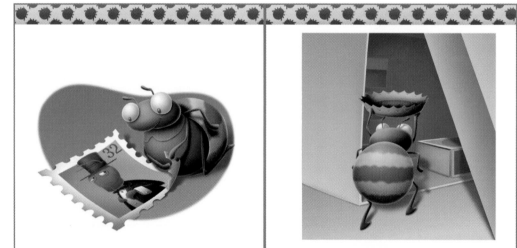

Yes, a rug can fit in the hut.
A cot, a jug, and a rug can fit.

226

Can Zig Bug get a cup in the hut?

227

Anthology pages 226–227

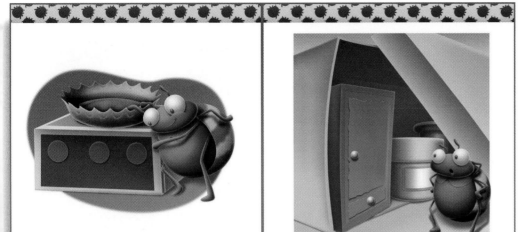

Yes, a cup can fit in the hut.
A cot, a jug, a rug, and
a cup can fit.

228

Can Zig Bug fit in the hut?

229

Anthology pages 228–229

Comprehension/Critical Thinking

1 What things has Zig Bug put in his hut? (shell, a thimble, a stamp, a bottle cap) **Noting Details**

2 ✓ Reread page 229, and look at the picture. Zig Bug has another problem, doesn't he? What is that problem? (He is not sure if he can fit inside the hut.) **Story Structure**

3 ✓ **Strategy Focus: Student Modeling** We've already summarized part of the story. What would you add to our summary? (Zig Bug has so many things in his hut that he may not fit.) **Summarize**

4 How could you use what you know about letters and sounds to help you figure out this word (*rug,* page 225)? (Blend the sounds /r/ /ŭ/ /g/.) **Phonics/Decoding**

DAY 3

Reaching All Students

English Language Learners

Building Vocabulary Have English speakers name the human object that Zig Bug uses as a *cup*. Show real *bottle caps.* Write the word and have children repeat after you. Talk about how bottle caps are used.

Learning to Read
Day 3

Comprehension/Critical Thinking

1. How does Zig Bug solve his problem?
(He squeezes as hard as he can until he is in.) **Story Structure**

2. **Strategy Focus: Student Modeling**
How would you end our summary of this story? (It's hard, but Zig Bug squeezes himself in.) **Story Structure**

Anthology pages 230–231

Revisiting the Text

Retelling the Story:

✓ Story Structure

Have children use what they learned about story structure to retell the story with partners. Remind them to tell who is in the story, where it takes place, what the problems are, and how the character solves them.

Do not quit, Zig Bug!
You can fit!

230

Zig Bug does fit!
A cot, a jug, a rug, a cup,
and Zig Bug fit in the hut!

231

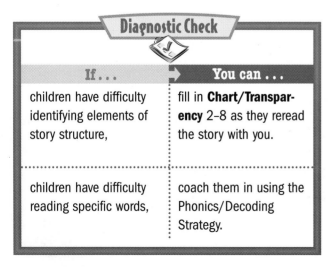

Diagnostic Check

If . . .	You can . . .
children have difficulty identifying elements of story structure,	fill in **Chart/Transparency** 2–8 as they reread the story with you.
children have difficulty reading specific words,	coach them in using the Phonics/Decoding Strategy.

Reaching All Students

Extra Support

Writing Support for Responding Page through the story with children. Have them identify each item that Zig Bug puts into his hut. List the items on the board: a nutshell, a thimble, a stamp, a bottle cap. Discuss how each thing is used by Zig Bug. Ask children to think of something else Zig Bug might need, such as a chair, a sofa, or a desk. Encourage children to look around the classroom to find some very small things—such as an art eraser or a paper-clip box—that might be used. Add these to the list, and have children refer to it as they respond.

Anthology pages 232–233

Pages within image:

Responding

Think About the Story

1 Was Zig Bug smart? Why?

2 What else could Zig Bug put in his hut?

3 Will Zig Bug be happy in his hut? Why?

232

Writing

Write a List

List the things Zig Bug put in his hut. Add some more things he could put in there.

233

Responding

▶ Think About the Story

Discuss the questions on Anthology page 232 and the starred question. Accept reasonable responses.

1 **Drawing Conclusions** Children will probably respond that Zig Bug was smart in furnishing his hut, using a nutshell for a cot, a thimble for a jug, and so on.

2 **Drawing Conclusions** Nothing else will fit in the hut. Zig Bug had trouble getting himself in.

3 **Drawing Conclusions** Answers will vary, but children will probably suggest that he will be happy, since he has everything he needs.

4 **Connecting/Comparing** What is the surprise in this story? (Zig Bug finds surprising new uses for ordinary things.)

▶ Comprehension Check

Practice Book page 96

Think About Zig Bug

Circle the answer for each question.

1. What is a cot for Zig Bug? (1 point)
2. What is a jug for Zig Bug? (1)
3. What is a rug for Zig Bug? (1)
4. What is a cup for Zig Bug? (1)
5. What is a hut for Zig Bug?
   A pot is a hut. **A box is a hut.** (1)

96 Theme 2: Surprise!
Assessment Tip: Total 5 Points   Read directions to children.

Reaching All Students
English Language Learners

Beginning/Preproduction Help children describe Zig Bug. You may want to guide them with questions such as: "How many legs does Zig Bug have? What color is he? Does he have big eyes or small eyes?"

Early Production and Speech Emergence Have partners work together to describe Zig Bug's home.

Intermediate and Advanced Have children say what the real objects are that Zig Bug uses in his hut. List the words for the human objects on the board or on chart paper.

Student Self-Assessment

Help children assess by asking:

- What did you do well while reading this story?
- Were any parts of the story hard to understand?

DAY 3

Phonics Review

Words with Short e

▶ **Reading Words with Short e**

Reviewing Consonants Display **Large Letter Cards** for all the consonants. Remind children that they know the sounds for these letters. Have children name each letter and say its sound.

Reviewing Short e Tell children that today they will read some words with consonant letters and the vowel *e*. Display **Large Letter Card** *Ee* and tell children to say the short *e* sound, /ĕ/.

Playing "Get That Word!" Invite children to play "Get That Word!" To play:

■ Randomly display the following word cards: *bed, beg, den, fed, get, jet, led, leg, men, net, pen, pet, red, set, ten, vet, wet, yes.*

■ Arrange children in two groups, or teams.

■ Team A chooses a word card and gives it to the first player on Team B. The child to whom the card is given must blend and read the word. If the child is successful, his or her team scores a point.

■ The team with the most points wins.

■ As children become more accurate, you may want to set a time limit for each turn.

Words with short e Using **Blackline Master** 201, prepare two word wheels for words with short *e* as shown below. Use the letters *d, m, t, p,* and *h* with *e* and *n*. Use *w, l, y, v, g,* and *s* with *e* and *t*.

Remind children how to turn the wheel to make words. Then have partners take turns displaying words and reading them. As one child reads the word, the other child can write it and practice spelling.

▶ Making Words

Place **Large Letter Cards** *a, e, e, h, l, n, p, t* in a pocket chart. Give each child a matching set of punchout letters and a tray. Name the letters on the cards as children hold up their matching cards. Tell children that they will use their letters to make some words. In the end they will use all their letters to make a big word that names a big animal.

Give the following directions for making words, and say the context sentences. Call on a child who makes the word correctly to display it with the **Large Letter Cards** in the pocket chart.

- *Take two letters and make* at. *(Look at the dog.)*

- *Add a letter to the beginning of* at *to make* pat. *(I gave my dog a pat on the head.)*

- *Change just the middle letter to change* pat *into* pet. *(Would you like to pet my cat?)*

- *Change just the last letter to change* pet *into* pen. *(The pen is on the desk.)*

- *Change just the middle letter to change* pen *into* pan. *(The pan is on the stove.)*

Extension/Challenge

- *Add a letter to* pan *to make* plan. *(I plan to build a tower with my blocks.)*

- *Add a letter to the end of* plan *to make* plant. *(The plant grew green and tall.)*

Big Word Ask if anyone has figured out the big word made with all the letters. (elephant)

Sort Have children sort the index cards for words with short *a* and words with short *e*.

Practice Have children read **I Love Reading Books,** Review Books 15–18.

• Instruction, T86–T88	• Reteaching, R8, R10

Suggestions for Daily Fluency Building

Extra Support	On Level	Challenge
Independent Reading	**Teacher-Supported Reading**	**Independent Reading**
• Reread On My Way Practice Reader: *Where Is Tug Bug?*	• On Level/Challenge Theme Paperback: *Spots*	• Check in with teacher after reading the Little Big Book: *Jasper's Beanstalk*
• Reread Anthology, Phonics Library, and I Love Reading Books selections		

Spelling and Phonics

Words with qu, j, z, *and Short* u

Review the letters and sounds for *qu, j, z* and short *u* using **Large Sound/Spelling Cards** *queen, jumping Jill, zebra,* and *umbrella*. Remind children how to write the letters *qu, j,* and *z* by modeling on the chalkboard.

■ Display the **Picture Cards** in random order, and have children write the letters that stand for the beginning sounds.

■ Display the **Picture Card** *jug.* Say the word slowly, and ask a child to spell the word orally as you model how to write it. Then have children write the word on their own.

Penmanship For children who need extra practice, model how to write *jug* again. Have children practice writing the word several times. You may want to have children practice writing *hug* and *bug.*

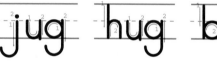

Two penmanship models (continuous stroke, ball and stick) are available in the **Practice Book** (pp. 198–205) and the **Teacher's Resource Blackline Masters** (pp. 143–194).

Vocabulary

Days of the Week

Turn to page 50 of *Jasper's Beanstalk.* Point to the word *Monday,* and read it for children. Tell them that Monday begins with a capital letter because it is a special name: the name of a day of the week.

Ask if children can name other days of the week. Write the words on the board as they are suggested. If children need prompting, page through *Jasper's Beanstalk,* pointing out the words *Tuesday, Wednesday,* and so on.

Have children make calendars to record what Jasper did each day during that first week. Children can write or draw to show what Jasper did each day.

Monday	Tuesday	Wednesday	Thursday	Friday	Saturday	Sunday
found a bean	planted	watered	dug, raked, sprayed, hoed	picked up slugs and snails	mowed	waited and waited

---

Grammar

Action Words

■ Display the **Picture Card** *sit*. Without naming the picture, ask if children know what *action* it shows. Ask a volunteer to do this same action. Then sit for the child.

■ Next, display this sentence:

> (child's name) *and I sit.*

Read the sentence. Tell children that *sit* is an action word, or verb. It tells what someone does.

■ Display these **Picture Cards**: *run, cut, mix, swim*. Ask children to name the action and to then pantomime doing that action.

■ Next, write these sentences on the board. Have children find the action word in each sentence.

Ben ran.

The men dig.

Dan and I jump.

Nan cut the fig.

Skill Finder
• Review, page T199

OBJECTIVES

Children
• identify action words

MATERIALS

• **Picture Cards** *bike, cut, mix, run, sit, swim*

·········· **Houghton Mifflin English** ··········
Correlated Instruction and Practice, pp. 119–120

DAY 3

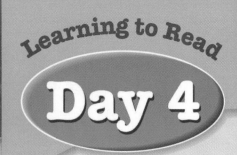

Learning to Read

Day 4

Day at a Glance

Learning to Read

Reading the Anthology, *T184–T191*

The Rope Tug

written by Veronica Freeman Ellis • art by Mary Lynn Carson
photography by Richard Haynes

- ✓ **Comprehension:**
  Story Structure

- ✓ **Reading Strategy:**
  Summarize

- ✓ **Applying Phonics
  and High-Frequency
  Words**

Word Work

Spelling and Phonics, *T192*

- Word Slides with Short *u*

- Penmanship

Vocabulary, *T192*

- Homographs

Writing & Language

Writing, *T193*

- Writing About Bugs

✓ = Tested Skill

Opening

Daily Message

Use the Daily Message for a quick review of high-frequency words, phonics, and language skills.

- ■ Read the message aloud, pointing to each word as it is read.

- ■ Call on children to find and circle examples of *qu, j, z.*

- ■ Call on other children to find the high-frequency words *and, you, the, does, he, I, too, It, is, They,* and *to.*

> Good morning, Boys and Girls!
>
> Did you enjoy the story about Zig Bug? Zig just doesn't quit, does he? I think you will like our next story, too. It is about some zany animals. They like to zig, tug, and jig.

Concepts of Print

- Remind children that names begin with capital letters. Have them point to the capital letter that begins a name.

- Point out that there are several commas in today's message. Mention that a comma shows where to pause briefly when reading a sentence aloud.

Routines

Daily Phonemic Awareness

Blending Phonemes: Categories

Play "Categories" with children to name things that hold other things.

- Say: *These things can hold other things. Listen: / c / / ŭ / / p /. Blend the sounds quietly. Raise your hand when you know what I named ... What's the word?* (cup)

- Continue with the words *jug, can, bag, pot, net,* and *kit.*

- You might have children blend words in other categories, such as ways to travel (*jet, jog*).

Daily Independent Reading

Remind children to practice reading the Word Pattern Board. They can also read:

- **Bibliography, pages T4–T5**

  Choose books from this list for children to read, outside class, for at least twenty minutes a day.

- **Books for Small-Group Reading, pages T156–T159**

- **Selections from the Phonics Library**

- **Reread I Love Reading Books, Review Books 15–18**

✏ Daily Prompt for Independent Writing

Use the prompt below, or allow children to write about a topic of their choice. Encourage them to use what they know about letters and sounds to record their ideas.

- Draw and write about your favorite animal.

turtle

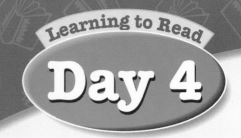
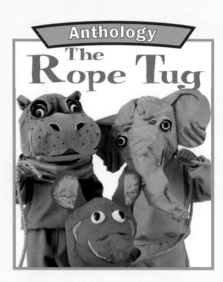

Anthology

The Rope Tug

Purpose • applying reading strategies, comprehension skills, phonics/decoding skills, high-frequency words, and critical thinking

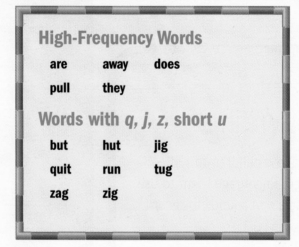

High-Frequency Words

are	away	does
pull	they	

Words with *q, j, z,* short *u*

but	hut	jig
quit	run	tug
zag	zig	

Preparing to Read

▶ ## Building Background

Acting in a Play Ask if children have acted out a story or been in a play. Encourage those who have to tell about their experiences. Ask what parts they played, and what the play was about.

▶ ## Developing Story Vocabulary

■ Elephant ■ Hippo ■ I'm ■ Narrator ■ outside ■ rope

Display **Chart/Transparency 2–10,** and use it to introduce children to the format of a play. Point out the characters and the setting. Explain that pictures of the characters are used to show who says what. Have children read the title. Then ask them to use the pictures of the characters to figure out the words Elephant and Hippo. Explain the role of the narrator. Read the play for children, pointing out who says what. Then have children take turns reading what each character says. Point to the underlined words, and ask children to identify them.

Practice Have children complete **Practice Book** page 97 as a class or with partners.

▶ ## Using "Get Set to Read"

Have children turn to Anthology pages 234–235. Explain that the words in the box are words they will read in the next story. Ask volunteers to read the words. Then have children read the sentences.

Anthology pages 234–235

Strategy & Skill Focus

 ## Strategy Focus:
Summarize

Have children turn to Anthology page 237. Read the selection title and the names of the author and the photographer. Point out that *The Rope Tug* is written as a play. Then have children turn to pages 238–239.

Teacher Modeling Point out that page 238 shows the cast of characters in the play, while page 239 shows the setting.

A play has characters, just as a story does. The characters are usually listed at the beginning of the play. A play is often acted out on a stage—with scenery to show what the setting is. I see a hut on the stage in this photo, so I think the setting may be in and around a hut.

Quick Write Ask children what they think the play is about. Have them record their predictions by drawing or writing in their journals.

Purpose Setting Ask children to think about characters, setting, problem, and solution as they read. This will help them summarize the play after reading. Remind children to also use their other reading strategies as they read the selection.

 ## Comprehension Skill Focus:
Story Structure

Point out that children have already identified the characters and the setting of *The Rope Tug*. Review that one character in a story usually has a problem, and the events of the story tell how the character tries to solve the problem. Point out that this problem-solution structure is also true of most plays.

The Big Tug

Elephant   Hippo   Narrator

Elephant and Hippo are <u>outside</u>.

Here is the <u>rope</u>.
Get set to tug.
Pull on three.

<u>I'm</u> big!   I can tug.

I'm big, too!   I can tug.

One, two, three!   GO!

 ### Teacher's Note

Strategy and Comprehension Skills Connection Focusing on the structure of a story is an excellent way for readers to prepare a summary of that story.

Focus Questions

Have children turn to Responding on page 252. Read the questions aloud and tell children to keep them in mind as they read *The Rope Tug*.

Reaching All Students
English Language Learners

Show children photos of a real hippo, elephant, and rat. Introduce the names; talk about relative sizes. Also introduce or review comparatives such as *bigger, biggest*, and *smaller, smallest* and the words *play* and *costume*. Tell children that this type of story is called a *play*. Refer to any plays the class may have seen. Also say that the children acting in this play are wearing *costumes* for these three animals.

DAY 4

Preparing to Read: *The Rope Tug*

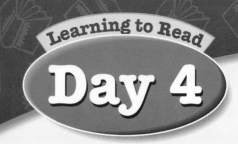

Learning to Read
Day 4

Reading the Anthology

Options for Reading

▶ **Universal Access** See the Classroom Management tips at the bottom of these pages for suggestions to meet individual needs during and after reading.

About the Author Veronica Freeman Ellis was born in Africa. She grew up hearing and telling stories like *The Rope Tug*. Many of her characters find ways to do great things.

Key to Underlined Words
Words with *q, j, z,* short *u* =====
High-Frequency Words ———
Story Vocabulary ———

Meet the Author
Veronica Freeman Ellis

Meet the Artist
Mary Lynn Carson

Meet the Photographer
Richard Haynes

236

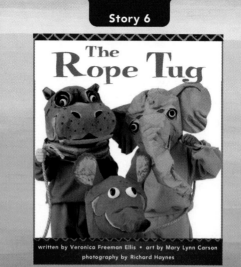

Story 6

The Rope Tug

written by Veronica Freeman Ellis • art by Mary Lynn Carson
photography by Richard Haynes

237

Anthology pages 236–237

Narrator

Elephant

Hippo

Rat

238

Elephant can get in the <u>hut</u>.
Hippo can get in the <u>hut</u>.

239

Anthology pages 238–239

Reaching All Students
Classroom Management

On Level

Partner Reading Partners can decide beforehand who will read which parts. After reading, children join the class to discuss: Comprehension/Critical Thinking, T187, T188, T189; Story Structure, T189; Think About the Story, T190.

Challenge

Independent Reading Children read the story and begin **Practice Book** page 98 before the class to discuss: Comprehension/Critical Thinking, T187, T188, T189; Story Structure, T189; Think About the Story, T190.

English Language Learners

Intermediate and Advanced
Read this selection as a group and have volunteers mime actions such as *tug, zig,* and *do a jig.* For English language learners at other proficiency levels, see Language Development Resources.

Rat can not get in.
Rat can not fit.
Let me in! Let me in!

240

You can not fit, Rat.
<u>Run</u> away, Rat!
Run, run, run!

241

Anthology pages 240–241

I can <u>pull</u> you outside.
I am not big, <u>but</u> I can tug.

242

You can not tug me, Rat.
You can not tug me, Rat.

243

Anthology pages 242–243

Comprehension/Critical Thinking

1. ✓ What is Rat's problem? (He can't fit in the hut with Elephant and Hippo.) **Story Structure**

2. ✓ Reread page 242. What does Rat say to try to solve his problem? (He says he can pull Elephant and Hippo out of the hut. Then he will fit.) **Story Structure**

3. ✓ **Strategy Focus: Teacher/Student Modeling** Let's summarize the story so far. Who are the animal characters? (Rat, Hippo, and Elephant) Look at the scenery. Where are the animals? (in and around a hut) What is Rat's problem? (He wants to get into the hut but won't fit. He comes up with a plan to get Elephant and Hippo out.) **Summarize**

4. How do you know this story is a fantasy? (Animals can't talk in real life. Only humans can talk.) **Fantasy and Realism**

5. How could you use what you know about letters and sounds to figure out this word (*hut*, page 239)? (Blend the sounds /h/ /ŭ/ /t/.) **Phonics/Decoding**

Revisiting the Text

Concepts of Print

Review the play format with children. Ask them to point to the picture that shows what the narrator says on page 240. Ask them to explain how to tell who says what on page 243.

DAY 4

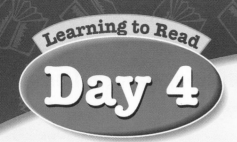

Learning to Read
Day 4

Comprehension/Critical Thinking

1 What do Hippo and Elephant tell Rat to get?
(a rope) **Noting Details**

2 What does Rat do with the rope? (He wraps it around several trees.) **Noting Details**

3 Why do you think he does this? (Hippo and Elephant may be strong, but they are probably not strong enough to pull down trees.) **Cause and Effect**

Revisiting the Text

Concepts of Print

Have children find and read aloud a sentence that asks a question on page 244. Have them find a sentence that ends with an exclamation mark on page 245. Point out that an exclamation mark shows that a sentence should be read with surprise or strong feeling.

Can you tug and pull me?
I am not big, but I can tug.

244

We are big!
We can pull you!
Get a big rope, Rat!

245

Anthology pages 244–245

Rat can get a big, big rope.

246

Rat can zig zag, zig zag.

247

Anthology pages 246–247

Diagnostic Check

If...	You can ...
children have difficulty identifying elements of story structure,	guide them in rereading the story, pausing to talk about characters, setting, problem, and solution.
children have difficulty summarizing the story,	have them retell it with partners or in small groups.
children have difficulty reading specific words,	coach them in using the Phonics/Decoding Strategy.

Reaching All Students
English Language Learners

Building Vocabulary Have children say the word and point to the *rope* on pages 246 and 247. Then have volunteers mime a *zig-zag* motion. Ask "Can Rat zigzag?" You may want to say that we often use the two words *zig* and *zag* together as *zigzag* and that this expresses movement back and forth. Have volunteers zigzag around the room.

Tug, tug, tug!
You can not win, Rat!
Tug, tug, tug!

248

They are big!
They tug and tug and tug,
but they can not pull Rat.

249

Anthology pages 248–249

I quit!
I quit!

250

Rat does a jig.
I win! I win!
I'm not big, but I can tug!

251

Anthology pages 250–251

Comprehension/Critical Thinking

1  How does Rat solve his problem?
(He tricks Elephant and Hippo into pulling a rope that's wrapped around trees. They tug so hard they fall out of the hut. Now there is room for Rat in the hut.)
Story Structure

2 **Strategy Focus: Student Modeling**
Tell me how you would summarize the last part of this story. (Rat's plan is to get the animals to tug on a rope that's wrapped around trees. They tug so hard that they fall out and he gets in.) **Summarize**

Revisiting the Text

Retelling the Story
Story Structure

After discussing the Comprehension/Critical Thinking questions, call on individuals to summarize the story by telling who the characters are, describing the setting, and telling what the problem is and how it is solved.

Reaching All Students
English Language Learners

Have volunteers demonstrate what it means to *do a jig*. Ask: "Who does a jig? Why does Rat do a jig?" As needed, help children complete the phrase "Rat does a jig because _____."

Student Self-Assessment

Help children assess by asking:
- What parts were easy to read? Which parts were hard?
- What did you do well as you read this story?

DAY 4

Responding

▶ Think About the Story

Discuss the questions on Anthology page 252 and the starred question. Accept reasonable responses.

1 Drawing Conclusions Perhaps they didn't think much of Rat and didn't want him around. They said he couldn't fit and told him to go away.

2 Cause and Effect He wrapped the rope around several trees so they couldn't pull him. When they fell out of the hut, he got in.

3 Critical Thinking Answers will vary.

4 Connecting/Comparing How is *The Rope Tug* like *A Hut for Zig Bug*? (Zig Bug has trouble fitting himself into his hut. Rat has a problem fitting because Elephant and Hippo are so big that there is no room left.)

▶ Comprehension Check

Practice Book page 98

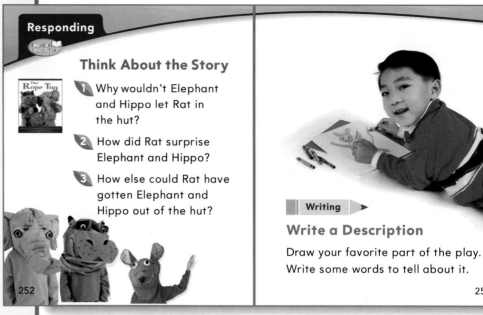

Responding

Think About the Story

1 Why wouldn't Elephant and Hippo let Rat in the hut?

2 How did Rat surprise Elephant and Hippo?

3 How else could Rat have gotten Elephant and Hippo out of the hut?

Write a Description

Draw your favorite part of the play. Write some words to tell about it.

252 / 253

Anthology pages 252–253

Reaching All Students
Extra Support

Writing Support for Responding Ask children to choose favorite parts and tell about them. List the page numbers of the parts mentioned on the board, and write some of the things children say. Suggest that children refer to the list as they draw and write about their favorite parts.

Reaching All Students
English Language Learners

Beginning/Preproduction Show the photos of each of the characters, and ask children to identify them. Then ask children to mime *tug*, *zigzag*, and *do a jig*.

Early Production and Speech Emergence Ask children to take turns reading the lines for the play. Help with pronunciation and intonation.

Intermediate and Advanced Ask groups of four children to plan their own presentation of this play.

Anthology pages 254–255

Way Down South

Way down South where
bananas grow,
A grasshopper stepped on
an elephant's toe.
The elephant said, with tears
in his eyes,
"Pick on somebody your
own size."

Anonymous

254 255

Poetry Link

▶ Skill: How to Read a Poem

Preview the illustration with children. Identify the animals as an elephant and a grasshopper. Point out the differences in their sizes.

Before you read, explain that this is a silly poem. Then read the title, and ask children to find those same three words in the first line of the poem.

Ask children to listen for rhyming words as you read the poem aloud. Then reread the poem. Stop at *toe* for children to supply the word that rhymes with *grow*. Stop at *eyes* for children to supply the words that rhymes with *size*.

Comprehension/Critical Thinking

1. What did the grasshopper do to make the elephant cry? (The grasshopper stepped on the elephant's toe.) **Cause and Effect**

2. What is so funny about this? (An elephant probably wouldn't even feel anything if a grasshopper stepped on its toe.) **Evaluate**

3. What did the elephant say to the grasshopper? (He told the grasshopper to pick on somebody his own size.) **Noting Details**

DAY 4

Suggestions for Daily Fluency Building

Extra Support	On Level	Challenge
Teacher-Supported Reading • Phonics Library	**Partner Reading** • Reread On Level Theme Paperback, *Spots* • Reread Anthology selections	**Partner Reading** • Reread Anthology selections • Literature Resources

Responding/Poetry Link   (T191)

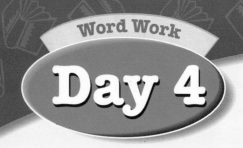
Day 4

OBJECTIVES

Children

- **Spelling and Phonics** build, read, write, and spell words with short *u*.

- **Vocabulary** learn and recall homographs

MATERIALS

Spelling and Phonics

- **Blackline Master** 197

Vocabulary

- **Picture Card** *can*

··· **Houghton Mifflin Spelling and Vocabulary** ···
Correlated Instruction and Practice, p. 89

Spelling and Phonics

Word Slides with Short u

Using **Blackline Master** 197, prepare two sets of word slides. One set will have the letters *b, d, h, j, m, r,* and *t* on the letter strip and *u* and *g* in the small boxes on the slide. The other set will have the letters *b, c, h, j, n,* and *r* on the letter strip and *u* and *t* in the small boxes on the slide.

Have children work with partners. Each child in the pair takes a different word slide. Have partners take turns forming three-letter words and blending the sounds to read them. After one child reads the word, the other child can write it and practice spelling. Have partners compare their lists, noting which words begin with the same consonants.

Penmanship For children who need extra practice, model how to write this sentence: *Zig Bug said, "I have a hut."* Have children write the sentence.

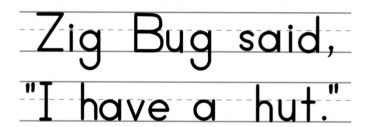

Two penmanship models (continuous stroke, ball and stick) are available in the **Practice Book** (pp. 198–205) and the **Teacher's Resource Blackline Masters** (pp. 143–194).

Vocabulary

Homographs

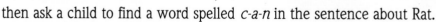

Display the **Picture Card** *can*, and this sentence: *Rat can tug.*

Tell children to watch as you write the picture name on the board. Write *can*, and then ask a child to find a word spelled *c-a-n* in the sentence about Rat.

Underline the word *can* in the sentence. Explain that the letters *c-a-n* spell words with two very different meanings. One names the object shown on the card. The other means "is able," as in *Rat is able to tug.*

Ask children which *can* belongs in this sentence: "Dan opened a _____ of soup." (Children should point to the picture of the can.)

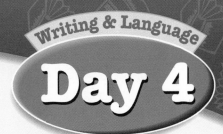

✏️ Writing

Writing About Bugs

Make available to children several books about bugs and/or insects, such as *Bugs! Bug! Bugs!* by Jennifer Dussling (DK Publishing, 1998) and *Big Bug Book* by Margery Facklam (Little, Brown; 1994, 1998). Allow children to browse through the books and to comment on the real, live bugs (or insects).

- Ask each child to choose a bug (or an insect) to write about.

- Talk about what to include, such as what the animal looks like, how big or little it is, and what it can do.

- If necessary, model how to write about a bug of your own choosing. (See example on the chart shown.)

- Assist children with writing, if need be. Allow them to dictate some sentences to you—but do encourage them to try writing on their own as well.

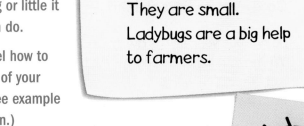

Ladybugs
Ladybugs are red.
They have black spots.
They are small.
Ladybugs are a big help
to farmers.

After children have shared their writing, arrange their work on a bulletin board display entitled "Best Bugs."

Have children complete **Practice Book** page 99.

Reaching All Students

English Language Learners

Have English language learners work in a group. Provide books on bugs and allow the children to decide on a bug for a group writing activity. Help children identify the name of the bug. Then brainstorm words they can use to describe their bug. Write their ideas on a word web with the name of the chosen bug in the center. Then ask each child to take a turn describing the bug. Write their sentences on chart paper.

OBJECTIVES

Children

- write about bugs

Practice Book page 99

Type to Learn™ Jr.

Students may use Type to Learn™ Jr. to familiarize themselves with the computer keyboard. ©*Sunburst Technology Corporation, a Houghton Mifflin Company. All Rights reserved.*

Portfolio Opportunity

Save a copy of each child's work as a sample of his or her writing development.

DAY 4

Learning to Read
Day 5

Day at a Glance

Learning to Read

Reading Instruction, *T196*

☑ Revisiting the Literature: *Story Structure*

Reading Check, *T197*

- **Phonics Library:** *Rug Tug*
- **I Love Reading Books, Books 19–22**

Word Work

Spelling and Phonics, *T198*

- Spelling Words with Short *u*
- Penmanship

Word Pattern Board, *T198*

Writing & Language

Grammar Review, *T199*

- Action Words

Listening and Speaking, *T199*

- Reader's Theater

☑ **= Tested Skill**

Opening

··

Daily Message

Use the Daily Message for a quick skill review.

■ Read the message aloud, pointing to each word as it is read.

■ Have children find and underline any words they can read.

> Good Morning, Boys and Girls!
>
> Do not put your things away yet! The day is just beginning. We have a lot to do today. At the end of the day, you will go home. You will go to the place where you live. But first, let's pull on our thinking caps and get to work.

Concepts of Print

Have children find a sentence that ends with an exclamation mark and shows strong feeling.

Count Them!

Have children count the sentences in this rather long message. Then have them count all the words they know!

Routines

....

Daily Phonemic Awareness

Blending Phonemes: Name the Picture

Tell children that they will play a guessing game.

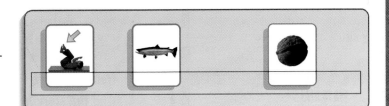

■ Hold up **Picture Card** *six* so that children can't see the picture. Say the picture name, segmenting the sounds: /s//ĭ//ks/. Repeat.

■ Have children guess the picture name by blending the sounds together, saying the word naturally to themselves, and raising their hands when they know the word.

■ When all hands are up, show children the picture so that they can check their responses.

■ Repeat this activity with **Picture Cards** *hen, feet, fish, fox, leg, nut,* and *ox.*

Daily Independent Reading

Have children read with partners.

■ Reread *The Bug Kit* or *Quit It, Zig!* from the Phonics Library.

■ Bibliography, pages T4–T5

   Choose books from this list for children to read, outside class, for at least twenty minutes a day.

■ Reread I Love Reading Books, Review Books 15–18

✏️ Daily Prompt for Independent Writing

Use the prompt below, or allow children to write about a topic of their choice. Encourage them to use what they have been learning about letters and sounds to record their ideas.

■ Draw and write about your favorite story in this theme.

> The best story is Hot Fox Soup.

MATERIALS
- **Blackline Masters** 32-34

Chart/Transparency 2–11

Surprise Stories

Story	Jasper's Beanstalk	A Hut for Zig Bug	The Rope Tug
Who?	Jasper	Zig Bug	Rat, Hippo, Elephant
Where?	outside, in a yard	in a house	in and around a hut
What?	grow a beanstalk	make a good home	let Rat in the hut
How?	give it time to grow	use small things	trick the animals

TRANSPARENCY 2–11
TEACHER'S EDITION PAGE T196

SURPRISE! Week 3, Day 5
Revisiting the Literature Story Structure

Revisiting the Literature

☑ *Story Structure*

Comparing Texts Review the elements of story structure: *characters, setting, problem, solution.*

> **Think Aloud**
>
> *Here are some things we've learned about the plan of a story. The characters are who the story is about. The setting is where the story takes place. One character often has a problem. I need to think about what the problem is, and how the character solves it.*

Display **Chart/Transparency** 2–11. Point out the title of the stories. Then point out the words in the first column that relate to story structure. Ask children to help you complete this chart.

For each story, have children tell:

- **who** the characters are,
- **where** the story takes place,
- **what** the problem is, and
- **how** the problem is solved.

Additional Practice

- Assign children to reread other selections from the week (On My Way Practice Reader and On Level/Challenge Theme Paperbacks, Phonics Library selections) and think about story structure in those stories.

- Children can demonstrate their understanding of the comprehension skill, story structure, through a retelling of the story *The Rope Tug* using the story characters on **Blackline Masters 32-33.**

Decodable Text

Reading **Phonics Library**

Surprise!

Reading Check

▶ Phonics-Decoding Strategy

Student Modeling Ask children to tell how they have used the Phonics/Decoding Strategy to read new words. Tell them that they should use what they know about letters, sounds, and words to read the next story. Choose a child to model how to use the strategy to read the title. Then have children read the story independently.

Coached Reading If children have difficulty decoding words like *cut* on their own, coach them with prompts such as these:

- ■ *What are the letters from left to right?* (c, u, t)

- ■ *What sound does each letter stand for?* (/k/, /ŭ/, /t/)

- ■ *Blend the sounds. What is the word?* (cŭŭŭt, cut)

- ■ *Does* cut *make sense in the story?*

Developing Fluency Encourage children to read aloud fluently and with expression. Model reading fluently, and coach children to read with feeling and expression as needed.

Assessment Options

Oral Reading Records You may wish to take an oral reading record as children read the **Phonics Library** book individually or in small groups.

Alternative Assessment Use **Blackline Master** 34 to assess individual children's phonics and high-frequency word skills.

Suggestions for Daily Fluency Building

Extra Support	On Level	Challenge
Partner Reading	**Independent Reading**	**Teacher-Supported Reading**
• Books from Bibliography	• Books from Bibliography	• Phonics Library
• Literature Resources	• Literature Resources	

Phonics Library

Purposes for decodable text

- • assessment
- • applying phonics skills
- • applying high-frequency words

Rug Tug
by Randolph Silva
illustrated by Laura DeSantis

Ten men can tug a big rug.

37

Ten men pull it to a tan hut.

38

It does not fit yet, but the ten men do not quit.

39

Cut! Cut! Zig, jig!
Ten men cut it. It can fit.

40

DAY 5

Home Connection

A take-home version of *Rug Tug* is available in the **Phonics Library Blackline Masters**. Children can take the story home to read with their families.

OBJECTIVES

Children

- **Phonics and Spelling** read, build, write, and spell words with short *u*
- **Word Pattern Board** review the Word Pattern Board

MATERIALS

- teacher-made cards with *but, cut, hut, jut, nut, rut; bug, dug, hug, jug, lug, mug, rug, tug*

···· **Houghton Mifflin Spelling and Vocabulary** ····
Correlated Instruction and Practice, p. 89

Diagnostic Check

If . . .	You can . . .
children need more practice in discriminating beginning sounds,	use **Back to School** pages or Daily Phonemic Awareness, pages T145, T161, T183, T195.

Spelling and Phonics
Spelling Words with Short u

Make and display cards with short *u* words that end with *g* and *t,* as shown under Materials. Call on volunteers to read the words.

- With scissors, cut *jug* into its individual letters. Mix up the letters and display them.

- Ask: **Which letter stands for the first sound in** jug? **... the second sound? ... the third sound? Write the word** jug.

- After children have written the word, check their spelling. Spell *jug* aloud as one child arranges the letters in the correct order.

- Choose other listed words and repeat the procedure.

Penmanship Model how to write *Here is a hut for a bug*. Monitor children's progress as they write the sentence.

Here is a hut for a bug.

Two penmanship models (continuous stroke, ball and stick) are available in the **Practice Book** (pp. 198–205) and the **Teacher's Resource Blackline Masters** (pp. 143–194).

Word Pattern Board

High-Frequency Words Tell children that today you will move this week's high-frequency words from the "New Words" section to the permanent Word Pattern Board.

- Review the "New Words" section with clap and spell. Remove each word as it is reviewed.

- Call on volunteers to move the words to the permanent Word Pattern Board. The class can chant the words are they are moved.

- Review the entire Word Pattern Board with clap and spell.

Vocabulary Speed Drills On index cards, write this week's new words and add a few decodable words that feature the week's phonics/decoding elements. At small group time, have children take turns holding up the cards for a partner to read. After this warm-up, display the cards as a list on a table and have individuals read them to you as quickly as they can.

Grammar Review

Action Words

Display **Chart/Transparency 2–12**. Tell children that these sentences are missing action words, or verbs.

- Display index cards with the words *dig, hug, jump,* and *ran*.

- Choose a child to read the first incomplete sentence. Ask the child to choose a verb from among the words on display to complete the sentence.

- Write the suggested verb on the line. Have children as a group read the sentence and decide if it makes sense. Help children conclude that the verb *ran* is an action word and that it makes sense in the sentence.

- Follow a similar procedure with the remaining sentences.

Coached Writing Dictate the following sentence: **Bug and Pig dig.** Have children write the sentence. Then ask them to find the action word in the sentence (*dig*).

Listening and Speaking

Reader's Theater

Explain that in Reader's Theater, readers take the parts of the characters in a play and read the lines they say. Ask children how many characters are needed for a Reader's Theater presentation of *The Rope Tug*. (four)

- Divide the class into groups of four. Have members of each group choose the parts they want to play—or assign the parts yourself.

- Have the actors practice reading their lines, both alone and with their groups.

- Review that in Reader's Theater, actors should speak in loud voices. They should also follow along carefully so they know when it is their turn to read a line.

- When children are ready, have groups take turns reading the play aloud for the class.

Reaching All Students

English Language Learners

Give English language learners ample time to practice their lines before presenting in front of the group. If possible, allow each child to read his or her lines to you, either individually or in the group of four, so that you can assist with pronunciation and intonation.

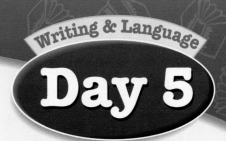

Writing & Language

Day 5

Chart/Transparency 2–12

Action Words

The fox ___ran___ to the den.

We ___dig___ a big rut.

I ___hug___ my cat.

They ___jump___ on the mat.

SURPRISE! Week 3, Day 5
Grammar Action Words

TRANSPARENCY 2–12
TEACHER'S EDITION PAGE T199

Copyright © Houghton Mifflin Company. All rights reserved.

·········· **Houghton Mifflin English** ··········
Correlated Instruction and Practice, pp. 119–120

DAY 5

MATERIALS

- **Large Sound/Spelling Cards:** *duck, elephant, fox, jumping Jill, kangaroo, lion, ostrich, queen, umbrella, volcano, worm, yo-yo, zebra*
- **Picture Cards:** *bed, box, boy, cup, dog, farm, fox, hen, hut, jet, jug, kit, leg, log, man, mop, nurse, ox, pot, pup, store, tub, up, vet, web, wig, yak, yard, zip, zoo*

Skill Reminder

Naming Words

Remind children that a naming word can name a person, animal, place, or thing. One at a time, display these **Picture Cards:** *bed, box, boy, cup, dog, farm, fox, hen, hut, jet, jug, kit, log, man, mop, nurse, ox, pot, pup, store, tub, vet, web, wig, yak, yard, zoo.*

Ask children to identify each card and to tell whether it is a person, animal, place, or thing. Then have children sort the cards.

People: *boy, man, nurse, vet*
Animals: *dog, fox, hen, ox, pup, yak*
Places: *farm, hut, store, yard, zoo*
Things: *bed, box, cup, jet, jug, kit, log, mop, pot, tub, web, wig*

Taught: *Grade 1, Theme 2*
Reviewed: *Grade 1, Theme 2*

Spiral Review

Phonics Skills: *Consonants:* d, w, l, x, y, k, v, q, j, z; *Short* o, e, u; *Blending Short* o, e, u *Words (VC, CVC)*

▶ Review

On the chalk ledge, display **Large Sound/Spelling Cards** *duck, lion, kangaroo, volcano, zebra, worm, yo-yo, fox, queen, jumping Jill.* Review what children have learned about the sound/spellings represented on the cards:

- Dd *stands for the /d/ sound,* Ll *for the /l/ sound,* Kk *for the /k/ sound,* Vv *for the /v/ sound, and* Zz *for the /z/ sound. These sounds can come at the beginning or at the end of words.*

- Ww *stands for the /w/ sound,* Yy *for the /y/ sound. These sounds can come at the beginning of words.*

- Xx *stands for the /ks/ sounds at the end of* fox. *The /ks/ sounds for x come at the end of words.*

- *In English, q is always followed by u;* qu *together stand for the /kw/ sounds.*

- Jj *may stand for the /j/ sound at the beginning of a word.*

Now display the *elephant, ostrich,* and *umbrella* cards. Remind children that *Ee, Oo,* and *Uu* are vowels and review these sound/spellings: *o,* /ŏ/ as in *ostrich* and *top; e,* /ĕ/ as in *elephant* and *bed; u,* /ŭ/ as in *umbrella* and *bug.*

▶ Apply

Distribute one or more of these **Picture Cards** to each child: *bed, box, cup, dog, fox, hen, hut, jet, jug, kit, leg, log, mop, ox, pot, pup, tub, up, vet, web, wig, yak, zip.* Write *bed* on the board. Have children read the word silently. The child who has the corresponding **Picture Card** should stand and read the word aloud. Repeat with the remaining cards. Then write *quit* and *quiz.* Have children read the words silently. Call on volunteers to use the words in oral sentences.

 Skill Finder Consonants *d, w, l, x, y, k, v, qu, j, z; Short o, e, u; Blending Short o, e, u Words (VC, CVC)* **Taught:** Gr. 1, Th. 2, T26–T28, T86–T88, T150–T152; **Reviewed:** Gr. 1, Th. 2, T114–T115, T178–T179, Th. 3, T54–T55; **Reteaching:** Gr. 1, Th. 2, R4, R6, R8, R10, R12, R14

Comprehension Skill: *Noting Details; Fantasy and Realism*

▶ **Review and Apply**

Remind children that in a story, both words and pictures include details about the story characters and events. Also remind them that some stories tell about things that could really happen, but if any part of a story is make-believe, then the story is called a *fantasy*.

Ask children whether *A Hut for Zig Bug* (Anthology pages 217–231) is a fantasy or a story that could really happen. (fantasy) Ask them what details let them know that the story is a fantasy. List their responses on the board. (Examples: Bugs don't have names; A real bug would not have its own hut; A real bug would not use a cot, jug, rug, or cup.) Then have children draw a detail from *The Rope Tug* (Anthology pages 237–251) that lets them know that this story is a fantasy. Allow time for children to share their drawings with the class.

High-Frequency Words

▶ **Review and Apply**

Have partners play Match That Word. Give pairs of children two sets of punchout word cards *five, four, in, once, three, two, upon, what, do, for, I, is, me, my, said, you, are, away, does, he, live, pull, they, where.* Have children shuffle all the cards and place them face down on a table in four rows of six.

Players take turns turning over two cards and reading the words aloud. If the two words match and are read correctly, the player keeps the cards and turns over two more cards. If the words do not match, it is the other player's turn to try to match two cards. The player with the most matches when all the cards have been picked up wins the game.

Noting Details
Taught: Gr. 1, Th. 2, T22, T38–T39, T50; **Reviewed:** Gr. 1, Th. 2, T70;
Reteaching: Gr. 1, Th. 2, R22

Fantasy and Realism
Taught: Gr. 1, Th. 2, T82, T98–T99; **Reviewed:** Gr. 1, Th. 2, T134;
Reteaching: Gr. 1, Th. 2, R24

High-Frequency Words
Taught: Gr. 1, Th. 2, T40, T100, T164; **Reviewed:** Gr. 1, Th. 2, T42, T72, T102, T136, T166, T198; **Reteaching:** Gr. 1, Th. 2, R16, R18, R20

MATERIALS

• **Anthology 1.1 Here We Go!**
• punchout word cards *five, four, in, once, three, two, upon, what, do, for, I, is, me, my, said, you, are, away, does, he, live, pull, they, where*

Skill Reminder

Capitalizing Names
Write your name on the board, and read it. Remind children that names begin with a capital letter. Have children revisit Anthology themes 1 and 2 to find the names of story characters. Have children take turns identifying a character and spelling its name, for example: *Pat Pig. Capital P, a, t. Capital P, i, g.* Write the names in a list on the board as children spell them.

Taught: *Grade 1, Theme 2*

Theme Assessment Wrap-Up

Integrated Theme Test — Integrated test of reading and writing skills: Phonics, comprehension strategies and skills, high-frequency words, and writing

Theme Skills Test — Tests discrete skills: Phonics, comprehension skills, and high-frequency words

▷ Assessing Student Progress

Formal Assessment The **Integrated Theme Test** and the **Theme Skills Test** are formal group assessments used to evaluate student performance on theme objectives. The **Theme Skills Test** may be used as a pretest or may be administered following the theme.

The **Integrated Theme Test** assesses students' progress as readers and writers in a format that reflects instruction. Decodable text passages test reading skills in context.

The **Theme Skills Test** assesses students' mastery of specific reading and language arts skills taught in the theme. Individual skill subtests can be administered separately.

The **Emerging Literacy Survey** can be administered or readministered individually to chart progress, to identify areas of strength and need, and to evaluate need for early intervention.

Using Multiple Measures Student progress is best evaluated through multiple measures, which can be collected in a portfolio. The portfolio provides a record of student progress over time and can be useful in conferencing with the student, parents, or other educators. In addition to the tests mentioned above, portfolios might include the following:

- Oral reading records
- Observation Checklist from this theme (See *Teacher's Resource Blackline Masters*)
- Student writing from lessons or activities in this theme
- Other writing, projects, or artwork
- One or more items selected by the student

▶ Assessing Student Progress *(continued)*

Using Assessment for Planning Instruction You can use the results of theme assessments to evaluate individual students' needs and to modify instruction during the next theme. For more detail, see the test manuals or the **Teacher's Assessment Handbook**.

Customizing Instruction

Student Performance Shows:	Modifications to Consider:
Difficulty with Decoding or Oral Fluency	**Emphasis:** Phonemic awareness and phonics; rereading for fluency **Resources:** Teacher's Edition: *Daily Phonemic Awareness, Phonics Reteaching lessons;* Lexia Quick Phonics Assessment CD-ROM; Lexia Phonics CD-ROM: Primary Intervention; Phonics Library; I Love Reading Books; On My Way Practice Readers; Anthology
Difficulty with Comprehension	**Emphasis:** Oral comprehension; strategy development; story comprehension; Teacher-Supported Reading **Resources:** Teacher's Edition: *Teacher Read Alouds, Reading the Big Book, Selection Comprehension questions*
Overall High Performance	**Emphasis:** Independent reading and writing; vocabulary development; critical thinking **Resources:** Teacher's Edition: *Think About the Story questions, Challenge notes, Challenge/Extension;* Theme Paperbacks; Book Adventure Website; Literature Resources; Challenge Handbook; Education Place Website

Theme Resources
Surprise!

Contents

Teacher Read Aloud

Jack and the Beanstalk

Once upon a time a boy named Jack lived with his mother in a tiny cottage. One day, Jack's mother sent him to the market to sell their cow. At the market, a man offered Jack five special beans for the cow.

"These beans will grow faster than any beans you've ever seen," rasped the man. Jack happily took the beans and gave the cow to the man.

When he arrived home, Jack showed the beans to his mother. "What good will these beans do?" she lamented. "We can't buy food with them. Oh well, we might as well plant them and have beans to eat."

Imagine her surprise when she awoke the next morning and discovered that a huge beanstalk had sprouted in the garden and stretched beyond the clouds!

"I must climb up and see just where the beanstalk goes," exclaimed Jack. Imagine his surprise when he saw that the beanstalk led to a magnificent castle!

Suddenly, Jack felt the earth tremble beneath his feet. A voice bellowed, "Fee, fi, fo, fum, I can smell a little one."

Terrified, Jack ran into the castle and hid behind a curtain. And just in time, too! In stormed a giant. After satisfying himself that no one was in his room, the giant set a cage onto a table and demanded, "Hen, hen, lay me an egg of solid gold, or you won't live to be another day old!" Frightened, the hen squawked and promptly laid a golden egg.

Turning his attention to a lavish meal, the giant gorged until he could eat no more and fell into a deep slumber. Jack tiptoed out from behind the curtain.

"Please, please, take me with you," clucked the hen.

Jack, feeling sorry for the bird, grabbed the cage and ran. The startled hen squawked loudly.

The giant, awakened by the commotion, lumbered to his feet and bellowed, "Fee, fi, fo, fum, there goes my hen with a little one!"

Trembling with fear, Jack raced to the beanstalk. Clutching the cage in one hand and gripping the beanstalk with the other, Jack half climbed and half slid down the beanstalk, all the while screaming, "Mother, save me!"

Ax in hand, Jack's mother ran to the beanstalk. As soon as Jack was home, she chopped until the beanstalk snapped. The giant, knowing he would be doomed if he fell to the ground, promptly leapt back to his castle. The hen, thrilled to be free, laid another golden egg, but this time it was for Jack and his mother.

Phonics Skills: Consonants *d, w, l, x*

 Reteaching

OBJECTIVES

Children

- recognize *d, w, l,* and *x* and the sounds they represent

- independently read words with *d, w, l, x*

MATERIALS

- **Large Sound/Spelling Cards** *duck, fox, lion, worm*

- **Picture Cards** *bed, box, cloud, desk, dime, dog, doll, fox, girl, lamp, leaf, leg, lemon, lion, mix, ox, pad, sad, seal, watch, wave, web, wig*

- **Anthology 1.1 Here We Go!,** pp. 133–145

- **I Love Reading Books,** Review Books 11–14

Teach

Display the **Large Sound/Spelling Cards** one at a time. Have children name each letter with you and say the letter sound: *d,* /d/; *w,* /w/; *l,* /l/; *x,* /ks/. Distribute the **Picture Cards** for initial *d,* initial *l,* and initial *w,* one card to each child. Say: *Find other children whose picture names begin with the same sound as yours. Everyone whose picture name begins with the same sound, stand together.*

Have children in each group name their cards, say the beginning sound, and name the letter that stands for that sound.

Next, distribute the **Picture Cards** for final *d,* final *l,* and final *x,* one card to each child. Have children stand with classmates whose picture names end with the same sound.

Have children in each group name their cards, say the ending sound(s), and name the letter that stands for the sound(s).

To help children differentiate among the consonants, point out the position of their lips and tongue, and have them feel for vibration of the voice box.

- /d/ — tongue tip starts behind upper teeth, then moves back; vibration

- /w/ — rounded lips, tongue behind lower teeth; vibration

- /l/ — tongue tip behind upper teeth; vibration

- /ks/ — combines /k/ and /s/; begin with back of tongue on top of mouth, no vibration and end with tongue at top of mouth, no vibration

Practice

Display **Picture Card** *dog* and have children identify it. Call on a child to tell what sound he or she hears at the

beginning of *dog.* Write *dog* on the board and have a child underline the *d.* Repeat with **Picture Cards** *web* and *leg.* Then display **Picture Cards** *bed, girl,* and *fox* and ask children what sound they hear at the end of each word.

Apply

Write *d, w, l,* and *x* on chart paper. Have children look for words that begin with *d, w,* and *l* or end with *d, l,* or *x* in **Anthology** selection *The Box.* Each time they find a word, ask children to say it aloud so you can write it in a word list under the appropriate letter. After the search has been completed, have volunteers read the words in the list.

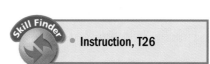

Skill Finder

- Instruction, T26

Diagnostic Check

If...	You can ...
children need more practice in the sounds for *d, w, l* and *x,*	• continue coached readings of **Anthology** selection *The Box* and have children read the story at home • have children read **I Love Reading Books,** Review Books 11–14

Phonics Skills: Consonants *d, w, l, x*

Challenge/Extension

Challenge
A Web of Words

Draw a large web on chart paper and hang it on the wall. Have children brainstorm a list of words with initial *d, w,* and *l,* and final *d, l,* and *x.* As children suggest each word, write the word on a strip of paper and hang it on the web. Then have children pick one word from the web and use it in a sentence.

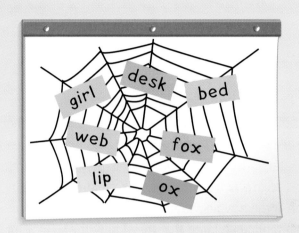

Acting out Words

Write the following words on index cards: *dance, walk, wiggle, wave, wash, listen,* and *leap.* Have children work in small groups. Give a card to one child at a time and whisper the word to that child. Have the child say the beginning sound of the word on the card and dramatize the word, while the other group members guess the word.

Phonics Skills: Blending Short *o* Words

Reteaching

OBJECTIVES

Children

- blend phonemes

- associate the short *o* sound with the letter *o*

- independently read short *o* words

MATERIALS

- **Large Sound/Spelling Card** *ostrich*

- **Large Letter Cards** *b, o, p, t, x, d, l, f*

- **Picture Cards** *box, cot, dot, fox, otter, ox, pot, log, hop*

- **Blending Routines Card 2**

- **Anthology 1.1 Here We Go!,** pp. 151–163

- **I Love Reading Books,** Review Book 10

Teach

Display **Large Sound/Spelling Card** *ostrich* and remind children that *o* often stands for the /ŏ/ sound. Have them say the sound after you, /ŏ/ - /ŏ/ - /ŏ/. Be sure that children have their mouths in the correct position as they say the sound. Hold up **Picture Card** *otter* and ask children to identify the picture. Ask them which sound *otter* begins with, /ŏ/ or /ă/. Then remind children that they know the sounds for the following letters, and say the sounds with them: *t*, /t/; *x*, /ks/; *d*, /d/; *l*, /l/; *p*, /p/; *b*, /b/.

Next, use the **Large Letter Cards** to model how to blend the word *pot* using **Blending Routine 2**. Have children say the sound for *p*, /p/, then say the sound for *o*, /ŏ/, then blend *pŏŏŏ*. Finally, have them say the sound for *t*, /t/, and blend *pŏŏŏt, pot*. Repeat with *got, hop*.

Remind children that they can make words by adding different letter sounds to the beginning and end of /ŏ/. Have children blend continuously *cŏŏŏd, cod; fffŏŏŏx, fox; lllŏŏŏt, lot; bŏŏŏx, box; rrrŏŏŏd, rod.*

Practice

Place **Large Letter Card** *o* on a chalk ledge and explain to children that they will spell some short *o* words. Then place **Picture Card** *box* on the chalk ledge and have a child choose the correct consonant cards to spell the word *box*. Repeat this procedure with **Picture Cards** *cot, dot, fox, ox, hop, log,* and *pot.*

Apply

Have partners take turns finding a word with short *o* in **Anthology** selection *Wigs in a Box*. Each time a child finds a word with short *o*, he or she should read aloud the word while you write it in a column on the board labeled short *o*.

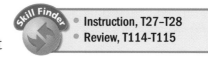

- Instruction, T27–T28
- Review, T114-T115

Diagnostic Check

If . . .	You can . . .
children need more practice with blending short *o* words,	• continue coached readings of **Anthology** selection *Wigs in a Box* and have children read the story at home • have children read **I Love Reading Books,** Review Book 10.

Phonics Skills: Blending Short *o* Words

Challenge/Extension

Filling a Box with Short *o* Words

Display a large box at the front of class. Have children brainstorm a list of short *o* words. As children suggest each word, write the word on a strip of paper and put it in the box. Then have children pick one word out of the box to read, use in a sentence, and illustrate.

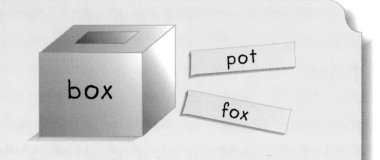

Challenge
Spellng Words with Short *o*

Have children use punchout letters to build as many words with short *o* as they can. Have children list their words and share them with a partner by using each of the words in a sentence.

 **Reteaching**

OBJECTIVES

Children

- recognize *y, k,* and *v* and the sounds they represent

- independently read words with *y, k, v*

MATERIALS

- **Large Sound/Spelling Cards** *kangaroo, volcano, yo-yo*

- **Large Letter Cards** *y, k, v*

- **Picture Cards** *hook, key, king, kiss, kit, kite, van, vane, vase, vest, vet, vine, yak, yam, yard, yarn, yellow, yolk, yo-yo*

- **Anthology 1.1 Here We Go!,** pp. 171–185

- **I Love Reading Books,** Review Books 16–18

Teach

Display the **Large Sound/Spelling Cards** one at a time. Have children name each letter with you and say the letter sound: *y,* /y/; *k,* /k/; *v,* /v/. Distribute the **Picture Cards** for initial *y,* initial *k,* and initial *v,* one card to each child. Say: *Find other children whose picture names begin with the same sound as yours. Everyone whose picture name begins the same, stand together.*

Have children in each group name their cards, say the beginning sound, and name the letter that stands for that sound.

Then display **Picture Card** *hook* and have children identify the picture. Ask a volunteer to tell what sound he or she hears at the end of *hook.* Write the word *hook* on the board and have a volunteer underline the final *k.*

To help children differentiate among the consonants, point out the position of their lips and tongue, and have them feel for vibration of the voice box.

- /k/ — back of tongue against roof of mouth; vibration

- /v/ — upper teeth on your lower lip; vibration

- /y/ — combination of vowel sounds long *e* and short *u*; begins with tongue at the middle of the mouth, vibration and ends with tongue at the bottom of the mouth, vibration

Practice

Display **Picture Cards** *yak, yarn, key, kite, hook, vet,* and *van* and write those words on the board. Read each word with children. Have a child underline the *y, k,* and *v* in each word and say the sound and then the word aloud. Call on another child to find the matching **Picture Card** for each word.

Apply

Have children find words with *y, k,* and *v* in **Anthology** selection *What Can a Vet Do?* Each time a child finds a word with *y, k,* or *v,* he or she should read the word aloud while you write it on the board. Have volunteers come to the board to underline the *y, k,* or *v* in each word.

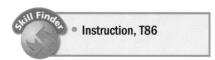
Skill Finder
- Instruction, T86

Diagnostic Check

If...	You can...
children need more practice in the sounds for *y, k,* and *v,*	• continue coached readings of **Anthology** selection *What Can a Vet Do?* and have children read the story at home • have children read **I Love Reading Books,** Review Books 16–18.

Phonics Skills: Consonants *y, k, v*

Challenge/Extension

Making Riddles

Have children work in pairs. Give each pair one of the following **Picture Cards**: *hook, key, king, kiss, kit, kite, van, vane, vase, vest, vet, vine, yak, yam, yard, yarn, yellow, yo-yo, yolk.* Have each pair of children make up a riddle about their **Picture Card** and have their classmates guess the word. For example: *My name begins with the sound of / k /. On a windy day, you can have fun flying me.* (kite)

UNIVERSAL ACCESS

Challenge
Finding Picture Cards

Hide **Picture Cards** for words with *y, k,* and *v* throughout the room. Display the corresponding **Word Cards** on the chalkboard. After each child finds a **Picture Card**, have him or her find the corresponding **Word Card** and hold the cards together at the front of the class. Have the child display both cards, say the word, and name the first or last letter of the word on the card.

Phonics Skills: Blending Short *e* Words

 Reteaching

OBJECTIVES

Children

- blend phonemes
- associate the short *e* sound with the letter *e*
- independently read words with short *e*

MATERIALS

- **Large Sound/Spelling Card** *elephant*
- **Large Letter Cards** *e, n, t, p, v, j, h*
- **Picture Cards** *egg, hen, ox, pen, pet, ten, vet, net, bed*
- **Blending Routines Card 2**
- **Anthology 1.1 Here We Go!,** pp. 191–209
- **I Love Reading Books,** Review Book 15

Teach

Display **Large Sound/Spelling Card** *elelphant* and remind children that *e* often stands for the /ĕ/ sound. Have them repeat /ĕ/ after you: /ĕ/-/ĕ/-/ĕ/. Be sure children have their mouths in the correct position as they say the sound. Hold up **Picture Card** *egg* and ask children to identify the picture. Ask them which sound *egg* begins with, /ĕ/ or /ŏ/. Repeat this procedure with **Picture Card** *ox.*

Next, use the **Large Letter Cards** to model how to blend the word *vet* using **Blending Routine 2**. Have children say the sound for *v*, /v/, then say the sound for *e*, /ĕ/, then blend *vĕĕ*. Finally, have them say the sound for *t*, /t/ and blend *vĕĕĕt, vet*. Repeat with *pet, men.*

Remind children that they can make more words by adding different sounds to the beginning and end of short *e*. Have children blend continuously *jĕĕĕt, jet; hĕĕĕnnn, hen; nĕĕĕt, net; pĕĕĕn, pen.*

Practice

Place **Large Letter Card** *e* on a chalk ledge and explain to children that they will spell some short *e* words. Then place **Picture Card** *hen* on the chalk ledge and have a child choose the correct consonant cards to spell the word *hen*. Repeat this procedure with **Picture Cards** *pen, pet, ten, vet, net,* and *bed.*

Apply

Have partners look for words with short *e* in **Anthology** selection *Hot Fox Soup*. Each time a child finds a word, he or she should say the word aloud so that you can write it in a short *e* word list on the board. Then give each pair a piece of paper divided in half vertically. Have partners each choose a different word from the word list and illustrate it on either side of the center line. Children can share their short *e* "partner pictures" with the class.

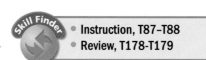

Skill Finder
- Instruction, T87–T88
- Review, T178-T179

Diagnostic Check

If . . .	You can . . .
children need more practice with blending short *e* words,	• continue coached readings of **Anthology** selection *Hot Fox Soup* and have children read the story at home • have children read **I Love Reading Books,** Review Book 15.

Phonics Skills: Blending Short *e* Words

Challenge/Extension

Fly the Rhyme Jet

Draw on chart paper the outline of a jet plane. Brainstorm words that rhyme with *jet*. Have each child write one of the words on a piece of paper. Then have each child read his or her word, use it in a sentence, and tape it to the jet.

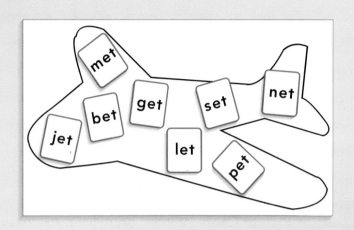

Challenge
Partner Riddles

Have partners use punchout letters to spell as many short *e* words as they can. Have them list their words. Then have them invent a riddle for one of the words they have made. Have each pair of children ask the riddle to the others in the group.

Phonics Skills: Consonants *q, j, z*

Reteaching

OBJECTIVES

Children

- recognize *qu, j,* and *z* and the sounds they represent
- read words with *qu, j,* and *z*

MATERIALS

- **Large Sound/Spelling Cards** *jumping Jill, queen, zebra*
- **Large Letter Cards** *q, u, j,* and *z*
- **Picture Cards** *jam, jar, jeans, jeep, jet, jug, queen, quill, quilt, zebra, zigzag, zip, zoo*
- **Anthology 1.1 Here We Go!,** pp. 217–231
- **I Love Reading Books,** Review Books 20–22

Teach

Display the **Large Sound/Spelling Cards.** Have children name each letter with you. Remind them that in English *q* is always followed by *u* in a word and that letters *qu* together stand for the /kw/ sound. Have children say the letter sounds with you: *qu,* /kw/; *j,* /j/; *z,* /z/.

Distribute the **Picture Cards** for initial *qu,* initial *j,* and initial *z,* one card to each child. Say: ***Find other children whose picture names begin with the same sound as yours. Everyone whose picture name begins the same, stand together.***

Have children in each group name their cards, say the beginning sound, and name the letter or letters that stand for that sound.

To help children differentiate among the consonant sounds, point out the position of their lips, teeth, and tongue, and have them feel for vibration of the voice box:

- /kw/ — combination of /k/ and /w/ sounds; begins with back of tongue against roof of mouth, vibration, and ends with rounded lips, tongue behind lower teeth; vibration
- /j/ — tongue against the roof of the mouth; vibration
- /z/ — tongue in the middle of the mouth, teeth closed; vibration

Practice

Display **Large Letter Cards** for *q, z, u, j,* and **Picture Card** *queen* on the chalk ledge. Have children identify the picture. Call on a child to tell what sound he or she hears at the beginning of *queen.*

Have a child hold up the correct **Letter Cards.** Point out again that the letters *qu* together stand for the /kw/ sounds. Repeat with **Picture Cards** *jam* and *zip.*

Apply

Have children look for words that begin with *qu, j,* and *z* in **Anthology** selection *A Hut for Zig Bug.* Each time a child finds a word with *qu, j,* or *z,* he or she should read the word aloud as you write it on the appropriate place on the board. Have children come to the board to underline the *qu, j,* or *z* in each word.

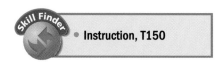

- Instruction, T150

Diagnostic Check

If . . .	You can . . .
children need more practice in the sounds for *qu, j, z,*	• continue coached readings of **Anthology** selection *A Hut for Zig Bug* and have children read the story at home • have children read **I Love Reading Books,** Review Books 20–22

Phonics Skills: Consonants *q, j, z*

Challenge/Extension

A Quilt of Paper

Divide children into three groups, *qu, j,* or *z*. Ask them to brainstorm a list of words that begin with their group's letter(s). Then give each child a square piece of paper. Have children write the letter(s) of their group on the top on their square. Have them choose a word that begins with the letter(s) on their square and illustrate it. Then help children attach the completed squares together to make a paper quilt.

Challenge
The Search for *qu, j,* and *z* Words

Have children make self-stick notes for *qu, j,* and *z*. Then have them look through books in the classroom library for words that begin with these letters. Have them attach the notes to the words they have found and then share their discoveries with the class.

Phonics Skills: Blending Short *u* Words

Reteaching

UNIVERSAL ACCESS

OBJECTIVES

Children
- blend phonemes
- associate the short *u* sound with the letter *u*
- independently read words with short *u*

MATERIALS
- **Large Sound/Spelling Card** *umbrella*
- **Large Letter Cards** *g, n, r, t, u*
- **Picture Cards** *bug, egg, hug, hut, nut, rug, under, up, run*
- **Word Cards** *bug, hug, hut, nut, rug, under, up, run*
- **Blending Routines Card 2**
- **Anthology 1.1 Here We Go!,** pp. 237–251
- **I Love Reading Books,** Review Book 19

Teach

Display **Large Sound/Spelling Card** *umbrella* and remind children that *u* often stands for the /ŭ/ sound. Have them repeat /ŭ/ after you: /ŭ/-/ŭ/-/ŭ/. Be sure children have their mouths in the correct position as they say the sound. Hold up **Picture Card** *under* and ask children to identify the picture. Ask them which sound *under* begins with, /ŭ/ or /ĕ/. Follow the same procedure with **Picture Cards** *egg* and *up*.

Next, use the **Large Letter Cards** to model how to blend the word *nut* using **Blending Routine 2**. Have children say the sound for *n,* /n/, then the sound for *u,* /ŭ/, then blend *nnnŭŭŭ*. Finally, have them say the sound for *t,* /t/ and blend *nnnŭŭŭt, nut.* Repeat with *mud, dug.*

Remind children that they can make words by adding different sounds to the beginning and end of short *u.* Have children blend continuously *cŭŭŭt, cut; hŭŭŭt, hut; hŭŭŭg, hug; bŭŭŭnnn, bun.*

Practice

In random order, display **Picture Cards** and corresponding **Word Cards** *bug, hug, hut, nut, rug, run, up.* Say *nut.* Have a volunteer find the matching **Picture Card** and **Word Card** and then read the word aloud. Repeat the procedure with *rug, hut, run, up, hug,* and *bug.*

Apply

Have children look for words with short *u* in **Anthology** selection *The Rope Tug.* Each time a child finds a word, ask him or her to read the word aloud and help you to write it on the board. Have all children repeat the word as the child at the board circles the *u.*

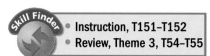

Skill Finder
- Instruction, T151–T152
- Review, Theme 3, T54–T55

Diagnostic Check

If . . .	You can . . .
children need more practice with blending short *u* words,	• continue coached readings of **Anthology** selection *The Rope Tug*, and have children read the story at home • have children read **I Love Reading Books,** Review Book 19.

Phonics Skills: Blending Short *u* Words
Challenge/Extension

A Short *u* Cut-Up

Distribute scissors and pieces of paper with the following words written randomly on the page: *bun, hut, hug, run,* and *nut.* Ask children to choose a short *u* word, cut it out, and paste it on an illustration they have drawn of the word.

Challenge
Word Slide for Short *u*

Prepare word slides using initial consonants to combine with short *u* and *g* to make words. Have children slide the letters, read the words, and write the words they have made on a short *u* word list.

High-Frequency Words

Reteaching

OBJECTIVES

Children

- read and write high-frequency words *five, four, in, once, three, two, upon, what*

MATERIALS

- **Letter Cards:** *a, c, e, e, f, h, i, n, o, p, r, t, u, v, w*
- Index cards for the High-Frequency words

Teach

Write *five, four, in, once, three, two, upon,* and *what* on the board. Read each word aloud while pointing to that word. On a second reading, encourage children to read along with you.

Place the **Letter Cards** in the chalk tray below the words. Ask, *How many letters do we need to spell the word* five? Assign one letter to each of four children, and tell them to come up and hold their letters for classmates to see. Have classmates spell the word together, clapping for each letter.

Write a sentence from the story, *Wigs in a Box* that contains the word *five,* for example, *"Pat Pig can find* five *wigs in the big box!"* Have children read the sentence together, and clap their hands when they read the word *five.* Repeat this procedure for the remaining words using sentences from both *Wigs in a Box* and *The Box.*

Practice

Ask the children to name the number words. If necessary, remind them that these words tell how many. Write each number word on a large index card, then write each remaining high-frequency word on a card.

Tell children you want to sort the words into two groups: words that *tell how many* (five, four, three, two) and words that *do not tell how many* (in, once, upon, what).

Have children read each word card and decide which group the card belongs in. Tape the words in two columns. When finished, have children read the lists together.

Apply

Have children match the High-Frequency Word Cards to the words in the story.

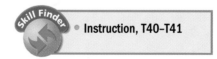

Skill Finder   • Instruction, T40–T41

Diagnostic Check

If...	You can...
children need more practice with the High-Frequency Words *five, four, in, once, three, two, upon, what,*	have them match High-Frequency Word Cards to the corresponding words on the Word Pattern Board.

Challenge/Extension

High-Frequency Words

Have children make a numeral book. Children can fold a sheet of paper to make a four- or eight-page book. Provide the following template. Children can use numerals, words, or drawings to complete their sentences.

I have one _____

I have two _____

I have three _____

I have four _____

I have five _____

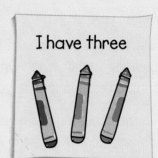

I have three

Challenge Activity

Have children make a one through five (or ten) number book. Children might want to write rhyming couplets and illustrate each page.

High-Frequency Words

Reteaching

OBJECTIVES

Children

- read and write high-frequency words *do, for, I, is, me, my, said, you*

MATERIALS

- **Letter Cards:** *a, d, e, f, i, l, m, o, r, s, u, w, y*

Teach

Write *do, for, I, is, me, my, said,* and *you* on the board. Read each word aloud while pointing to that word. On a second reading, encourage children to read along with you.

Place the **Letter Cards** in the chalk tray below the words. Ask, *How many letters do we need to spell the word* do? Assign one letter to each of two children, and tell them to come up and hold their letters for classmates to see. Have classmates spell the word together, clapping for each letter.

Write a sentence from the story, *What Can a Vet Do?* that contains the word *do,* for example, *A vet can do a lot.* Have children read the sentence together, and clap their hands when they read the word *do.* Repeat this procedure for the remaining words, using sentences from both *Hot Fox Soup* and *What Can a Vet Do?* that contain a high-frequency word.

Practice

Write each High-Frequency Word on a large index card and distribute the cards to children. Write a sentence from one of the stories that uses each new word. Leave a blank for the word from the high-frequency list. Have children read each sentence along with you. Have the children decide who has the missing word. Have that child bring up the word and tape it in the blank space.

Apply

Have children match High-Frequency Word Cards to the words in the story.

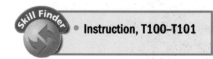

Skill Finder • **Instruction, T100–T101**

Diagnostic Check

If . . .	You can . . .
children need more practice with the High-Frequency Words,	have them match High-Frequency Word Cards to the corresponding words on the Word Pattern Board.

High-Frequency Words
Challenge/Extension

High-Frequency Words

Have children write the words on large index cards, leaving some space between each letter. Have them cut apart the letters in each word. Tell them to mix the letters up, then arrange them to spell the words in the list. Draw the outline of a vat or pot on the chalkboard. Children might want to assemble their letters to make words and then put the words in the pot to make alphabet soup.

Challenge Activity

Have children write a story using as many of the High-Frequency Words as possible. Encourage children to illustrate their stories and share their work with the rest of the class.

High-Frequency Words

 **Reteaching**

OBJECTIVES

Children

• read and write high-frequency words *are, away, does, he, live, pull, they, where*

MATERIALS

• **Letter Cards:** *a, a, d, e, e, h, i, l, o, p, r, s, t, u, v, w, y*

Teach

Write *are, away, does, he, live, pull, they,* and *where* on the board and read each word. On a rereading, have children read the words along with you. Then distribute the **Letter Cards.** Draw three squares on the board, and tell children that you need their help to spell the word *are.* You might want to emphasize the use of *are* in a sentence to be certain they understand the word's meaning, for example, *We* are *learning to read lots of new words.*

> *The word* are *has three letters. Who will come up and help me identify the letters in the word? Who has the letters* a, r, *and* e? *Stand up here and I'll write the word* are *in the boxes.*

Lead children in a cheer to help them remember the word. Clap on each letter and syllable as children spell and say the word together: *a-r-e, are!* Then tell children to jump when you point to each of their cards. Lead a new "hop-it" cheer *a-r-e, are!*

Repeat the procedure for the words *away, does, he, live, pull, they,* and *where.*

Practice

Give children these sentence frames. Have them complete the sentences by drawing or writing to fill in the blanks.

Are you_____?

Where does_____live?

They are away in the _____.

He is _____.

Apply

Have children show and read their sentences to the class. Then ask children to exchange and read one another's sentences.

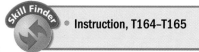

Skill Finder • **Instruction, T164–T165**

Diagnostic Check

If . . .	You can . . .
children need more practice with the High-Frequency Words,	have them repeat the Practice activity with different sentence frames.

High-Frequency Words

Challenge/Extension

High-Frequency Words

Have children work together to make a word chain. Have them begin by writing their new high-frequency words on strips of paper, linking and pasting them together to form a chain. Then have them extend their word chains by writing words that they have learned in the last several stories. Tell children to see how long they can make their word chains to show how many new words they can read and write.

Challenge Activity

Children can make up a dialogue between Hippo and Elephant and Rat, after Hippo and Elephant find out that Rat has tricked them. Children can use pictures or quotations to show what the characters are saying. Have children act out their "script" of what the animals say.

Comprehension Skills: Noting Details

Reteaching

Children

- note details in a story
- identify details in pictures

Teach

Begin the lesson by using three similar but not identical items to discuss the skill of noting details. For example, you might ask three children to volunteer the use of their jackets, book bags, or lunch boxes. As you display the items, ask children to look closely as you describe details about the jackets, for example: *I am looking at a jacket that has a zipper. Which jacket is it? I am looking at a jacket that has brown trim around the sleeves.*

Explain to children that writers often create small details to help the reader get a picture of story characters and events. Explain that illustrators often do the same thing. They include details in their art to help the viewer further understand a character or event.

Practice

Discuss the story *Wigs in a Box* by Valeria Petrone. Begin by having children look at the illustration on page 152. Invite them to describe what they see in the drawing and ask them what details help them to know that the story takes place at a carnival or a fair. (tents, game booth, and balloons) Have children read the text on this page together. Ask, *How can you tell that the animals are going to play a game?* Lead them to understand that the word *win* and the picture clues (booth, ball, bat, and prize) can help them understand that the animals will play a game.

Explain to children that looking at picture clues and reading words carefully can help them to note details when they read.

Apply

Have children work in small groups of five. Ask children to look carefully at the illustrations in the story and to find details in the drawings. Ask, *How does the artist use details to make each animal look different so that we know what kind of animal it is? What features does the artist give each of the animals?* Invite children in each group to choose one of the story animals and to draw a picture of it. Tell them to pay close attention to the details the artist uses in the drawings as they draw their own pictures.

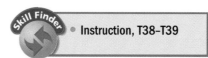

Skill Finder • Instruction, T38–T39

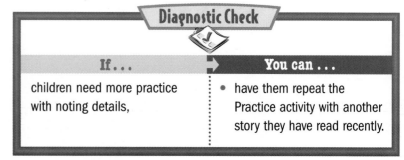

Diagnostic Check

If...	You can ...
children need more practice with noting details,	• have them repeat the Practice activity with another story they have read recently.

Comprehension Skills: Noting Details
Challenge/Extension

Challenge
Science
Drawing Details

Small Group or Paired Activity Have children draw pictures of a lake in summer and a lake in winter. Remind children that they must carefully visualize what the lake would look like in the two seasons, noting the details that would change for each season.

Ask, *What details will you include in the picture to show that the water is liquid or frozen? How will you show the trees to be different in the two seasons? What other details can you use to show the change of seasons?* Then provide drawing tools. Some children might want to label their pictures.

Language Arts
Describing Objects

Small Group or Paired Activity Have children play a game in which they imagine that Pat Pig has other objects in the box. Then have them begin each new round of the game with the words, *I am thinking of something that is in Pat Pig's box.* Have them choose a classroom object and use words to describe it as classmates guess what it is they are thinking of. You might want to have the children draw the item first so that they look carefully at the object in order to focus on its details.

Social Studies
Describing Places

Independent Activity Ask children to think about places in their community. Then have them consider how they might describe these places to others. For example, children might ask themselves, "What shops and buildings are in my community? How many swings does my favorite park have?" Then have children draw a picture of a place in their community, labeling the special details. Invite them to title their drawings.

Comprehension Skills: Fantasy and Realism

Reteaching

Teach

Explain to children that you are going to tell them two short stories and that they should listen carefully to see if they can tell which one is real and which one is make-believe.

Story 1: This morning I woke up, got dressed, and ate breakfast. I fed my goldfish and my dog.

Story 2: Two hundred years ago, I lived on the planet Jupiter. When I was hungry, I reached out and ate some stars.

Ask children which story they think is real and could happen in real life. Ask them why it might be true. (We wake up in the morning, we get dressed and eat breakfast. We feed our pets. These are things that happen every day.) Then ask them which story is not true. Repeat the story if necessary. Ask them why they think the second story is not true. (People don't live to be 200 years old. We live on Earth. We can't eat stars.) Explain that the second story is make-believe. Tell children that another word for make-believe is *fantasy*. And another word for stories with events that could happen in real life, and with characters who act and talk like we do in real life, is *realism*.

Practice

Revisit the story *Hot Fox Soup* by Satoshi Kitamura. Direct the children to look at the illustrations and listen as you read pages 192 and 193. Ask them to tell you which parts of the story are realistic, that is, what parts could really happen. (camping, woods, cooking supplies, fire) Then ask them what makes this story fantasy or make-believe. (Fox is acting human, he is wearing an apron, he is walking on two feet, he is talking and cooking.) Continue through the story, identifying fantasy and realism elements.

Apply

Have children act out some of the story actions by taking the parts of Fox, Hen, Pig, and Ox. Provide cards for each child with the words *Yes* on one and *No* on the other. As volunteers act out the roles of the story animals, have classmates tell whether the action could really happen or not by holding up their cards.

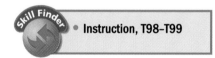

Skill Finder
- **Instruction, T98–T99**

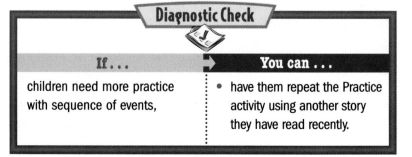

Diagnostic Check

If . . .	You can . . .
children need more practice with sequence of events,	• have them repeat the Practice activity using another story they have read recently.

Challenge/Extension

Science
Real and Fantasy Animals

Small Group Activity Have children work together to brainstorm a list of wild animals that they might find in a forest. Have them divide a sheet of paper in half. Ask them to label the left side of the paper, *Real*, and the right side of the paper *Not Real*. On the left, have children draw a picture of something the wild forest animal might do; on the other side have them draw a picture of something the wild forest animal could not do.

Social Studies
Discussing Animals

Paired Activity Explain to children that many cultures use animal characteristics to tell stories about human behavior. Ask, "What other stories with animals do you know? In what ways do these animals behave like people?" What are some things people can do that real animals can't do?

Challenge
Language Arts
Writing a Fantasy Story

Independent Activity Have children work in pairs to make up a story about a wild animal that moves from the forest or desert to a big city. Have them write about what the animal likes or does not like about the city. Children can illustrate their stories and share them with the rest of the class.

Comprehension Skills: Story Structure

Reteaching

Children

- identify the setting, characters, and plot of a story

- use a story map to identify the elements of a story

Teach

Ask children if they know the well-known children's fairy tale, *Goldilocks and the Three Bears*. If they don't know the story, tell it to them. Then ask them questions such as the following:

- *Who are the characters in the story?* (Goldilocks and the three bears)

- *Where does the story take place?* (the woods, the home of the three bears)

- *What happens in the story?* (Goldilocks explores the house of the three bears.)

Explain to children that many stories include these elements: *characters*, the people or animals; a *setting*, the place and time the story happens; and a *plot*, events in the story, often with a story problem and solution. You might want to write the words *Character* (Who?), *Setting* (Where?), and *Plot* (What happens?) on the chalkboard.

Practice

Discuss the story *The Rope Tug* by Veronica Freeman Ellis. Begin by asking children to identify the characters in the story. Allow them to look through the pages of the story to be certain they have identified each of the characters. Write the word *Character* on the board or chart paper and list the names of the story characters. Continue in this same way as children identify the *Setting* and story *Plot*. If children are uncertain about the setting or plot, encourage them to look at the illustrations for clues.

Apply

Assign children the roles of Hippo, Elephant, and Rat. Have other children draw the setting on the chalkboard. Then ask a child to tell the plot of the story while the story characters act it out. When finished, work with children to complete a story map. Some children may want to draw pictures to indicate their responses.

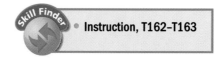
Skill Finder   • **Instruction, T162–T163**

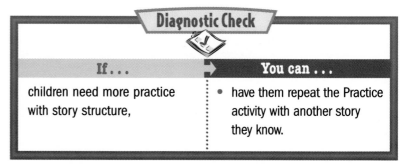

Diagnostic Check	
If . . .	**You can . . .**
children need more practice with story structure,	• have them repeat the Practice activity with another story they know.

Comprehension Skills: Story Structure
Challenge/Extension

Challenge
Science
A Realistic Story

Small Group Activity Have students make up a realistic story about life on a farm or in a ranch community. Have them think about the characters, the setting, and the plot. The story should tell what it is like to take care of the animals that live there. Children can perform their story as a play or record it on audiocassette tape.

Social Studies
A Map of a Story Setting

Small Group or Paired Activity Divide children into small groups or pairs. Have each group develop a setting for a story. Tell them that their setting can be a city, a farm, an ocean, or a mountain town. Direct the groups to work together to draw a map of their story setting. Have them label their maps and tell the kind of story that might take place in this setting.

Language Arts
A Story Map

Independent Activity Provide each child with a story map graphic organizer. Have them use it to develop an idea for a story. Tell them to think about a story they would like to write, perhaps, a story about an animal character that lives in a human setting. Then have them think about what events might take place in their story. Children can use pictures or words to record ideas on their story map. Then have children use the story map to retell their story in an oral presentation.

Information and Study Skills

Following Instructions

Children
- identify times when they follow instructions
- follow instructions

MATERIALS

- **Blackline Master 10**
- paper, pencils
- crayons

Teach

Tell children that following instructions is a part of many things they do each day. Following instructions can help them learn to make things, or remember how to do something or go somewhere. Share some things that you have done by following instructions, such as going to a friend's house or baking a cake. Ask children to share times they have had to follow instructions.

Discuss some important things to keep in mind when following instructions.

- Listen to or read the instructions carefully.
- Think about what should be done.
- Follow the instructions in the correct order.

Practice

Give children a piece of paper. Tell them to listen carefully before they follow each step of your instructions. Repeat each step if requested to do so. Do not tell children that they will draw a box.

- *Pick up your pencils and follow my directions carefully.*
- *First, draw a straight line across the top of the page.*

- *Next, start at the end of that line and draw a straight line halfway down along the side of the piece of paper.*

- *Now start at the end of the second line and draw a straight line across the paper.*

- *Next, start at the end of the third line and draw a straight line up to where your first line started.*

- *What did you draw?* (a box)

Apply

Have partners take turns giving and following directions on how to color the characters on **Blackline Master 10**. Circulate as children work to be sure they are following directions. Then ask:

- *Why is it important to follow instructions carefully?*

Mary Had a Little Lamb

Traditional

Brightly

Mar - y had a lit - tle lamb, lit - tle lamb, lit - tle lamb,

Mar - y had a lit - tle lamb, its fleece was white as snow.

2. And ev'rywhere that Mary went, Mary
   went, Mary went,
   And ev'rywhere that Mary went, the lamb
   was sure to go.

3. It followed her to school one day, school
   one day, school one day,
   It followed her to school one day, which
   was against the rule.

4. It made the children laugh and play,
   laugh and play, laugh and play,
   It made the children laugh and play, to
   see a lamb at school.

Polly, Put the Kettle On

English Traditional Song

Lightly

Pol - ly, put the ket - tle on, Pol - ly, put the ket - tle on,

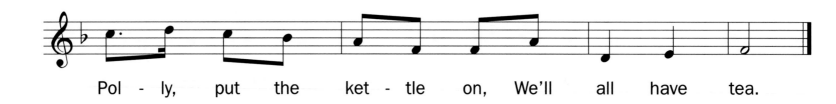

Pol - ly, put the ket - tle on, We'll all have tea.

The Giants

by Isabel Carley

Slow and steady

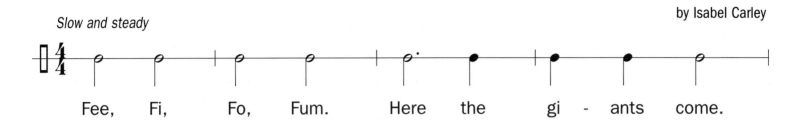

Fee, Fi, Fo, Fum. Here the gi - ants come.

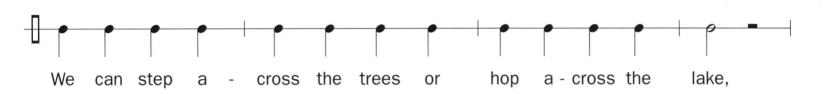

We can step a - cross the trees or hop a - cross the lake,

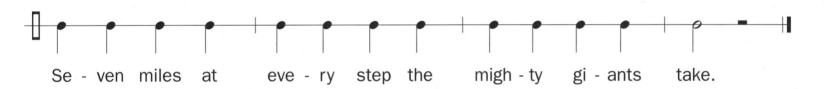

Se - ven miles at eve - ry step the migh - ty gi - ants take.

Divide the class into two groups, and let half the class say
the rhyme with body rhythm and/or rhythm instruments
while the other half moves like giants. Reverse assignment.

Word List

Theme 2; Week 1

➤ **Phonics Skills:** Consonants *d, w, l, x;* Short *o* words
➤ **High-Frequency Words:** five, four, in, once, three, two, upon, what

Day 1
Phonics Library: *Dot Fox*

Phonics Practice Words: Dot, Fox, got, hot, lot, wig, *fan, ran*

High-Frequency Words: *a*

Day 2
Phonics Library: *Bob Pig and Dan Ox*

Phonics Practice Words: Bob, box, Dan, lot, Ox, **and**, *big, can, fit, Pig*

High-Frequency Words: in, what, *a*

Day 3
Anthology: **The Box**

Phonics Practice Words: box, Don, Dot, fox, got, lot, top, wig, **and**, *big, can, fit, hat, pig, tan*

High-Frequency Words: in, once, what, *a, find, on, one, the*

Day 4
Anthology: **Wigs in a Box**

Phonics Practice Words: box, Dog, Don, Dot, Fox, got, lot, Ox, wig, win, *big, can, Cat, Fat, fit, hit, it, Pat, Pig, sat, Tan*

High-Frequency Words: five, four, in, three, two, upon, what, *a, find, one, the*

Story Vocabulary: ball, shelf, thanks, wigs

Day 5
Phonics Library: *Once Upon a Dig*

Phonics Practice Words: Bob, dig, Dot, Fox, lot, *can, Pig*

High-Frequency Words: once, upon, *a, find*

Theme 2; Week 2

➤ **Phonics Skills:** Consonants *y, k, v;* Short *e* Words
➤ **High-Frequency Words:** do, for, I, is, me, my, said, you

Day 1
Phonics Library: *Not Yet!*

Phonics Practice Words: get, Hen, kit, Peg, ten, van, yet, *can, fit*, **not**, *tan*

High-Frequency Words: *in*, one, the, two

Day 2
Phonics Library: *Big Ben*

Phonics Practice Words: Ben, Ken, set, vet, yet, *Big, can, Dan, got, pat, sit*

High-Frequency Words: for, I, **is**, me, said

Day 3
Anthology: **What Can a Vet Do?**

Phonics Practice Words: Ben, get, kit, Ned, pen, pet, van, vet, wet, yes, *Big, bit, can, cat, fix, in, lot, Mom*, **not**, *pat, sit, tan*

High-Frequency Words: do, for, **is**, my, *a, here, jump, the, to, what*

Challenge Word: Chapter

Day 4
Anthology: **Hot Fox Soup**

Phonics Practice Words: get, hen, kit, let, met, vat, wet, yes, yet, *big, box, can, dig, fit, fix, fox, got, hot*, **in**, *it, lit*, **not**, *ox, pig, ran*

High-Frequency Words: I, **is**, me, my, said, you, *a, we, what*

Story Vocabulary: fire, noodle, soup, wanted

Day 5
Phonics Library: *Get Wet, Ken!*

Phonics Practice Words: Ken, get, van, wet, yet, *big, can, got, it*, **not**, *tan*

High-Frequency Words: do, I, my, you

Theme 2; Week 3

➤ **Phonics Skills:** Consonants *q, j, z;* Short *u* Words
➤ **High-Frequency Words:** are, away, does, he, live, pull, they, where

Day 1
Phonics Library: *The Bug Kit*

Phonics Practice Words: bug, but, Jen, quit, zag, zig, *big, can, get, got, it, kit, ran, red*

High-Frequency Words: *a, said, the*

Day 2
Phonics Library: *Quit It, Zig!*

Phonics Practice Words: big, but, Jan, mug, quit, rug, tut, Zig, *big, get, hot, it, red, sat, set, wet*

High-Frequency Words: are, away, they, *a, on, the*

Day 3
Anthology: **A Hut for Zig Bug**

Phonics Practice Words: Bug, cup, fun, hut, jug, quit, rug, up, Zig, **and**, *box, can, cot, fit, fix, get, in*, **not**, *yes, yet*

High-Frequency Words: does, he, live, where, *a, do, for, have, here, the, you*

Day 4
Anthology: **The Rope Tug**

Phonics Practice Words: but, hut, jig, quit, run, tug, zag, zig, *am*, **and**, *big, can, fit, get*, **in**, *let*, **not**, *Rat, win*

High-Frequency Words: are, away, does, pull, they, *a, I, me, the, we, you*

Story Vocabulary: Elephant, Hippo, **I'm**, Narrator, outside, rope

Day 5
Phonics Library: *Rug Tug*

Phonics Practice Words: but, cut, hut, jig, quit, rug, tug, zig, *big, can, fit, it, men*, **not**, *tan, ten, yet*

High-Frequency Words: does, pull, *a, do, the, to*

This list includes all words in Phonics Library and Anthology selections for Theme 2. Words in regular type apply skills for the week; words in italics apply previously taught skills. High-Frequency Words are practiced in Phonics Library and Anthology selections and in Practice Book and Word Pattern Board activities; each is practiced at least six times in the week it is taught. Challenge words include some known phonics elements and some that are unfamiliar.

High-Frequency Words

Word	Taught as High-Frequency Word Theme/Week	Decodable Theme/Week
a	1/3	1/1
*able	10/3	n/a
about	8/1	n/a
*above	10/2	n/a
*afraid	7/2	n/a
after	9/2	10/1
again	7/1	n/a
*against	10/2	n/a
all	3/2	n/a
*already	10/2	n/a
*also	3/3	n/a
always	8/2	n/a
and	1/2	5/2
*animal	3/1	n/a
any	7/2	n/a
are	2/3	n/a
*arms	8/2	10/2
around	9/1	n/a
away	2/3	n/a
*baby	9/3	n/a
*bear	7/2	n/a
because	8/1	n/a
been	6/3	n/a
before	9/2	n/a
*began	10/1	n/a
*begin	10/2	n/a
*bird	3/1	10/1
blue	3/3	7/3
*body	8/2	n/a
both	7/1	n/a
*break	10/1	n/a
brown	3/3	8/2
*build	7/3	n/a
*butter	8/3	10/1
buy	9/2	n/a
by	6/1	9/1
call	3/2	n/a
*car	4/3	10/2
carry	8/3	9/1
*caught	10/2	n/a
*children	4/1	n/a

Word	Taught as High-Frequency Word Theme/Week	Decodable Theme/Week
*climb	6/1	n/a
cold	3/1	n/a
*color	3/3	n/a
come	4/1	n/a
could	5/2	n/a
*cow	6/2	8/2
*dance	9/1	n/a
*divide	10/1	n/a
do	2/2	n/a
does	2/3	n/a
done	9/2	n/a
*door	6/2	n/a
down	4/3	8/2
draw	8/1	9/3
eat	3/2	6/2
*edge	9/3	n/a
eight	8/2	n/a
*else	9/1	n/a
*enough	9/3	n/a
*evening	6/3	n/a
*ever	9/1	10/1
every	3/2	n/a
*eye	10/3	n/a
fall	3/1	n/a
*family	4/1	n/a
far	6/3	10/2
*father	4/1	n/a
find	1/3	n/a
first	3/2	10/1
five	2/1	5/3
*flower	3/1	10/1
fly	5/3	9/1
*follow	7/2	8/2
for	2/2	10/1
*forest	6/3	10/1
found	6/1	8/2
four	2/1	n/a
*friend	4/2	n/a
full	3/1	n/a
funny	3/3	9/1
*garden	9/3	10/2

Word	Taught as High-Frequency Word Theme/Week	Decodable Theme/Week
*girl	4/2	10/1
give	5/3	n/a
go	1/1	6/1
goes	6/3	n/a
*gone	7/1	n/a
good	5/3	7/2
green	3/3	6/2
grow	5/1	7/1
*happy	8/1	9/1
*hard	7/1	10/2
have	1/3	n/a
he	2/3	6/2
*head	10/1	n/a
*hear	4/3	n/a
her	5/3	10/1
here	1/2	n/a
hold	4/3	n/a
*horse	6/2	10/1
*house	5/2	8/2
how	5/2	8/2
*hungry	6/3	n/a
hurt	4/3	10/1
I	2/2	2/2
*idea	7/2	n/a
in	2/1	1/3
is	2/2	1/3
jump	1/2	4/3
kind	8/3	n/a
know	4/2	7/1
laugh	10/1	n/a
*learn	4/3	n/a
light	5/1	7/3
like	3/3	5/3
little	5/3	n/a
live	2/3	n/a
long	5/1	5/2
look	3/1	7/2
*love	4/1	n/a
many	3/3	n/a
me	2/2	6/2
*minute	10/2	n/a

Word	Taught as High-Frequency Word Theme/Week	Decodable Theme/Week
*more	5/1	10/1
*morning	6/1	10/1
*most	7/2	n/a
*mother	4/1	n/a
my	2/2	9/1
*near	6/3	n/a
never	3/2	n/a
not	1/2	2/1
now	6/2	8/2
*ocean	9/1	n/a
of	3/1	n/a
off	9/2	n/a
old	7/3	n/a
on	1/1	2/1
once	2/1	n/a
one	1/3	n/a
only	9/3	n/a
open	9/1	n/a
or	7/1	10/1
*other	5/1	n/a
our	5/3	8/2
out	6/1	8/2
over	5/2	n/a
own	5/2	7/1
*paper	3/2	n/a
*part	8/1	10/2
*people	4/1	n/a
*person	8/3	n/a
*picture	4/1	n/a
*piece	7/3	n/a
play	4/2	6/3
*present	10/3	n/a
pretty	9/2	n/a
pull	2/3	n/a
put	8/3	n/a
read	4/2	6/2
*ready	8/2	n/a
right	5/1	7/3
*room	5/1	7/3
said	2/2	n/a
saw	8/3	9/3

Word	Taught as High-Frequency Word Theme/Week	Decodable Theme/Week
*school	9/2	n/a
*second	10/1	n/a
see	3/1	6/2
seven	8/2	n/a
shall	3/2	5/1
*sharp	9/3	10/2
she	4/2	6/2
*shoe[s]	7/3	n/a
*shout	6/1	8/2
show	6/1	7/1
sing	4/2	5/2
small	5/1	n/a
so	5/2	6/1
some	3/3	n/a
soon	6/3	7/3
start	7/3	10/2
*sure	10/1	n/a
*table	6/2	n/a
*talk	9/1	n/a
*tall	7/2	n/a
*teacher	8/1	10/1
the	1/1	6/2
their	4/3	n/a
there	6/2	n/a
these	5/1	6/2
they	2/3	n/a
*though	9/1	n/a
*thoughts	10/3	n/a
three	2/1	6/2
*through	6/2	n/a
*tiny	8/1	n/a
to	1/3	n/a
today	4/2	n/a
together	9/3	n/a
too	1/2	7/3
try	5/3	9/1
*turn	7/1	10/1
two	2/1	n/a
under	7/3	10/1
upon	2/1	n/a
very	7/3	n/a

Word	Taught as High-Frequency Word Theme/Week	Decodable Theme/Week
walk	4/3	n/a
*wall	6/2	n/a
want	7/1	n/a
warm	8/2	n/a
was	5/3	n/a
wash	9/2	n/a
*watched	9/3	n/a
*water	7/2	n/a
we	1/2	6/2
*wear	7/3	n/a
were	8/3	n/a
what	2/1	n/a
where	2/3	n/a
who	1/3	n/a
why	3/2	9/1
work	8/3	n/a
*world	5/2	n/a
would	4/3	n/a
write	4/2	5/3
you	2/2	7/3
your	4/1	n/a

* - Words from the 800 Base Words of Highest Frequency of Occurrence in the American Heritage Computerized Study of the Vocabulary of Published Materials Used in Public Schools. Words without asterisks are from the Dolch list.

Technology Resources

American Melody
- P. O. Box 270
- Guilford, CT 06473
- 800-220-5557

Audio Bookshelf
- 174 Prescott Hill Road
- Northport, ME 04849
- 800-234-1713

Baker & Taylor
- 100 Business Court Drive
- Pittsburgh, PA 15205
- 800-775-2600

BDD Audio
- 1540 Broadway
- New York, NY 10036
- 800-223-6834

Big Kids Productions
- 1606 Dywer Ave.
- Austin, TX 78704
- 800-477-7811
- www.bigkidsvideo.com

Blackboard Entertainment
- 2647 International Boulevard
- Suite 853
- Oakland, CA 94601
- 800-968-2261
- www.blackboardkids.com

Books on Tape
- P. O. Box 7900
- Newport Beach, CA 92658
- 800-626-3333

Filmic Archives
- The Cinema Center
- Botsford, CT 06404
- 800-366-1920
- www.filmicarchives.com

Great White Dog Picture Company
- 10 Toon Lane
- Lee, NH 03824
- 800-397-7641
- www.greatwhitedog.com

HarperAudio
- 10 E. 53rd St.
- New York, NY 10022
- 800-242-7737

Houghton Mifflin Company
- 222 Berkeley St.
- Boston, MA 02116
- 800-225-3362

Informed Democracy
- P. O. Box 67
- Santa Cruz, CA 95063
- 831-426-3921

JEF Films
- 143 Hickory Hill Circle
- Osterville, MA 02655
- 508-428-7198

Kimbo Educational
- P. O. Box 477
- Long Branch, NJ 07740
- 900-631-2187

The Learning Company (dist. for Broderbund)
- 1 Athenaeum St.
- Cambridge, MA 02142
- 800-716-8506
- www.learningcompanyschool.com

Library Video Co.
- P. O. Box 580
- Wynnewood, PA 19096
- 800-843-3620

Listening Library
- One Park Avenue
- Old Greenwich, CT 06870
- 800-243-4504

Live Oak Media
- P. O. Box 652
- Pine Plains, NY 12567
- 800-788-1121
- liveoak@taconic.net

Media Basics
- Lighthouse Square
- P. O. Box 449
- Guilford, CT 06437
- 800-542-2505
- www.mediabasicsvideo.com

Microsoft Corp.
- One Microsoft Way
- Redmond, WA 98052
- 800-426-9400
- www.microsoft.com

National Geographic Society
- 1145 17th Street N. W.
- Washington, D. C. 20036
- 800-368-2728
- www.nationalgeographic.com

New Kid Home Video
- 1364 Palisades Beach Road
- Santa Monica, CA 90401
- 310-451-5164

Puffin Books
- 345 Hudson Street
- New York, NY 10014
- 212-366-2000

Rainbow Educational Media
- 4540 Preslyn Drive
- Raleigh, NC 27616
- 800-331-4047

Random House Home Video
- 201 E. 50th St.
- New York, NY 10022
- 212-940-7620

Recorded Books
- 270 Skipjack Road
- Prince Frederick, MD 20678
- 800-638-1304
- www.recordedbooks.com

Sony Wonder
- Dist. by Professional Media Service
- 19122 S. Vermont Ave.
- Gardena, CA 90248
- 800-223-7672

Spoken Arts
- 8 Lawn Avenue
- P. O. Box 100
- New Rochelle, NY 10802
- 800-326-4090

SRA Media
- 220 E. Danieldale Rd.
- DeSoto, TX 75115
- 800-843-8855

Sunburst Communications
- 101 Castleton St.
- P. O. Box 100
- Pleasantville, NY 10570
- 800-321-7511
- www.sunburst.com

SVE & Churchill Media
- 6677 North Northwest Highway
- Chicago, IL 60631
- 800-829-1900

Tom Snyder Productions
- 80 Coolidge Hill Road
- Watertown, MA 02472
- 800-342-0236
- www.tomsnyder.com

Troll Communications
- 100 Corporate Drive
- Mahwah, NJ 07430
- 800-526-5289

Weston Woods
- 12 Oakwood Avenue
- Norwalk, CT 06850-1318
- 800-243-5020
- www.scholastic.com

Lesson Planning Support

Teacher's Book, page T26

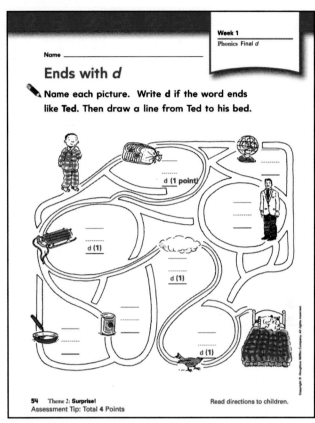

Teacher's Book, page T26

Teacher's Book, page T26

Teacher's Book, page T26

Lesson Planning Support *(Continued)*

Teacher's Book, page T27

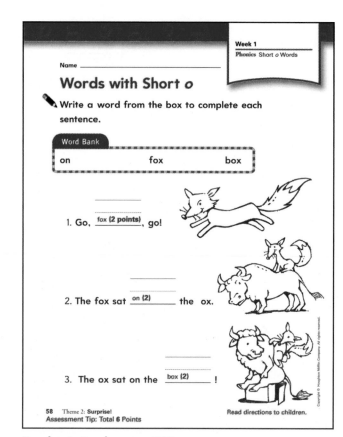

Teacher's Book, page T28

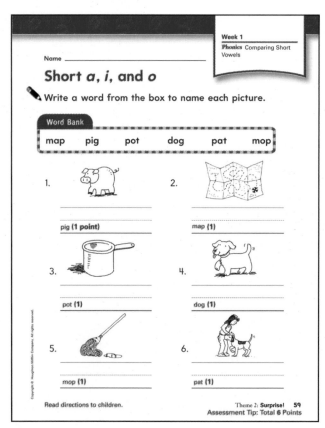

Teacher's Book, page T28

Teacher's Book, page T30

R38   THEME 2: **Surprise!**

Teacher's Book, page T39

Teacher's Book, page T40

Teacher's Book, page T40

Teacher's Book, page T40

Lesson Planning Support *(Continued)*

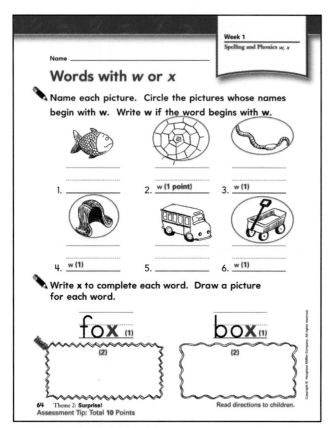

Teacher's Book, page T42

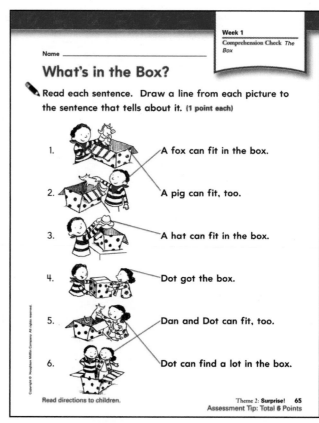

Teacher's Book, page T51

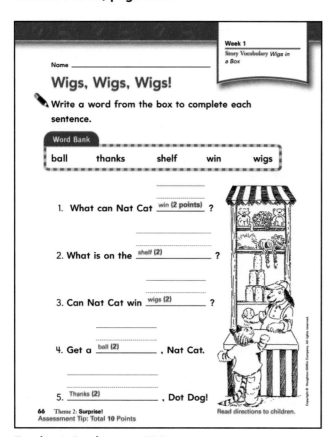

Teacher's Book, page T59

Teacher's Book, page T59

Teacher's Book, page T64

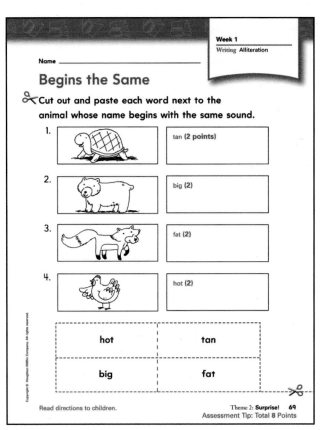

Teacher's Book, page T67

Teacher's Book, page T70

Teacher's Book, page T86

Lesson Planning Support *(Continued)*

Teacher's Book, page T86

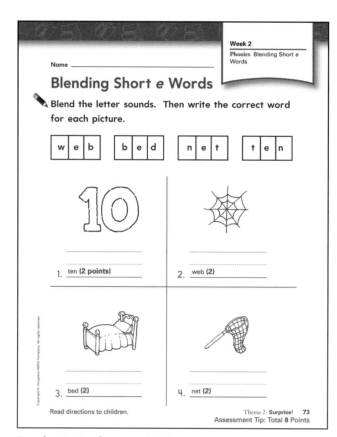

Teacher's Book, page T87

Teacher's Book, page T88

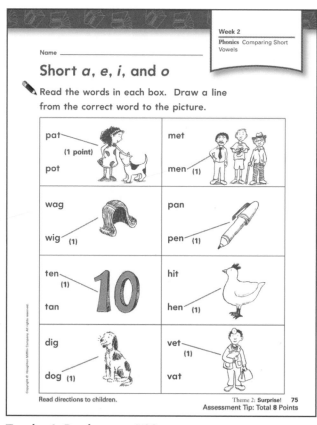

Teacher's Book, page T88

THEME 2: **Surprise!**

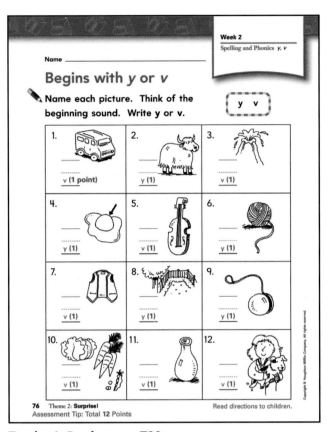

Teacher's Book, page T90

Teacher's Book, page T99

Teacher's Book, page T100

Teacher's Book, page T100

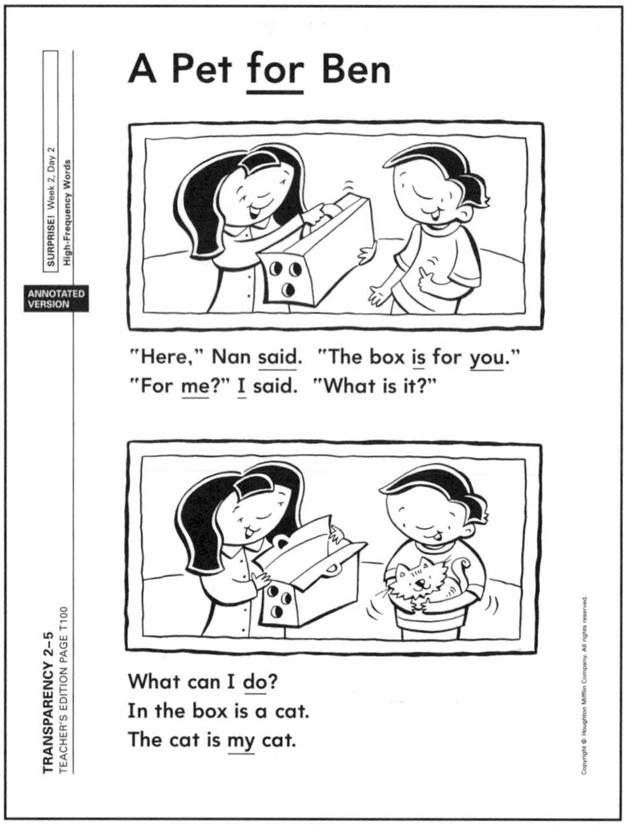

SURPRISE! Week 2, Day 2
High-Frequency Words

ANNOTATED VERSION

A Pet for Ben

"Here," Nan said. "The box is for you."
"For me?" I said. "What is it?"

What can I do?
In the box is a cat.
The cat is my cat.

TRANSPARENCY 2–5
TEACHER'S EDITION PAGE T100

Copyright © Houghton Mifflin Company. All rights reserved.

Teacher's Book, page T100

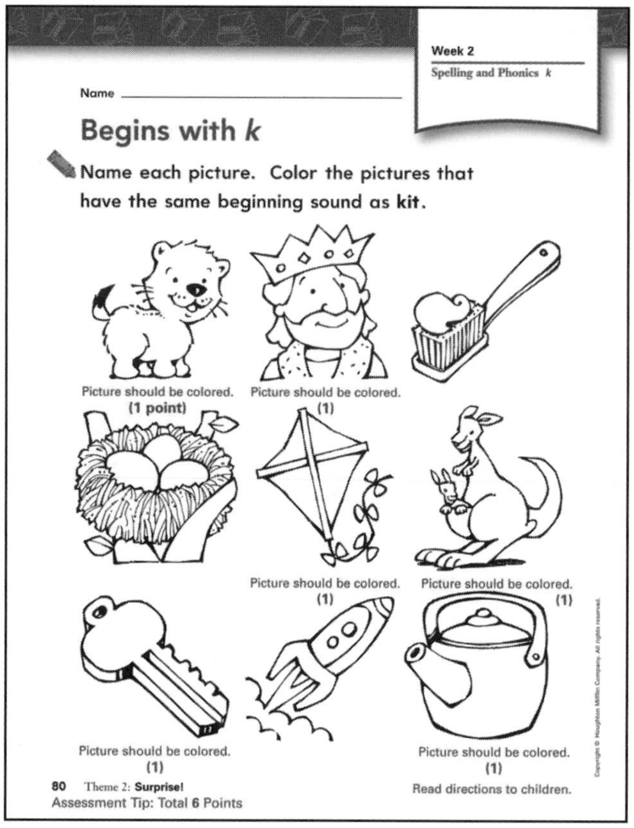

Week 2
Spelling and Phonics *k*

Name

Begins with *k*

Name each picture. Color the pictures that have the same beginning sound as **kit**.

Picture should be colored. (1 point)
Picture should be colored. (1)
Picture should be colored. (1)
Picture should be colored. (1)
Picture should be colored. (1)
Picture should be colored. (1)

80 Theme 2: **Surprise!**
Assessment Tip: Total 6 Points
Read directions to children.

Copyright © Houghton Mifflin Company. All rights reserved.

Teacher's Book, page T102

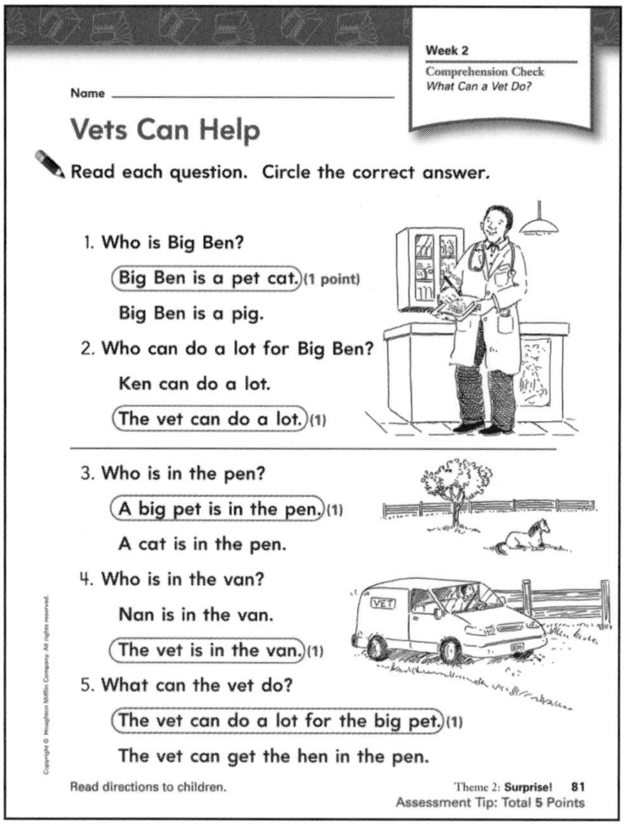

Week 2
Comprehension Check
What Can a Vet Do?

Name

Vets Can Help

Read each question. Circle the correct answer.

1. Who is Big Ben?
   (Big Ben is a pet cat.) (1 point)
   Big Ben is a pig.
2. Who can do a lot for Big Ben?
   Ken can do a lot.
   (The vet can do a lot.) (1)
3. Who is in the pen?
   (A big pet is in the pen.) (1)
   A cat is in the pen.
4. Who is in the van?
   Nan is in the van.
   (The vet is in the van.) (1)
5. What can the vet do?
   (The vet can do a lot for the big pet.) (1)
   The vet can get the hen in the pen.

Read directions to children.
Theme 2: **Surprise!** 81
Assessment Tip: Total 5 Points

Copyright © Houghton Mifflin Company. All rights reserved.

Teacher's Book, page T113

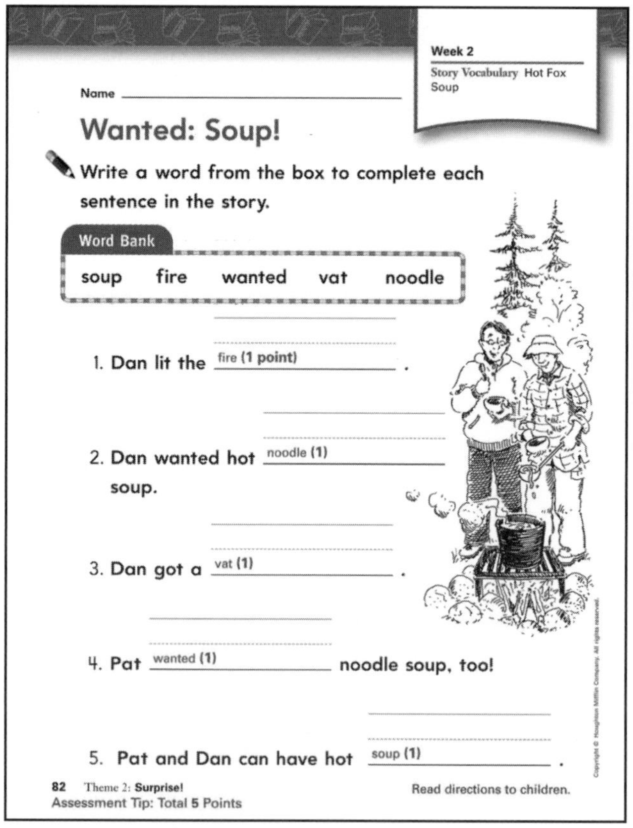

Week 2
Story Vocabulary Hot Fox Soup

Name

Wanted: Soup!

Write a word from the box to complete each sentence in the story.

Word Bank

soup fire wanted vat noodle

1. Dan lit the fire (1 point).
2. Dan wanted hot noodle (1) soup.
3. Dan got a vat (1).
4. Pat wanted (1) noodle soup, too!
5. Pat and Dan can have hot soup (1).

82 Theme 2: **Surprise!**
Assessment Tip: Total 5 Points
Read directions to children.

Copyright © Houghton Mifflin Company. All rights reserved.

Teacher's Book, page T121

Noodle Soup

ANNOTATED VERSION

Kit Cat <u>wanted</u> soup.

Nat Rat wanted <u>soup</u>, too.

Kit Cat wanted <u>noodle</u> soup.

Nat Rat wanted hot noodle soup.

Kit Cat got a <u>vat</u>, and Nat Rat lit a <u>fire</u>.

"Is the soup hot yet?" said Nat Rat.

"It is <u>too</u> hot for me," said Kit Cat.

"You can have it!"

Teacher's Book, page T121

Name _____

Put Them in Order!

✂ Cut out and paste the sentences in the order that they happened in the story.

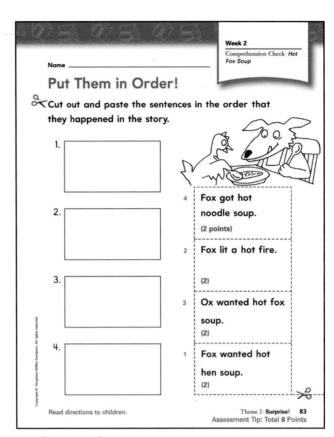

1. [   ]

2. [   ]

3. [   ]

4. [   ]

4 Fox got hot noodle soup.
(2 points)

2 Fox lit a hot fire.
(2)

3 Ox wanted hot fox soup.
(2)

1 Fox wanted hot hen soup.
(2)

Read directions to children.

Theme 2: **Surprise!**   83
Assessment Tip: Total 8 Points

Teacher's Book, page T128

Name _____

An Animal Fact

✏ Draw a picture of an animal.

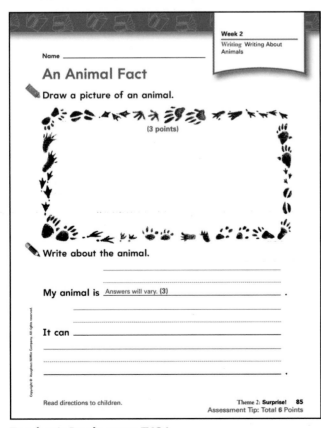

(3 points)

✏ Write about the animal.

_____

My animal is Answers will vary. (3) _____ .

_____

It can _____

_____

_____

Read directions to children.

Theme 2: **Surprise!**   85
Assessment Tip: Total 6 Points

Teacher's Book, page T131

Naming Words

ANNOTATED VERSION

The ___vet___ can do a lot for a pet.

The ___fox___ ran to the den.

The ___box___ is for the hat.

Teacher's Book, page T137

Lesson Planning Support *(Continued)*

Teacher's Book, page T150

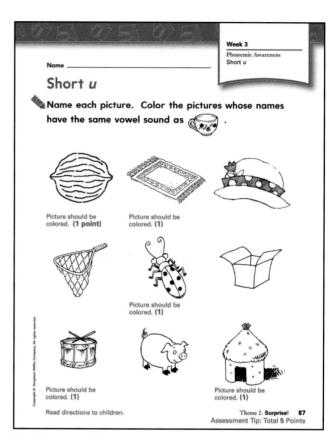

Teacher's Book, page T151

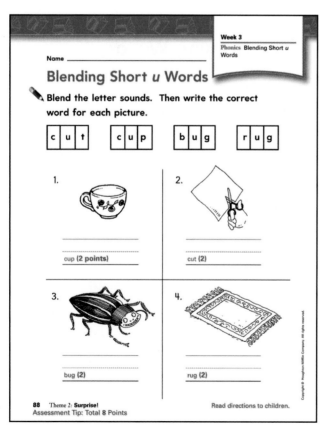

Teacher's Book, page T152

Teacher's Book, page T152

Teacher's Book, page T154

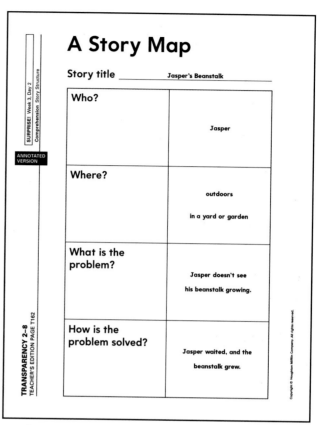

Teacher's Book, page T162

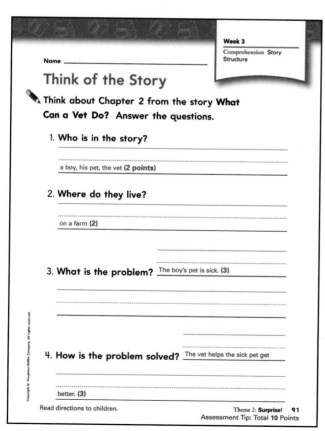

Teacher's Book, page T163

Teacher's Book, page T164

Teacher's Book, page T164

Teacher's Book, page T164

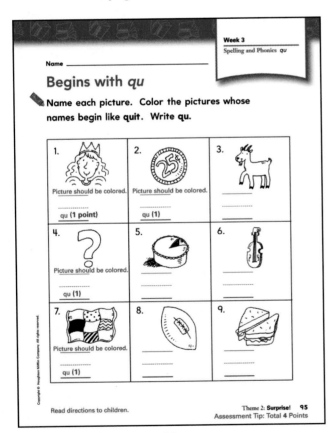

Teacher's Book, page T166

Teacher's Book, page T177

Tug Away!

✎ Read the words in the box. Write the correct word to finish each sentence in the play.

Name _____

Word Bank

| rope | I'm | outside |

_____

Narrator: We are outside (2 points)
Get set for the big tug.

_____

Elephant: I have a rope (2) _____ .
I am big, and I can tug Hippo.

_____

Hippo: I'm (2) _____ big, too.
I can tug a lot.
I can get Elephant to quit!

Read directions to children.
Theme 2: **Surprise!** 97
Assessment Tip: Total 6 Points

Teacher's Book, page T185

Who Is It?

✎ Circle the name that completes each sentence correctly.

Name _____

1. ___ can not get in the hut.
(Rat) (1 point)   Elephant   Hippo

2. ___ can get a big rope.
Hippo   Elephant   (Rat) (1)

3. Hippo and ___ tug, tug, tug.
(Elephant) (1)   Rat   Hippo

4. But they can not pull ___ .
Hippo   (Rat) (1)   Elephant

5. Elephant and ___ quit.
(Hippo) (1)   Elephant   Rat

6. ___ does a jig.
Elephant   Hippo   (Rat) (1)

98   Theme 2: **Surprise!**
Assessment Tip: Total 6 Points
Read directions to children.

Teacher's Book, page T190

The Big Tug

Elephant   Hippo   Narrator

ANNOTATED VERSION

Elephant and Hippo are <u>outside</u>.

Here is the <u>rope</u>.
Get set to tug.
Pull on three.

<u>I'm</u> big!   I can tug.

I'm big, too!   I can tug.

One, two, three!   GO!

TRANSPARENCY 2-10
TEACHER'S EDITION PAGE T185

Teacher's Book, page T185

Name _____

What a Bug!

✎ Draw a picture of a bug.

(3 points)

✎ Write about the bug.

My bug is Answers will vary. (3) _____ .

It has _____

Read directions to children.
Theme 2: **Surprise!** 99
Assessment Tip: Total 6 Points

Teacher's Book, page T193

Lesson Planning Support *(Continued)*

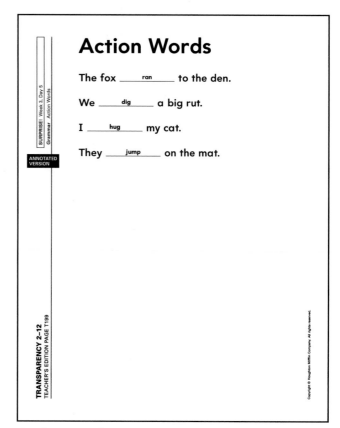

Surprise Stories

Story	Jasper's Beanstalk	A Hut for Zig Bug	The Rope Tug
Who?	Jasper	Zig Bug	Rat, Hippo, Elephant
Where?	outside, in a yard	in a house	in and around a hut
What?	grow a beanstalk	make a good home	let Rat in the hut
How?	give it time to grow	use small things	trick the animals

Teacher's Book, page T196

Action Words

The fox ____ran____ to the den.

We ____dig____ a big rut.

I ____hug____ my cat.

They ____jump____ on the mat.

Teacher's Book, page T199

Acknowledgments

Acknowledgments

For each of the selections listed below, grateful acknowledgment is made for permission to excerpt and/or reprint original or copyrighted material, as follows:

Poetry

"At Night" from *Out in the Dark and Daylight,* by Aileen Fisher. Copyright © 1980 by Aileen Fisher. Used by permission of Marian Reiner for the author.

"Cats" by Jacquiline Kirk. Copyright © by Jacquiline Kirk. Reprinted by permission of the author.

"Here Is the Beehive" from *Hand Rhymes,* collected and illustrated by Marc Brown. Copyright © 1985 by Marc Brown. Published by Dutton Children's Books, a division of Penguin Putnam Inc.

"Riddle" from *The Llama Who Had No Pajama: 100 Favorite Poems,* by Mary Ann Hoberman. Copyright © 1973 by Mary Ann Hoberman. Reprinted by permission of Harcourt Inc.

"There was a small pig who wept tears . . ." from *The Book of Pigericks: Pig Limericks,* by Arnold Lobel. Copyright © 1983 by Arnold Lobel. Reprinted by permission of HarperCollins Publishers.

"Together" from *Embrace: Selected Love Poems,* by Paul Engle. Copyright © 1969 by Paul Engle. Reprinted by permission of Random House, Inc.

Credits

Photography

CA4 (frog) JH Pete Carmichael/ImageBank. **CA5** (hat, school bus) © 2001 PhotoDisc. (butterfly) Artville. (shuttle) Comstock KLIPS. (caterpillar) © Michael & Patricia Fogden/CORBIS. **3** (t) image Copyright © 2000 PhotoDisc, Inc. **7** (t) image Copyright © 2000 PhotoDisc, Inc. **12** (icon) image Copyright © 2000 PhotoDisc, Inc. **12–13** Jo Browne/Mick Samee/Tony Stone Images. **16** Courtesy Lynn Munsinger. **27** (cat) Artville. **30** Courtesy NB Westcott. **44** Artville. **46–7** Artville. **50** Courtesy Lisa Campbell Ernst. **64** (l) American Images Inc/FPG International. (r) Jeri Gleiter/FPG International. **68** (t) Lawrence Migdale. (b) Mark Gardner. **82** images Copyright © 2000 PhotoDisc, Inc. **84–5** Telegraph Colour Library/FPG International. **88** Andrew Yates/Mercury Pictures. **89** Dennis Gray/Mercury Pictures. **104** images Copyright © 2000 PhotoDisc, Inc. **108** Sharron McElmeel. **124** images Copyright © 2000 PhotoDisc, Inc. **125** (r) image Copyright © 2000 PhotoDisc, Inc. **128** (icon) image Copyright © 2000 PhotoDisc, Inc. **128–9** Mauritius/Nawrocki Stock Photo Inc. **132** (t) Jon Crispin/Mercury Pictures. (b) Courtesy Cynthia Jabar. **150** Courtesy Valeria Petrone. **170** (t) Kindra Clineff. (b) Courtesy Anne Kennedy. **186** image Copyright © 2000 PhotoDisc, Inc. **190** Courtesy Farrar, Straus and Giroux. **210** image Copyright © 2000 PhotoDisc, Inc. **216** Courtesy Bernard Adnet. **236** (t) Jesse Nemerofksy/Mercury Pictures.

Assignment Photography

CA1 (t) Joel Benjamin. (b) Tony Scarpetta. **CA2** (t) Allan Landau. **CA3** Tony Scarpetta. **CA4** (t) Allan Landau. (b) Tony Scarpetta. **CA5** Joel Benjamin. **66–67, 69–81** Joel Benjamin. **26–7, 45, 65, 83, 105, 125** (l), **146–7, 164–5, 166–7, 187, 211, 232–3, 253** David Bradley Photographer. **234–5, 236** (m&b), **237–252** Richard Haynes.

Illustration

14–25 Lynn Munsinger. **28–43** Nadine Wescott. **48–63** Lisa Campbell Ernst. **70–81**(r) Rob Dunlavey. **86–103** John Ceballos. **106–123** David McPhail. **126–127** Stef De Reuver. **130–145** Cynthia Jabar. **148–163** Valerie Petrone. **166–167** Tammy Smith. **168–185** Anne Kennedy. **188–209** Satoshi Kitamura. **212–213** Matt Novak. **214–231** Bernard Adnet. **234–251** Mary Lynn Carson. **254–255** Keiko Motoyama.

263

Acknowledgments

For each of the selections listed below, grateful acknowledgment is made for permission to reprint original or copyrighted material, as follows:

JASPER'S BEANSTALK, by Nick Butterworth and Mick Inkpen. Copyright © 1993 by Nick Butterworth and Mick Inkpen. Published by arrangement with Simon & Schuster Children's Publishing Division and Hodder and Stoughton Children's Books, London. The right of Nick Butterworth and Mick Inkpen to be identified as the authors of this work has been asserted under the United Kingdom Copyright, Designs, and Patents Act 1988.

MINERVA LOUISE AT SCHOOL, by Janet Morgan Stoeke. Copyright © 1996 by Janet Morgan Stoeke. Reprinted by arrangement with Dutton Children's Books, a division of Penguin Putnam Inc.

TO BE A KID, by Maya Ajmera, and John D. Ivanko. Developed by SHAKTI for Children, Box 99350 Duke Station, Durham, NC 27708. Copyright © 1999 by SHAKTI for Children. Published by arrangement with Charlesbridge Publishing, Watertown, MA. All rights reserved.

Photographer Credits: 8 (t) John D. Ivanko; (l) Steven G. Herbert; (r) Elaine Little; 9 (tl) Stephen Chicoine; (r) John D. Ivanko; (bl) Mary Altier; (br) Elaine Little; 10 (l) Elaine Little; (tr) Mary Altier; (br) Siteman/Monkmeyer; 11 (l) Elaine Little; (tr) Isaiah Mosteller; (bl) Jon Warren; 12 (l) John D. Ivanko; (br) Elaine Little; 13 (tl), (tr), (bl) John D. Ivanko; (br) Jane Lombardo; 14 (l) John D. Ivanko; (r) Steve Macauley; 15 (tl) Steve Macauley; (tr) Elaine Little; (br) John Moses; (bl), (c) Maya Ajmera; 16 (l), (tr) Elaine Little; (br) John D. Ivanko; 17 (tl) Michelle Burgess; (tr) Mary Altier; (br) John D. Ivanko; (bl) MacPherson/Monkmeyer; 18 (l) John D. Ivanko; (tr) Elaine Little; (br) Maya Ajmera; 19 (tl) Richard A. Foster; (r) Lisa Ponzetti; (bl) John D. Ivanko; 20 (l) Gretchen Young; (r) Elaine Little; 21 (l) Watson/Childreach; (r) John D. Ivanko; 22 (l) Stephen Chicoine; (tr) Robert Hitzig; (br) International Public Affairs Branch of the Australian DFAT; 23 (tl) Christine Drake; (r) Elaine Little; (bl) John Warren.

Houghton Mifflin Edition, 2001
Copyright © 2001 by Houghton Mifflin Company. All rights reserved.

No part of this work may be reproduced or transmitted in any form or by any means, electronic or mechanical, including photocopying and recording, or by any information storage or retrieval system without the prior written permission of the copyright owner unless such copying is expressly permitted by federal copyright law. With the exception of nonprofit transcription in Braille, Houghton Mifflin is not authorized to grant permission for further uses of this work. Permission must be obtained from the individual copyright owner as identified herein. Address requests for permission to make copies of Houghton Mifflin material to School Permissions, Houghton Mifflin Company, 222 Berkeley Street, Boston, MA 02116.

Printed in the U.S.A.

ISBN 0-618-06630-6
123456789-AK-05 04 03 02 01 00

Index

Boldface page references indicate formal strategy and direct skill instruction.

T